ENTREPRENEURSHIP IN NINETEENTH-CENTURY BRAZIL

Entrepreneurship in Nineteenth-Century Brazil

The Formation of a Business Environment

Sérgio de Oliveira Birchal
Lecturer in Economics and Business
UNA School of Business
Belo Horizonte
Brazil

First published in Great Britain 1999 by
MACMILLAN PRESS LTD
Houndmills, Basingstoke, Hampshire RG21 6XS and London
Companies and representatives throughout the world

A catalogue record for this book is available from the British Library.

ISBN 0–333–72468–2

First published in the United States of America 1999 by
ST. MARTIN'S PRESS, INC.,
Scholarly and Reference Division,
175 Fifth Avenue, New York, N.Y. 10010

ISBN 0–312–21716–1

Library of Congress Cataloging-in-Publication Data
Birchal, Sérgio de Oliveira, 1959–
Entrepreneurship in nineteenth-century Brazil : the formation of a
business environment / Sérgio de Oliveira Birchal.
  p. cm.
Based on the author's thesis (Ph. D.)—University of London [date
not given].
Includes bibliographical references and index.
ISBN 0–312–21716–1 (cloth)
1. Entrepreneurship—Brazil—Minas Gerais—History—19th century.
2. Minas Gerais (Brazil)—Economic conditions. 3. Industries–
–Brazil—Minas Gerais—History—19th century. I. Title.
HC188.M6B57   1998
338'.04'09815109034—dc21   98–34841
                                                CIP

This book is printed on paper suitable for recycling and made from fully managed and
sustained forest sources.

10   9   8   7   6   5   4   3   2   1
08 07 06 05 04 03 02 01 00 99

Printed and bound in Great Britain by
Antony Rowe Ltd, Chippenham, Wiltshire

In memoriam Father Joaquim Birchal

Contents

List of Tables

Acknowledgements

Special acknowledgement is due to Colin M. Lewis who gave unsparingly of his time in advising and counselling me throughout the research and the writing of this book. Many people have helped me with their kind comments on different chapters: I am specially grateful to Maria Cláudia de Lima Birchal, Joaquim Birchal, Maria Izabel de O. Birchal, Norah Gray, Margaret Wimble, Domingos Antônio Giroletti, Aloysio Sá Freire de Lima, and Aida Sena de Lima. With much gratitude I recall the assistance of Wilson Suzigan, Colin Barber, Alisson Mascarenhas Vaz, José Waldemar Teixeira, Almir Pita, Indiana Pinheiro, Luiz Bresser Pereira, and Luiz Antônio Valle Arantes. Many other people who are too numerous to mention here helped me in many ways and I am grateful to them all. José Alencar Gomes da Silva, Décio M. Mascarenhas, José Augusto Bahia, Maria Lúcia Prado Costa and Fernando Xavier (Dango) deserve special thanks.

SÉRGIO DE OLIVEIRA BIRCHAL

Abbreviations

AT&T	American Telephone & Telegraph Company
CCC	Companhia Cedro e Cachoeira
CCM	Companhia Cachoeira de Macacos
CIM	Companhia Industrial Mineira
CME	Companhia Mineira de Eletricidade
CTS	Companhia de Tecidos Santanense
CUI	Companhia União e Indústria
FTR	Fábrica de Tecidos do Rink
SPR	São Paulo Railway
WEC	Westinghouse Electric Company
CFTC	Companhia de Fiação e Tecidos Corcovado
CNFE	Companhia Nacional de Forjas e Estaleiros
CPIB	Companhia Progresso Industrial do Brasil
EFCB	Estrada de Ferro Central do Brasil
FFTC	Fábrica de Fiação e Tecelagem Carioca
FTPG	Fábrica de Tecidos Pau Grande
FTSC	Fábrica de Tecidos de São Christóvão
FTSJ	Fábrica de Tecidos São João
FTSL	Fábrica de Tecidos São Lázaro
SAIM	Sociedade Anônima Industrial Machadense
CFLCL	Companhia Força e Luz Cataguazes-Leopoldina
CFTCI	Companhia de Fiação e Tecidos Confiança Industrial
CFTSF	Companhia de Fiação e Tecidos São Félix
FFTTA	Fábrica de Fiação, Tecidos e Tinturaria Alliança
FFTTB	Fábrica de Fiação, Tecidos e Tinturaria Bomfim
EFDPII	Estrada de Ferro Dom Pedro II
RJTLPC	Rio de Janeiro Tramway, Light and Power Company Ltd.
SJDRMC	St John del Rey Mining Company
SPTLPC	São Paulo Tramway, Light and Power Company

Introduction

The nineteenth century witnessed the consolidation of industrial capitalism and the widening of the development gap between the first industrial countries and latecomer economies such as Brazil. However, the question of underdevelopment was overlooked by many contemporary economists, who assumed that the historical experience of countries such as England would repeat itself elsewhere. It was only more recently that the problem of the development of latecomer economies began to be studied as a problem in its own right. Economic development in backward countries was not only a unique and specific process, but also did not necessarily follow the same path taken by more advanced economies. In other words, differences were observed in the pace and substance of development in latecomer economies in contrast to the first industrial countries, and it was recognized that these were due to the distinct nature of the historical process of development of backward countries. Hence, it is important to ask to what extent the process of economic development of nineteenth-century Minas Gerais repeated the historical experience of more advanced economies, and in which respects was the *mineiro** experience peculiar and unique?

Furthermore, for much of the nineteenth-century the Brazilian economy has been generally regarded as a coffee-export economy. Indeed, the coffee sector was by far the most dynamic in Brazil during this period and has commanded the attention of many economic historians. Coffee was not only the main Brazilian cash crop, but coffee capital also financed to a large extent the early process of industrialization, the construction of the infrastructure, and many other businesses such as banking and trade. Consequently, the major coffee-growing areas of the country, Rio de Janeiro and São Paulo, have tended to be the subject of most studies dealing with economic development in Brazil. This has led to a tendency to overgeneralize from the experiences of the coffee sector, a process which neglects (or minimizes) important

---

* *Mineiro* relates to the people or things belonging to Minas Gerais.

xv

socioeconomic differences amongst regional economies in
southern and central Brazil during the nineteenth century.
Minas Gerais, for example, had a much more varied economy
than Rio de Janeiro and São Paulo with areas dedicated to
mining, ranching, manufacturing, the production of food-
stuffs for internal consumption, as well as the production of
coffee for export in the mid-nineteenth century. Thus, some
questions pose themselves: how distinct was the business
environment in Minas Gerais from that of São Paulo and
Rio de Janeiro? How far can generalizations based on the
experiences of the two principal coffee provinces/states be
applied to the case of Minas Gerais? Very little attention has
been given to these questions and very little has been written
on the business environment in Brazil to date. In providing
answers to these questions this research will make a contribution to a better understanding of the overall historical process
of development in Brazil.

The purpose of this book is to make a contribution to the
study of economic development and business formation in
latecomer economies by studying the development of a business environment in nineteenth-century Minas Gerais. The
focus of the work is on non-agricultural enterprises. The
business environment is defined as the conditions or circumstances in which people make production and commercial
decisions about their businesses. Thus, it is possible to say
that different periods of human history witnessed different
business environments, such as the feudalist, mercantilist or
capitalist. Yet, within these specific modes it is possible to
identify different business environments for each stage of
development; for example, competitive capitalism at the
beginning of the nineteenth century, and mature or mono-
polist capitalism at the end of the century. Finally, regarding
place, different business environments can be distinguished
from region to region or from country to country.

*   *   *

The book is divided into four chapters. The first chapter
reviews Brazilian and *mineiro* economic history in the nineteenth century, and provides a general background for the
book. Chapter 2 analyses the debate about the emergence of

the entrepreneur in the Brazilian economic historiography. With foreigners constituting a smaller proportion of its population compared with that of São Paulo and Rio de Janeiro, and coffee very much confined to the southern regions of Minas Gerais, Chapter 2 also investigates the social and ethnic background of *mineiro* entrepreneurs and the origin of their capital.

Chapter 3 assesses the degree of structural development of *mineiro* firms in the nineteenth century and relates it to the prevailing business environment. It examines the scale and scope of activities and the administrative structure of several *mineiro* firms in order to assess their degree of organizational maturity.

Chapter 4 investigates the process of technology transfer to Minas Gerais, the reliance on foreign technical knowledge, and restrictions on the development of native technology. As production of new technologies during the nineteenth century was limited to a small number of more advanced countries, less-developed regions such as Brazil relied heavily on imported technology to promote economic development. Therefore, Chapter 4 examines the process of technology transfer in nineteenth-century Minas Gerais, and discusses the dependence of various firms on imported technical knowledge and the limits to the development of an indigenous technology during this period. It also discusses how *mineiro* entrepreneurs managed to absorb and modify these technologies.

1 Nineteenth-Century Brazilian and *Mineiro* Economic History

INTRODUCTION

During the nineteenth century, Brazil went through a number of social and political changes which had a great impact on the economic structure of the country: it became independent from Portugal, slavery was abolished, and the Republic was proclaimed. At the same time, a new economic pole based on coffee growing emerged in the centre-south region – replacing the north-eastern sugar economy as Brazil's main economic centre. This change had a profound impact. Meanwhile, Minas Gerais became largely an agro-pastoral economy after the gold-mining boom, which had characterized its economy for most of the eighteenth century, faded.

This chapter identifies changes in the social, institutional and economic structures of Brazil and Minas Gerais which have a bearing upon the 'business environment'. Brazil started the nineteenth century as a Portuguese colony whose main export, sugar, was produced mainly in the north-eastern region. At the beginning of that century, the *mineiro* economy was depressed and in contrast with the rich and sumptuous recent past there was misery and poverty. At the end of the nineteenth century, coffee was Brazil's main cash crop and it had come to serve as a basis for the development of capitalism. Minas Gerais, however, was fragmented, and each sub-region developed in a different way – the north was backward and the south developed rapidly.

NINETEENTH-CENTURY BRAZIL

From the discovery of Brazil in 1500 to its independence in 1822, the promotion of exports was the central concern

1

of the Portuguese crown because exports were the principal means by which monopoly profits were extracted from the colony. Brazil was thus transformed into an agricultural colony supplying tropical products, with the exception of the century-long gold rush which began shortly before 1700. Timber (mainly Pau Brasil) was the first main export, followed by sugar. Sugar remained Brazil's main cash crop throughout the colonial period, although from the late seventeenth century onwards sugar exports fell in value and Brazil lost her virtual monopoly of world production. By the end of the eighteenth century, Portugal stimulated the diversification of production in her colonies with some success. As a result, and partly due to interruptions in the Caribbean trade between 1776 and 1815, sugar revived and the export of other commodities grew significantly.[1]

The Brazilian economy, at the beginning of the nineteenth century might be described as a series of economic systems or, to quote Furtado, an archipelago.[2] The main areas – the sugar and the gold economies – were mutually connected whereas the others were nearly isolated. Connected with the sugar nucleus was the cattle-breeding economy of the north-east. The mining nucleus was linked with the southern cattle-breeding hinterland, the latter spreading from São Paulo to Rio Grande do Sul. These two systems were in turn loosely connected by the São Francisco river. There were two autonomous centres, Maranhão and Pará, in the northern region of the country. The former had enjoyed the initial advantage of careful attention from the Portuguese government, which had established a highly capitalized trading company responsible for financing the development of the region. The latter lived exclusively on the forest-extractive economy organized by the Jesuit fathers – which decayed after the Portuguese persecution of them in the last decades of the eighteenth century – and was based on exploitation of the Indian labour force. Although Maranhão constituted an autonomous system it was connected with the sugar nucleus by the cattle-breeding periphery. Thus, whereas Pará existed as a totally isolated nucleus, the three main economic nuclei – the sugar nucleus, the mining nucleus and Maranhão – were linked by the vast cattle-breeding hinterland.[3]

With the French invasion of Portugal in 1808, the Portuguese court was transferred to Rio de Janeiro, a fact which represented a major stage in the evolution of Brazil towards independence. Of even greater significance was the end of the monopoly of colonial trade and the elimination of Lisbon as an entrepôt for Brazilian imports and exports. On his arrival in Brazil, Dom João – the Prince Regent – opened Brazil's ports to direct trade with all friendly nations, which in practice, at least until the end of the Napoleonic Wars, meant trade with England. He also revoked all decrees prohibiting manufacturing in the colony, exempted industrial raw materials from import duties, encouraged the invention or introduction of new machinery, and offered direct subsidies to the cotton, wool, silk and iron industries.[4] However, in 1810, as the price for British protection of what remained of the Portuguese colonial empire, Britain was granted the position of a privileged power with extraterritorial rights and preferential tariffs at extremely low levels. For much of first half of the nineteenth century, the 1810 treaties seriously hampered the autonomy of the Brazilian government in the economic sector mainly by reducing its capacity to generate revenue from taxing imports.[5]

With the liberation of Portugal and the end of the war in Europe, the then King Dom João VI was soon forced to return to Portugal, leaving his son Dom Pedro I behind in Rio as Prince Regent. Independence in 1822 was the result of a conflict of interests between the Brazilian landowning class and the Portuguese overseas merchants, but produced few innovations in the economic structure of the country. Thus, colonial structures (like slavery and plantations) and with them the dependent nature of the export trade, remained largely intact. The landowning class strengthened its power, while English merchants replaced the Portuguese in the international trade sector though not necessarily in domestic commerce. At the same time, several revolts erupted challenging the authority of the central government. These revolts were reactions against the socially and economically disaggregative effects of neo-colonialism.[6] They also reflected the weakness of the new Brazilian government in both political and economic terms. In political terms, the various sub-groups of the Brazilian élite could not agree how to best organize the country. Those linked to the Rio economy advocated a more centralized system, whereas the long-established rural oligarchies fought for provincial power. Furthermore, independence in 1822 was incomplete since the movement for independence from Portugal was led by a Portuguese prince, whose commitment to sever all family and dynastic ties with the formal colonial power was doubted by many leading Brazilian figures. In economic terms, Brazil lacked a cash crop which would give her a stronger and wider economic basis, and the price paid for independence proved too expensive. Political stability was only finally achieved in the 1840s when the country enjoyed certain prosperity based on exports of coffee, and the dominant class reached relative agreement on fundamental issues.[7]

After independence, the new Brazilian government also faced increasing financial difficulties caused mainly by the unequal commercial treaty of 1810, renewed in 1827, which was the price that Britain exacted for the recognition of Brazilian independence. Until the middle of the 1840s, economic policy in Brazil was marked by a struggle against constant deficits in the balance of payments and scarcity of fiscal resources. As indicated above, according to the commercial treaties of 1810 and 1827, England was granted extraterritorial rights and a general 15 per cent *ad valorem* customs tariff. This situation created serious difficulties for the Brazilian government since the taxing of imports was the usual means whereby primarily producing countries, like Brazil, collected their basic revenues. As a fiscal apparatus to collect any other form of taxes (such as income and property) was almost non-existent, the only alternative was to tax exports. However, in a slave-based economy this would have meant a reduction in the profits of the great landlords, and the new (post-independence) government was pledged to abandon 'mercantilist' taxes that had been used to finance administration during the colonial period. Thus, restricted to customs duties as the sole source of revenue and means of sustenance, and without any further means of increasing its revenue, the central government found itself in serious financial difficulties until the denunciation of the treaties with England in 1844, when the increasingly irksome and economically debilitating commercial treaties expired, liberating tariff policy and strengthening the government's revenues.[8]

When Brazil became independent from Portugal it had an overwhelmingly rural population of between four and five million. This relatively small population was scattered over a vast territory, but was heavily concentrated in the coastal provinces – from the provinces of the north-east (with 40–45 per cent of the total population) to the provinces of the south, including Rio de Janeiro and São Paulo. The only inland province with a large population was Minas Gerais as a result of the gold rush in the first half of the eighteenth century. At this time, the *mineiro* population still accounted for 20 per cent of the total population, though it was mostly located in the south of the province adjoining the province of Rio de Janeiro. Less than a third of Brazil's population was white, the majority being black or mulatto. At least 30 per cent were slaves, of whom three-quarters were concentrated in only five of the 18 provinces – Maranhão, Pernambuco, Bahia, Minas Gerais and Rio de Janeiro. In many of these areas slaves constituted the majority of the population.[9]

For the greater part of the history of Brazil, African slavery was the dominant form of labour. Brazil imported more Africans than any other colony or country in the New World, receiving around 38 per cent of the 9.6 million Africans brought to the American continent during the history of the Atlantic slave trade. For almost the whole colonial period (1500–1822), the number of slaves surpassed that of the non-slave population. In the middle of the eighteenth century, slaves made up more than 60 per cent of the total population, a percentage which decreased to about a third around 1800, as shown in Table 1.1. During this period slaves constituted almost all the workers in the important regional systems of production of primary products for export, these systems characterizing this phase of the Brazilian economic history; that is, sugar in the north-east in the sixteenth and seventeenth centuries, and gold panning and diamond mining in Minas Gerais and Goiás in the eighteenth century.[10]

Table 1.1   Slave population in relation to the total population
in Brazil, 1800–1900

Years	Slaves	Total population
1800	1 000 000*	3 000 000*
1823	1 147 515	3 960 866
1850	2 500 000	8 020 000
1872	1 510 806	10 112 061
1887	723 419	
1890		14 333 915

* Estimated.

Source: C. Prado Júnior, *História Econômica do Brasil*, 36th
edn (São Paulo, 1988), p. 358.

In the nineteenth century (until the abolition of slavery in
1888), although slaves lost their absolute and relative importance in the total population, slavery continued to dominate
the main economic activity of the century, coffee-growing on
the farms of Rio de Janeiro, São Paulo, Minas Gerais and
Espírito Santo.[11] Furthermore, slaves were to be found
throughout rural Brazil in stockraising, in cereal production,
in the cultivation of basic staples for local consumption, and in
subsistence agriculture.[12] Slaves were also employed in technical positions on sugar and coffee farms and in sugar mills –
that is, as 'factory' hands. In addition, several industrial
enterprises (shipyards, textile industries, metal industries,
candle factories, and so forth) also employed a considerable
number of slaves.[13] Slaves were also employed as domestic
servants, as stevedores and porters in the docks, as water and
refuse carriers, as transporters of people, and as masons and
carpenters. There were also slave prostitutes and some were
even beggars.[14] Religious houses and hospitals owned slaves,
and the State owned and hired slaves for the building and
maintenance of public works.[15] Until the first serious efforts
were made to end the African slave trade, in the late 1840s,
slaves were both available and cheap.[16]

The trans-Atlantic slave trade was declared illegal by treaty
with Britain in 1826, effective from 1830. During the three
years 1827–30, in anticipation of the abolition of the trade,

175 000 slaves were imported. As a consequence, in the years immediately after 1831 very few slaves entered the country as the market was glutted; demand and prices fell off. However, the temporary end of the slave trade coincided with the rapid expansion of coffee plantations in the Paraíba Valley, where coffee farms were worked by slaves. Moreover, slave mortality was so high in Brazil that regular new supplies from Africa were required. Soon the demand for slaves revived, especially in the coffee regions of the centre-south, and the slave trade was gradually reorganized after 1830. In 1839, the British government adopted tougher measures to curb the Brazilian slave trade which was then growing very quickly. Therefore, from 1839 to 1842 – partly as a result of these initiatives and partly as a result of the temporary glut on the market following the huge slave imports of the late 1830s – imports into Brazil fell to less than a half of their previous level. Even so, in the second half of the 1840s the slave trade began to revive once again after several years of reduced activity. Nevertheless, by the early 1850s the trans-Atlantic slave trade was finally brought to an end as a result of strong British pressure and the enforcement of the Eusébio de Queiroz law of 4 September 1850, which declared the slave trade equivalent to piracy.[17]

After the suppression of the slave trade in 1850 the slave population began to decline, mainly because of the continuing high rate of mortality. Nevertheless, the decline in slave numbers in coffee districts was at first offset by an internal traffic. Slaves were sold from the less-productive north-eastern sugar provinces and from urban areas to the coffee-growing areas in south-eastern Brazil.[18]

By the middle of the century, coffee had become the main Brazilian export and its participation in the value of the major Brazilian exports increased from then onwards. At the same time, the price of sugar continued to fall and its participation in exports decreased steadily. It is the differences in the fate of these two commodities (coffee and sugar) which basically explains the shifting distribution of the slave population from the northern to the southern part of the country.[19]

Although it had been introduced into Brazil at the beginning of the eighteenth century, coffee acquired commercial

importance only at the end of that century with the disorganization of production in the French colony of Haiti.[20] The
climate and soil of south-eastern Brazil were very suitable for
coffee growing, and coffee beans were easy to transport and
store. Furthermore, there was no need for complex industrial
processes to prepare them for the market.[21] When coffee
became commercially important its production was concentrated in the hilly regions around the city of Rio de Janeiro,
where there was a relatively abundant supply of labour and,
given the proximity of the port, there were no transport
problems.[22] During the early decades of the nineteenth century, coffee cultivation spread up the Paraíba Valley. By the
middle of the century, it started to move towards the north of
the province of São Paulo.[23]

In the first decade of Brazil's independence, coffee already
accounted for 18 per cent of exports by value, taking third
place after sugar and cotton. In the 1830s coffee moved into
the lead, comprising more than 40 per cent of the country's
exports by value. In the 1850s coffee was responsible for
nearly half of all Brazilian export earnings. At the same
time, Brazil's share of world coffee output rose from a little
under 20 per cent in the 1820s to over 40 per cent in the
1840s, when the country became by far the world's largest
producer. From then on, Brazilian coffee production
accounted for around 50 per cent of world coffee output
during the third quarter of the last century, and for 75 per
cent at the beginning of the twentieth century.[24]

The second half of the nineteenth century was a period of
great transformation in Brazilian economic history, following
the first half of the century which was a period of adjustment
to the new situation created by independence from Portugal.
The economic, financial, social and political crisis, which
began with the transfer of the Portuguese crown in 1808
and independence in 1822, lasted until the end of the first
half of the century, and the seed of transformation sowed
during this period was to mature and produce its fruits only
in the second half of the nineteenth century.[25] Thus, during
the last part of the century several important phenomena
changed the social and economic structure of the country:
the building of the railway network, which began in 1852
and which by the end of the century had expanded to

more than 9000 kilometers of line; the abolition of slavery in 1888 and the arrival of a large number of immigrants in the southern parts of the country; the proclamation of the Republic in 1889; and the beginning of the process of industrialization.[26]

In the 1850s, Brazil enjoyed a period of economic prosperity which lasted until the financial crisis of 1857. As a consequence of the end of the slave trade and the resultant transfer of funds from this trade to the domestic economy, the more liberal monetary policy applied since the beginning of the decade and a good export performance due to increasing international demand for tropical products, the economy grew rapidly.[27] Furthermore, in 1850 Brazil was given her first commercial code, which updated and integrated a variety of laws and regulations dating back to the colonial period. By newly codifying commercial relations regarding partnerships, contracts and bankruptcies, business activity was boosted.[28] A large number of new companies were established during the 1850s including 62 factories, 17 banks, 20 shipping companies, eight railways, eight mining enterprises, four colonization companies, 23 insurance companies, two gas companies, and three urban transport companies.[29] Not long afterwards the government began to guarantee interest on capital invested in railways, bolstering the efforts of the planters to link Brazil more closely to the overseas markets.[30]

In the early 1860s, Brazil faced a greater crisis than that of 1857 as a result of the more restrictive monetary policy implemented by the conservative Cabinet then in government. In the aftermath of the crisis of 1857, the liberal administration failed to create an adequate financial structure to support economic growth either in the rural or in the manufacturing sectors. The financial chaos that followed created the conditions for the takeover by the so-called metallists, conservative politicians who advocated rigid monetary control.[31] During the same period a more restrictive commercial code was adopted, forcing all would-be companies to obtain preliminary government approval.[32] The 1864 crisis was followed by the Paraguayan War,[33] whose cost was greater than could have been predicted. Sustaining the war effort more than doubled public expenditure between 1864/65 and 1866/67, and the money supply rapidly increased. Nevertheless, wartime inflation stimulated the domestic economy which had been flat since the early 1860s,[34] and the ten-year period 1870–80 was one of the most prosperous in Brazilian history. The number of industrial, commercial, and – most of all – agricultural enterprises increased rapidly. The number of banks and all sorts of financial institutions also multiplied and the State – and to a lesser extent foreign capital – invested in large enterprises, such as railways, ports and the urban infrastructure.[35]

The first population census taken in Brazil in 1872 shows that there were approximately 10 million inhabitants. Slaves represented just over 15 per cent of the total population, in sharp contrast to the situation at the end of the eighteenth century when they represented more than half of the total population.[36] Furthermore, in the following decades they were to be more and more concentrated in coffee provinces of the south-east (São Paulo, Rio de Janeiro, and Minas Gerais). However, from 1870 onwards the supply of slaves, who in 1872 constituted about 20 per cent of the economically active population and about 70 per cent of plantation labour, was certainly precarious and the labour issue called for an urgent solution.[37] As growth in Brazil consisted merely of increasing utilization of the available factor – land – through the incorporation of greater quantities of labour, the supply of slaves was a key factor. However, alternatives to slave labour were very limited.[38]

The growing free Brazilian population appeared to be a great potential source of labour: in most provinces free people had outnumbered slaves since the early nineteenth century.[39] Brazilian free workers, white and coloured, participated in various activities in the export sector. In addition, they were employed to clear forest, to build roads, to cart, to assist at harvest time, and to grow subsistence crops for the plantation. In other words, although not fully available for regular work, the free Brazilian population constituted a potential source of occasional labour. Nevertheless, despite the fact that Brazilian workers (white and coloured, free and freed) were perceived by many as a viable alternative of labour, their wide and large-scale employment demanded complex reforms in the law, which were very controversial and of uncertain political and economic costs.[40]

Difficulties in recruiting domestic free labour on a large scale and growing certainties about the end of slavery stimulated attempts to attract immigrants. At the beginning of the 1880s it was obvious that the abolition of slavery was imminent, and growing external and internal pressure resulted in several laws which gradually ended slavery. Thus, in 1888, slavery was finally abolished.[41] What was feared by the large landowners as an economic catastrophe – after the failure of the earlier experiments in immigrant labour many southern farmers predicted a chronic shortage of labour and economic ruin for themselves after abolition – eventually proved to be a smooth transition from slave to free labour. Most freed slaves accepted wage and sharecropping contracts on nearby or even on the same estates.[42] More significantly, in the last quarter of the century European immigrants began to come to Brazil in increasing numbers, and during this period immigration amounted to more than 800 000.[43] At the beginning of the 1880s an immense wave of Italian, Spanish and Portuguese workers began to migrate to Brazil, and they went mainly to the coffee-growing regions, subsidized by state and federal governments.[44] São Paulo was the state which absorbed the larger number of immigrants.[45] Until the First World War the number of immigrants entering Brazil was kept as high as possible because they often tended to move from agriculture to other activities after a while, or to return to their home countries.[46]

During the second half of the nineteenth century, coffee was by far the most successful Brazilian product in the international market, and the second and third quarters of the century were basically the period of early growth for the coffee economy.[47] In the late 1850s, coffee production in Rio de Janeiro accounted for the greatest part of Brazilian coffee export, and by the last quarter of the century the great fertile plateau of São Paulo became the main source of coffee production. The arrival of the railway, the input of foreign investments in the decade after 1885, and the cheap money of the Republican provisional government stimulated new planting in São Paulo, doubling the number of Brazilian coffee plantations.[48] Low prices discouraged potential competitors and Brazil supplied more than half of the coffee sold in the international market. As Brazil's other exports did not enjoy similar success in world trade the Brazilian economy, until the 1930s, was characterized by a very high dependence on the performance of the price of a single export product – coffee.[49]

At the beginning of the twentieth century, the Brazilian government became engaged in the enormous task of stabilizing the price of its main product in the world market. In the late 1890s, coffee prices were depressed and the Brazilian coffee growers faced the effects of the internal deflationary policy that was imposed by the funding loan of 1898.[50] Between 1901 and 1904 coffee export revenue in Brazilian currency fell at the rate of 5.92 per cent a year. Facing the possibility of bankruptcy, Brazilian coffee growers organized themselves into a powerful pressure group and compelled the government to intervene in the international coffee market.[51]

In 1906, three of the main coffee-producing states – São Paulo, Minas Gerais and Rio de Janeiro – and the federal government agreed to support coffee prices, but the federal and state governments of Rio de Janeiro and Minas Gerais withdrew leaving São Paulo to act alone. Coffee producers from Minas and Rio were not as adversely affected by the coffee crisis as their *paulista** counterparts. Furthermore, the financial risks for both states (Minas Gerais and Rio de Janeiro) to participate in the scheme would be proportionally greater due to their smaller budgets. The so-called 'valorization' scheme involved the raising of funds to purchase surplus coffee at a price remunerative for Brazilian producers. Coffee was then stored and stocks used to regulate prices. The whole operation was financed by European and US banks through the intercession of coffee importers.[52] Later, the federal government finally agreed to guarantee the loans, and prices did begin to rise again. However, this policy diverted resources from other sectors of the economy, ignored the issue of productivity, and encouraged foreign competitors to expand their production.[53]

If in the past the Brazilian economy had relied on sugar and gold to promote its economic development, for much of the nineteenth century it relied heavily and almost exclusively on coffee. However, if in the former cases the result was economic stagnation after each specific economic boom, in the latter the

---

Paulista relates to the people or things belonging to São Paulo.

result was economic modernization. The coffee economy became the centre of a rapid process of capital accumulation, and it was as part of this process of accumulation that Brazilian industry was born.[54] In São Paulo, for example, coffee capital created the 'coffee export complex', which included the production and processing of coffee, the transport system (railways, ports and so on), the export and import trade and the banking system.[55] Thus, the coffee economy created the fundamental prerequisites for the emergence of industrial capital and large-scale industry. These conditions included capital accumulation for investment in the industrial sector, the formation of a free-labour market, the creation of an internal market for industrial goods, and the capacity to import wage goods, raw materials and machinery.[56]

Although the emergence of the first industries date to the 1860s and 1870s, the first industrial upsurge took place only between 1880 and 1890. From its origin, Brazilian industry developed unevenly through the various regions of the country and tended to concentrate in the coffee region; especially in Rio de Janeiro, São Paulo and Minas Gerais.[57] The very first products to be manufactured were those whose weight-to-cost ratio was so high that even with the most rudimentary technique they cost less to produce in Brazil than to buy from Europe. At least until the 1920s, with very few exceptions, only those goods that were quite bulky and intrinsically low in value were being produced. Furthermore, they were fashioned either from local raw materials or from semi-processed imported materials which would have been much bulkier if fully transformed before shipment. Nevertheless, even this rudimentary stage of pre-1920 industrialization involved a wide range of goods. Almost every kind of construction material was domestically produced by 1920, as well as shoes, beer, soft drinks, furniture, pots and pans, flour, boilers, hats, stonework and coarse textiles.[58] Furthermore, most of the industries which emerged in the period previous to the First World War were mainly complementary or subsidiary to the export sector – from whom they also depended for the import of raw materials and other inputs such as machinery and equipment – especially coffee.[59] Their activities included the processing of coffee, cotton, meat and oil seeds, the milling of sugar, small mechanical workshops for maintenance services, the packing, assembling and finishing of goods, or the adapting of foreign products to the local market, and the production of textiles.[60]

To sum up, during the nineteenth century Brazil became independent from Portugal, the Republic was proclaimed, slavery was abolished, European immigrants entered the country in large numbers and a free-labour market emerged, coffee became the main export, the economy diversified and the coffee economy created the basis for the development of industry in Brazil. Nevertheless, the process of social and economic development of each Brazilian region differred in varied degrees and respects from the general pattern described in this section. Thus, the next part of this chapter will examine the social and economic history of Minas Gerais during the nineteenth century, pointing out those changes that have a bearing upon the 'business environment'.

NINETEENTH-CENTURY MINAS GERAIS

Minas Gerais is a landlocked territory the size of France, with a variety of landscapes. Its frontiers do not define a coherent geographical region and Minas Gerais was not a natural economic unit. The rivers form several disconnected systems, and there are several mountain ranges which divide sub-regions, imposing huge barriers to communications and transport. Thus, during the last century Minas had a disarticulated pattern of growth which was largely determined by geographical considerations. The Triângulo – which was juridically linked to São Paulo until 1816 – and the South zones were logical extensions of the São Paulo hinterland, to which they were linked economically and culturally. Most of the northern region of Minas Gerais is geographically part of the Brazilian *sertão*, stretching into Ceará in north-eastern Brazil. It was formerly administered from Salvador, the capital of Bahia, until the middle of the eighteenth century and all of its exports passed through Salvador until this century. The western region was part of the colonial cattle frontier, extending from Bahia to Goiás. The Mata zone, in south-eastern Minas, was linked economically with the port of Rio de Janeiro and was part of Rio de Janeiro's hinterland from the coffee boom of the 1830s. The central part of Minas was the seat of provincial and, later, state government, whose authority over the other zones was weakened until the 1930s by poor communications and lack of economic influence. Thus, the more developed regions in the southern part of Minas Gerais (Triângulo, Mata, and South) were historically linked to São Paulo and Rio de Janeiro, whereas the less-developed northern part was a backwater of Bahia.[61]

The occupation of the territory was directly linked to the discovery of gold at the end of the seventeenth century, mainly in the central part of Minas Gerais. Gold production reached its peak around the 1760s and after that began to decline slowly.[62] In the 1800s, production was less than half the level of the 1760s, and in the 1820s the decay of the gold-mining economy was beyond doubt. Several different factors contributed to the decay of the eighteenth-century *mineiro* gold economy: production was restricted to alluvial gold deposits because of the requirements or difficulties of underground gold-mining; lack of slave labour; heavy duties levied on goods entering Minas Gerais making the cost of living very expensive; and the low standards of the prevailing methods of production.[63] With the progressive decay of the gold-mining economy during the last quarter of the eighteenth century, the economy of Minas Gerais went through a great transformation. During this period there was an important expansion of craft production, mainly of textiles and iron. However, this incipient production had its development hindered by the Portuguese colonial government which prohibited it in 1785. Furthermore, a large proportion of the population of the decaying gold-mining area turned to subsistence activities, moving from the central part of Minas towards the northern and western parts – where a cattle-raising economy emerged – and towards the southern parts – where dairy production developed.[64]

With the arrival of the Portuguese royal family in Brazil in 1808 there were several attempts to revive the economy of the central part of Minas Gerais by the establishment of an iron industry. Although the attempt to produce iron on a large scale in the Metalúrgica zone failed, mainly because of restricted markets, several small iron foundries of limited economic importance emerged. Their production was small and the greater part of their output was consumed locally.[65] Nevertheless, during the first years of the nineteenth century agriculture replaced gold as the main economic activity of Minas Gerais. Rural production, either for the *mineiro* or for the Brazilian and international markets, increased in importance. Gradually agriculture shifted from a predominantly subsistence to market-orientated activities. The main products of this period were coffee, corn, sugar, tobacco, cotton, rice, manioc and beans.[66]

Coffee spread into the Mata and the South zones, where it adapted very well to the soil and the climate. It became an important *mineiro* item of trade for the first time in 1819 when more than 95 per cent of the output was produced in Matias Barbosa, a district situated in the Mata zone close to Juiz de Fora.[67] In 1842–3, coffee was the third largest *mineiro* item of trade by value,[68] and from the 1850s onwards, it became the main item of trade.[69] In the 1860s, the construction of the União e Indústria turnpike, and later of the D. Pedro II railway (EFDPII), helped to open up new areas for coffee, guaranteeing the expansion of production.[70]

Nevertheless, coffee production was not very representative of the economic life of Minas Gerais as a whole. Throughout the Empire (1822–89), coffee production was confined mainly to a relatively small part of the Mata zone close to the border with the province of Rio de Janeiro. Until the early 1870s, the *mineiro* coffee economy employed less than 15 per cent of the non-slave population, and only a quarter of the slave population. Furthermore, the area covered by coffee plantation represented less than 4 per cent of the territory of the province. In the 1880s the South zone became a coffee-growing area, but it was only after the disorganization of coffee production in the Mata zone as a result of the abolition of slavery in 1888 that coffee production in the South zone became important. More representative of the *mineiro* economic life was the production of non-coffee products in the huge area outside the coffee-growing area where the majority of the slave and non-slave population lived.[71]

Cattle-raising, for example, was the second traditional economic activity in Minas Gerais, and was well-adapted to extensive ranching specially in the northern part and in the Triângulo zone.[72] After the decay of the eighteenth-century gold economy, cattle-raising became the most important economic activity in Minas Gerais until the 1840s when it was surpassed by coffee-growing.[73] From then onwards, beef on the hoof, meat and animal products were the second largest item of trade of the province.[74]

As mentioned above, until the end of the eighteenth century the establishment of industries was prohibited by the Portuguese colonial government. When the Portuguese crown was transferred to Brazil in 1808 this legal impediment was revoked. However, obstacles of a different nature then became obvious, such as lack of capital and credit, lack of suitable means of transport, small and scattered markets, and lack of a large and reliable workforce. These factors hindered the industrial development of Minas Gerais.[75] Nevertheless, a few industrial sectors such as mining, iron-working, textiles and food industries did develop during the nineteenth century, and were concentrated mostly in the developed southern half of Minas Gerais.[76]

Although the gold-mining boom was over at the beginning of the last century, hopes of new discoveries persisted. During the first decades of the nineteenth century the primitive and disordered gold-mining activity of the end of the eighteenth century was replaced by foreign mining companies using 'state of the art' technology. Some of these foreign companies, such as the British-owned Saint John Del Rey Mining Company and the Imperial Brazilian Mining Association, became large-scale enterprises.[77] The former, which exploited the mine at Morro Velho, was the largest single industrial employer in Minas Gerais until the 1930s and the only one to survive among the nine Brazilian and foreign-owned gold-mining companies active in 1900. Furthermore, prospecting for diamonds and semiprecious stones still provided a precarious livelihood for a few thousand people.[78]

The isolation of Minas Gerais and the high price of imports allowed the *mineiro* iron industry to develop numerically and geographically for six decades after the 1820s. Initially, changes in the process of gold-mining boosted the industrial production of iron, and underground gold mines constituting important consumers of iron goods during this period. Later on, the consumer market for iron products grew and the agricultural sector and muletrains became important consumers. In the 1880s, the industry suffered two lethal blows: the end of its geographical isolation with the arrival of the railway in the central part of Minas Gerais, and the abolition of slavery; the latter depriving the small foundries of their major competitive advantage against foreign competition.[79] With the proclamation of the Republic, the small foundries disappeared and a few major ironworks were built but with little success. Minas was doomed to await until the 1930s when iron and steel products led the second *mineiro* industrial boom and several chaorcoal-based steel plants began production.[80]

The first sustained industrial upsurge in Minas Gerais began with the establishment of the textile industry.[81] However, the development of this industry was preceded in the first half of the last century by a flourishing domestic textile production, a legacy of colonial times.[82] It was only in the 1870s that the first successful textile mills began to emerge in response to a set of favourable conditions: expanding local markets, exchange devaluations, cheap raw materials, high import tariffs and high freight rates.[83] The *mineiro* textile industry grew rapidly until the late 1920s; in 1907 it was the largest industrial sector, contributing 40.2 per cent of the total value of industrial production and accounting for 62.9 per cent of capital invested in *mineiro* industry, and employing 50 per cent of the *mineiro* industrial workforce.[84]

In 1907 the food industry was the second largest industrial sector, accounting for 32.6 per cent of the value of industrial production, 18.9 per cent of the capital invested in the *mineiro* industry, and 17.3 per cent of the *mineiro* industrial workforce. Nevertheless, the industry was made up of small factories employing on average six people.[85]

Another important economic sector in nineteenth-century Minas Gerais was transport. In the late 1850s, the Companhia União e Indústria built 144 kilometres of carriageway linking the southern part of Minas Gerais to the province of Rio de Janeiro. The construction of the turnpike pre-dated railways, and it was a time when the bulk of the transport of people and goods was made on the back of animals.[86] During this period, Juiz de Fora grew and became a large coffee entrepôt in Minas Gerais.[87]

The first phase of railway construction in Minas Gerais began in the 1870s. In 1869 the EFDPII (later Central do Brasil) reached the Mata zone, and in the late 1880s arrived in the central part of the province.[88] Several other small lines were built during this period in the Mata zone. All these early railways received concessions (guaranteed interest payments on invested capital) from the provincial and Imperial governments, and several were built by coffee planters either by themselves or in conjunction with British capitalists. Between 1875 and 1899, a total of 3500 kilometres of track was laid in Minas Gerais, most of it in the south. Nevertheless, by the late 1890s several of these private lines were taken over by the government, as coffee prices declined and could no longer support the high freight rates these railways needed to work profitably. Later, 21 railways of the Mata zone were incorporated into the British-owned Leopoldina system. From 1900 onwards, the federal government dominated railway construction until the 1920s when the state government became actively involved.[89]

It is important to point out that despite all of its economic transformation during the nineteenth century, Minas Gerais at the end of this period continued to be divided into disarticulated and autonomous sub-regions, each having developed in a different way with particular histories and specific problems.[90] In the 1880s the Triângulo became a modern agro-pastoral economy. In contrast the northern region, with the exception of a diamond rush which was over by 1830, followed the tracks of a seventeenth-century ranching economy and its cities stagnated on the margins of vast latifundia until the arrival of the railway at the beginning of the twentieth century. The cattle trade was the main activity of the western region whose towns had been linked by ancient cattle trails and later by railways. The Mata and South zones developed a coffee-based agriculture, which financed their mid-nineteenth-century rise. After the proclamation of the Republic these two zones became the most important regions in terms of wealth, population and political power. Throughout the nineteenth century the central part of Minas lost ground to both the Mata and the South zones. The long decline of the central region only came to an end in the 1920s, when the growth of consumer industries, banks and commerce gave the new political capital (Belo Horizonte) an economic base.[91]

Compared with the southern half, the backward north – with the exception of the Triângulo zone – lagged behind in towns and transport. The south had a well-articulated network of towns and transport routes which were created mainly during the great coffee boom and railway-construction phase in 1850–1900. With a large population and a good transport system, the Mata and the South were the most urbanized zones of Minas Gerais. Nevertheless, most *mineiros* lived in isolated rural areas. In 1920, only 11 per cent of the *mineiro* population lived in urban centres: if cities smaller than 5000 are left out, the urban population was only 5 per cent.[92]

Thus, during the nineteenth century the *mineiro* economy was transformed into an agro-pastoral economy following the decay of the eighteenth-century gold-mining economy. In the 1830s, the gold-mining industry became dominated by foreign-owned large-scale enterprises exploring underground mines. Until the coffee boom of the middle of the last century, cattle-raising was the main economic activity in Minas Gerais. From the 1850s onwards, coffee became the main *mineiro* item of trade. Nevertheless, the coffee economy was restricted to the southern part of the province, adjoining Rio de Janeiro, and its impact on the *mineiro* economy as a whole was not comparable to that of the coffee economy in São Paulo. In the last quarter of the century the first industries began to emerge, mainly the textile industry which was the largest industrial sector until the 1920s, just as in the rest of Brazil. It was during this period also that the first phase of railway construction took place. Nevertheless, nineteenth-century Minas Gerais was sharply divided into two halves: the developed south and the backward north. The central part was the seat of the provincial – and later the state – government, but exerted very little influence over the rest of Minas Gerais. Most of the other sub-regions were more closely linked, economically and culturally, to São Paulo, Rio de Janeiro, or Bahia.

2 The Entrepreneur

INTRODUCTION

This chapter examines the debate about the entrepreneur in the Brazilian economic historiography. It aims at challenging the widely accepted view that the *paulista* and, to a lesser extent, *carioca** experiences can be applied to other parts of Brazil. The work compares the social background and origin of the capital of *mineiro*, *carioca*, and *paulista* entrepreneurs in nineteenth-century Brazil. The analysis of the *mineiro* entrepreneur reveals that, in contrast with their counterparts in São Paulo and Rio de Janeiro, they were mainly recruited from the local élite constituted basically by Brazilians. Furthermore, although the sources of capital (mainly agriculture and trade) used by *mineiro* entrepreneurs were not very distinct from those used by their *paulista* and *carioca* counterparts, they differed in their nature with coffee and import–export activities playing a smaller role.

A BRIEF REVIEW OF THE LITERATURE

Drawing on the Brazilian economic historiography, this section considers the debates about the emergence of the Brazilian entrepreneurial class and the origins of the industrial entrepreneuriat as a prelude to an analysis of the formation of the *mineiro* entrepreneurial class.

The Brazilian economy in the late eighteenth century was overwhelmingly agricultural and pastoral and, moreover, export-oriented. To speak of entrepreneurs at that time is to speak of *senhores de engenho* (sugar planters and mill-owners) and other plantation owners. During the colonial period there was a clear distinction between the rural aristocracy, most of whom were Brazilians, and merchants, most of whom were foreigners.[1] With the development of the coffee economy in the early 1820s, a new entrepreneurial class

---

Carioca relates to the people or things belonging to Rio de Janeiro.

21

destined to play an important role in the future economic development of the country began to emerge. This new class was initially made up of local entrepreneurs who had accumulated some capital in commercial activities – mainly provisioning the city of Rio de Janeiro which was the main Brazilian consumer market – and who later turned towards coffee production.[2]

Comparing the processes of the formation of the ruling classes in the sugar and coffee economies some fundamental differences can be pointed out. When the ruling class of the sugar economy was formed, commercial activities were controlled by groups established either in Portugal or in the Low Countries. The men in charge of production lacked any perspective of the sugar economy as a whole, as the production and commercial phases were separated.[3] The formation of the coffee economy occurred under quite different conditions. From the beginning the ruling class was composed of men with business experience, as mentioned above, and production and trading interests were interrelated. The new coffee-entrepreneurial class was thus formed through a struggle for land, for labour supply, for internal means of transport, for marketing at the ports, for official contacts, and for financial and economic policies. These entrepreneurs indeed took advantage of their proximity to the capital of the country and soon took control of the government. But what particularly differentiates them from the other pre-existing dominant groups is the fact that they had a clear concept of their own interests and utilized that control to attain their objectives.[4]

However, during the first half of the nineteenth century no significant industrial class emerged. Although Rio de Janeiro and other Brazilian cities were full of establishments making soap, candles, cotton thread, clothing, hats, snuff, cigars, furniture and ironware, the textile and food-processing industries which were to form the basis of Brazil's early industrial growth did not appear until after 1840. Indeed there was no significant industrial growth until the 1870s. Furthermore, there is some controversy over the debate about the social and economic origins of the *paulista* industrial entrepreneurial class. Two main approaches may be identified in this debate. The first, the 'bourgeois immigrant' approach,[5] which argues that in the promotion of industrial-ization in São Paulo the most important role was played by importers and immigrants, or the so- called bourgeois immigrant. The second, the 'latecomer capitalism' approach,[6] which argues that in São Paulo coffee-planters constituted the social group from which emerged the industrial bour-geoisie.

To sum up, according to the Brazilian economic historio-graphy the modern Brazilian capitalist entrepreneur emerged only in the second decade of the last century with the expansion of the coffee economy, first in the Paraíba valley and then in western São Paulo. This coffee-entrepre-neurial class established the economic and social basis for the emergence of a further stage of capitalist development in Brazil. Industrialization was promoted by both the so-called bourgeois immigrant and coffee planters. However, most of what has been written so far about the social and economic origins of the Brazilian entrepreneuriat has been based mainly on evidence of the experience of São Paulo and, to a lesser extent, Rio de Janeiro. Nevertheless, there is evidence suggesting that the pattern of entrepreneurial development in other parts of Brazil, like Minas Gerais, was somewhat different.

THE *MINEIRO* ENTREPRENEUR

An important aspect in the study of the entrepreneur is the question of their availability. While classic economic theory devotes much attention to factor availability, it does not con-sider the supply of entrepreneurial talent. The general view is that there will be an ample supply of entrepreneurs as long as there is a suitable legal framework, a free market and free-dom of enterprise. Generally speaking, however, the supply of new entrepreneurs is influenced by the groups from which they come, by general social influences and attitudes towards entrepreneurship, and by economic considerations.

In many societies the pool of entrepreneurial talent is composed of the families, the associates and – occasionally – the workers of existing entrepreneurs. In less-developed countries a large proportion of early industrial and commercial entrepreneurs were drawn from the rural sector. Possibly this was due to the farming traditions of independence and self-sufficiency handed down from generation to generation. Often the children of farmers could count on financial support when setting-up in business, as the case of the Mascarenhas family to be described later illustrates so well. Also, small early manufacturing enterprises were often established in the countryside.[7]

The general social attitude towards entrepreneurship is another major influence on the supply of entrepreneurs. Social influences that derive from the educational system, literature and arts in general, religion and politics affect the supply of entrepreneurs. Weber, for example, explored the influence of religion on the general attitude towards entrepreneurship in Western Europe. On the economic side, institutions, laws or regulations which affect opportunities for entrepreneurs can also be regarded as having an effect on the supply of entrepreneurship. The availability of means of transport or the willingness of financial institutions to provide funds to new or aspiring entrepreneurs are obviously significant.[8]

In this section we examine the social, ethnic and economic origins of nineteenth-century *mineiro* entrepreneur. It compares the main social and economic influences on the process of the formation of the *mineiro* and the Brazilian entrepreneurial classes. First we investigate the social and ethnic background of the *mineiro* entrepreneur, with a focus on an analysis of the social groups from which the *mineiro* entrepreneurs emerged. We then examine the main economic influences on the formation of the *mineiro* entrepreneurial class, in other words the main sources of capital available to would-be entrepreneurs.

Social Background

In considering the social and ethnic origins of entrepreneurs, we focus on the entrepreneurial formation in the main coffee-growing and non-coffee-growing regions of Minas Gerais (mainly the southern and central parts respectively), and on four different economic sectors – iron, transport, textiles and electricity generating industries.

As shown above, the social group constituted by importers and immigrants, the so-called bourgeois immigrant, had a large influence on the formation of the *paulista* entrepreneurial class.[9] The importance of immigrants is also widely acknowledged, even in the case of the primitive Brazilian entrepreneurial class.[10] Regarding the formation of the *mineiro* entrepreneurial class, the participation of immigrants was much more limited. Immigrants had a small but relevant participation in the establishment of the *mineiro* iron industry and had a large participation in the entrepreneurial class of the Mata zone, a major coffee-growing area, but elsewhere immigrants are hardly observed.

In the iron sector, foreign entrepreneurs were important during the first three-quarters of the last century. Two of the most successful foundries during this period were established by foreigners. The Patriótica foundry was set up by Eschwege, a German engineer, who came to Minas Gerais in 1811 with the permission of the Portuguese Prince D. João IV for whom he had previously worked in the Figueiró dos Vinhos foundry in Portugal. He was reckoned to be a man of great knowledge, having written extensively about natural sciences.[11] Thus, it is reasonable to conclude that he had a more elaborated background and can be classified as a bourgeois immigrant, as defined by Dean.[12] The São Miguel de Piracicaba foundry was founded by Monlevade, a French engineer who came to Brazil in 1817.[13] Other foundries, smaller and less important, were also established by foreigners.[14] Furthermore, foreigners and their descendants participated in the establishment of the larger foundries which began to dominate the *mineiro* iron industry in the last quarter of the last century. The Esperança foundry was established in 1888 by three Brazilians (Amaro da Silveira, Henrique Hargreaves and Carlos da Costa Wigg) and a Swiss metallurgist (Alberto Gerspacher). Later José Gerspacher (son of Alberto Gerspacher, who operated both mills) and Carlos da Costa Wigg established the Burnier foundry in 1892.[15]

Thus, foreign entrepreneurs had a small but relevant participation in the establishment of the *mineiro* iron industry. This seems due to the technological know-how that these foreigners possessed, which was not available in the form of machinery as was the case for the textile industry.[16] Nevertheless, from the evidence presented above and bearing in mind that the estimated number of foundries in Minas Gerais during the period 1821–93 was never smaller than 30,[17] it is clear that most of the foundries belonged to Brazilians.

The participation of immigrants was much larger within the entrepreneurial class of the Mata zone. Here it is widely accepted that foreign residents played a key role in the process of industrialization.[18] The flow of immigrants to the region began in the 1850s with the establishment of an immigrant colony by the Companhia União e Indústria (CUI). Most of the immigrants were Germans, who were later responsible for the first industrial upsurge of Juiz de Fora. In the late 1880s a large number of Italians arrived in Juiz de Fora, several of whom subsequently established tanneries and factories making hats, shoes, furniture and so on.[19]

Moreover, as shown in Table 2.1, immigrants owned more than 66 per cent of the total number of industries established in Juiz de Fora during the period 1858–1912, which seems to corroborate Lydall's view – presented above – that immigrants are one of the major sources of new entrepreneurs.[20] German immigrants were particularly well represented and owned the largest number of the industrial establishments (43 per cent). Furthermore, it is important to point out that although nearly half of the Germans who came to Juiz de Fora were Catholics, those who became industrialists during the period 1858–1912 were mainly Protestants.[21] This seems to corroborate Weber's theory of the influence of the

Table 2.1 Juiz de Fora: nationality of factory owners, 1858–1912

Origin	No. of establishments	%
Germans	28	43.1
Brazilians	19	29.3
Italians	14	21.5
English	01	1.5
Other	02	3.1
No information available	01	1.5
Total	65	100.0

Source: Adapted from L.A.V. Arantes, 'As Origens da Burguesia Industrial em Juiz de Fora, 1858/1912', Universidade Federal Fluminense, unpublished M.Sc. thesis, Niteroi, 1991, p. 160.

Protestant ethic on the formation of the spirit of capitalism. The figures presented in Table 2.1 provide undisputable evidence of the importance of immigrants in the formation of the entrepreneurial class of the Mata zone, especially in the city of Juiz de Fora. Furthermore, contrary to what some authors observed in São Paulo,[22] the immigrant who became an industrialist in Juiz de Fora usually did not fit into the 'bourgeois immigrant' concept, most had initially come to Brazil to work as labourers, craftsmen or farm hands and were attracted by the prospect of owning a piece of land.[23]

Despite the importance of immigrants in the establishment of the iron industry and in the formation of the entrepreneurial class of the Mata zone, the *mineiro* entrepreneurial class was nevertheless largely constituted by Brazilians, even in the Mata zone. As shown in Table 2.1, Brazilians were responsible for the establishment of nearly a third of the industries founded in Juiz de Fora in the period 1858–1912. Brazilian industrialists not connected with the coffee economy owned just over 26 per cent of the total number of industries, and Brazilian farmers had a small participation owning just over 3 per cent of the industries established in Juiz de Fora.[24]

One of the most important enterprises set up by farmers of the Mata zone was the Companhia União e Indústria (CUI). The company was established by Mariano Procópio Ferreira Lage, a farmer born in Barbacena, and several other farmers of the region,[25] as illustrated by the following remark made in the company report of 1857:

> I would like to acknowledge the services rendered to the company by two of its shareholders... They are the Commendador José Antonio da Silva Pinto and Lino José Ferreira Armond. The Commendador José A. da Silva Pinto has advanced large amounts of money to the Company...- has hired out to the company more than a hundred slaves from his own stock, who are working on the construction of the turnpike between Mathias and the bridge over the Parahybuna river. Moreover, he has suffered several losses caused by the construction of the section which passes through his farm, destroying stables, etc., and has refused any kind of indemnification.[26]

Thus, it seems that the CUI was established by local farmers interested in improving the means of transport for their production, as was the case with several of the first railways in the province of São Paulo.[27]

The textile industry, which was mostly concentrated in the central part of Minas Gerais, was established almost exclusively by Brazilian entrepreneurs drawn from a few families or a small circle of friends. As shown in Table 2.2, the mills founded during the 1870s were established by local entrepreneurs. The Cedro mill, for example, was founded in 1872 by three brothers – Antônio Cândido, Caetano, and Bernardo Mascarenhas – born in Taboleiro Grande, Minas Gerais.[28] During the same year, Franciso José de Andrade Botelho, born in Carrancas, Minas Gerais, set up the Brumado mill.[29]

Table 2.2 Minas Gerais: nationality of the main promoters and shareholders of the textile mills established in the 1870s

Mill	Main promoters and shareholders	Nationality
Cedro	Antônio Cândido Mascarenhas	Brazilian
	Caetano Mascarenhas	Brazilian
	Bernardo Mascarenhas	Brazilian
Brumado	Franciso José de Andrade Botelho	Brazilian
SAIM	Azarias de Souza Dias	Brazilian
Biribiry	Santos family	Brazilian
Cachoeira	Pacífico Mascarenhas	Brazilian
	Victor Mascarenhas	Brazilian
	Francisco Mascarenhas	Brazilian
	Luis Augusto Vianna Barbosa	Brazilian
União Itabirana	Information not available	n.a.

Note: (n.a) information not available.

Sources: Compiled from P. Tamm, *Uma Dinastia de Tecelões*, 2nd edn, (Belo Horizonte, 1960), pp. 64–9; G. Guimarães, *Francisco José de Andrade Botelho* (Belo Horizonte, 1950), p. 14; M.L.P. Costa, *A Fábrica de Tecidos de Machado, 1871–1917* (Belo Horizonte, 1989), p. 25; M.T.R.O. Versiani, 'The Cotton Textile Industry of Minas Gerais, Brazil: Beginnings and Early Development, 1868–1906', University of London, unpublished Ph.D. thesis, 1991, pp. 50–1; G.M. Mascarenhas, *Centenário da Fábrica do Cedro, 1872–1972* (Belo Horizonte, 1972), pp. 93–118; S.J. Stein, *Origens e Evolução da Indústria Têxtil no Brasil, 1850–1950* (Rio de Janeiro, 1950), p. 216.

The Sociedade Anônima Industrial Machadense (SAIM) was organized in 1875 by 24 people, most of whom were local businessmen. Among them, Azarias de Souza Dias, the main promoter and shareholder, was born in Santo Antônio do Machado, Minas Gerais.[30] The Biribiry mill was established in 1876 by the bishop of Diamantina, Minas Gerais, João Antônio dos Santos, two of his brothers (Antônio Felício, and Joaquim Felício dos Santos), his nephew and another partner.[31] The Cachoeira mill was founded in 1877 by three other brothers of the founders of the Cedro mill (Pacífico, Victor, and Francisco de Paula Mascarenhas), who were also born in Taboleiro Grande, and one of their brothers-in-law (Luiz Augusto Vianna Barbosa) born in Matozinhos, Minas Gerais.[32] There is evidence that the União Itabirana mill, founded in 1876, was organized and financed by local people. A report of the Comissão Parlamentar de Inquérito observed that the União Itabirana mill had this name owing to the fact that most of its shareholders came from the city of Itabira, Minas Gerais.[33]

As shown in Table 2.3, during the 1880s textile mills continued to be founded by Brazilians, mainly local entrepreneurs. In 1880, the Filatório Montes Claros was established by a small group of locals connected by ties of kinship and friendship. The major shareholders were two brothers, Manoel and Donato Rodrigues from Grão Mogol, Antônio Narciso Soares born in Bocaiúva, Gregório Velloso from Montes Claros itself, and Angelo de Quadros Bittencourt born in the province of Bahia.[34] There is no information about the founders of the Marzagão mill established in Sabará in 1880.[35] Similarly, there is no information about the date when the Cassú mill was established nor about its founders, but given the name of the company, Borges, Irmãos & Co., it is reasonable to believe that the mill belonged to Brazilians.[36] The same can be said about the owners of the Bom Jardim mill, established in 1883 by the partnership Pereira Murta & Co.,[37] and about the owners of the Viçosa mill, established in Viçosa by Mello & Reis Company.[38]

The São Sebastião mill was established in 1884 by Antônio Gonçalves da Silva Mascarenhas, father of the Mascarenhas brothers, founders of the Cedro and the Cachoeira mills, who was born in Curral d'El Rey in Minas Gerais.[39] Very little is known about the founders of the São Vicente mill established

Table 2.3 Minas Gerais: nationality of the main promoters and shareholders of the textile mills established in the 1880s

Mill	Main promoters and shareholders	Nationality
Cassú	Borges, Irmãos & Co.	n.a.
Marzagão	Companhia Industrial Sabarense	n.a.
Filatório Montes	Manoel Rodrigues	Brazilian
Claros	Donato Rodrigues	Brazilian
	Antônio Narciso Soares	Brazilian
	Angelo de Quadros Bittencourt	Brazilian
	Gregório Velloso	Brazilian
Bom Jardim	Pereira Murta & Co.	n.a.
São Sebastião	Antônio Gonçalves da Silva Mascarenhas	Brazilian
Viçosa	Mello & Reis Co.	n.a.
Industrial Mineira	Andrew Steele	English
	John Steele	English
	Peter Steele	English
	William Moreth	English
	Henry Whittaker	English
São Vicente	Information not available	n.a.
União Lavrense	Information not available	n.a.
Cachoeira dos Macacos	João da Matta Teixeira	Brazilian
	Jeronymo Francisco França	Brazilian
	Américo Teixeira Guimarães	Brazilian
Santa Bárbara	Pedro da Matta Machado	Brazilian
	Augusto da Matta Machado	Brazilian
	Francisco F. Corrêa Rabelo	Brazilian
	Pedro José Verciani	Brazilian
	João Antônio L. de Figueiredo	Brazilian
	Antônio Moreira da Costa	Brazilian
Paulo Moreirense	Information not available	n.a.
Mascarenhas	Bernardo Mascarenhas	Brazilian
Pedreira	Information not available	n.a.
São Roberto	Quintiliano Alves Ferreira	Brazilian
Industrial Ouro Preto	Information not available	n.a.

Note: (n.a.) information not available.
Sources: Compiled from Versiani, *op.cit.*, pp. 75–92; Tamm, *op.cit.*, p. 25; A.M. Vaz, *Cia. Cedro e Cachoeira: História de uma Empresa Familiar, 1883–1987* (Belo Horizonte, 1990), pp. 102–3; N.A.M. Freitas, 'Cia. Têxtil Cachoeira dos Macacos: Empresa que deu Origem a uma Cidade', Fundação Mineira de Arte Aleijadinho/Escola Superior de Artes Plásticas, mimeo., Belo Horizonte, 1990, p. 17; N.L. Mascarenhas, *Bernardo Mascarenhas: o Surto Industrial de Minas Gerais* (Rio de Janeiro, 1954), pp. 123–5.

in 1885 in Pau Grosso. However, shortly after its establishment the mill was acquired by the Companhia Cedro e Cachoeira (CCC), founded by the Mascarenhas family.[40] The Companhia Cachoeira de Macacos (CCM) was established in 1886 by a group of locals brought together by Américo Teixeira Guimarães.[41] He was born in Inhaúma, Minas Gerais, and was the son of the main shareholder, João da Matta Teixeira.[42] Little information is available about the União Lavrense mill, apart from the fact that it was established in 1886. Nevertheless, there is evidence that most of its first shareholders lived in the city of Rio de Janeiro – there was pressure to transfer the headquarters of the company from Lavras to Rio de Janeiro.[43]

The founders of the Santa Bárbara mill, established in 1886, were a small and local group of friends and relatives born in the county of Diamantina where the mill was set up, namely, the three brothers Alvaro, Pedro and Augusto da Matta Machado, their brothers-in-law Francisco Ferreira Corrêa Rabelo, Pedro José Verciani, and João Antônio Lopes de Figueiredo, and Antônio Moreira da Costa.[44] There is no information about the founders of the Paulo Moreirense mill, established in 1887, nor about the founders of the Pedreira mill, founded in 1888.[45] The Tecelagem Mascarenhas mill was organized in 1888 in Juiz de Fora by Bernardo Mascarenhas, who was born in Taboleiro Grande, as mentioned above.[46]

The São Roberto mill was founded in 1888 by Quintiliano Alves Ferreira, the Baron of São Roberto, who was a local businessman.[47] Although there is little information about the establishment of the Industrial Ouro Preto mill, it seems that the mill was set up by capitalists from Rio de Janeiro.[48] The Industrial Mineira mill was one of the few textile mills established by foreigners during the 1880s: it was established in Juiz de Fora in 1884 by Englishmen – Andrew Steele, John Steele, Peter Steele, William Moreth and Henry Whittaker.[49] It is interesting to point out that with the exception of the Industrial Mineira mill, the SAIM and the Tecelagem Mascarenhas mill, all of the firms set up before the end of the 1880s were established in non-coffee-growing areas.

Most of the textile mills organized during the 1890s were also founded by Brazilians, as shown in Table 2.4. The Companhia de Tecidos Santanense (CTS) was set up in Santana do

Table 2.4 Minas Gerais: nationality of the main promoters and
shareholders of the textile mills established in the 1890s

Mill	Main promoters and shareholders	Nationality
Santanense	Manoel José de Souza Moreira	Brazilian
	Manoel Gonçalves de Souza Moreira	Brazilian
	Augusto Gonçalves de S. Moreira	Brazilian
	Antônio Pereira de Mattos	Brazilian
São Joanense	Antônio Moreira da Costa Rodrigues	n.a.
Itabira do Campo	Information not available	n.a.
Pitanguense	Luiz Augusto Barbosa	Brazilian
	Francisco Bahia da Rocha	n.a
	Sérgio Mascarenhas Barbosa	Brazilian
	Antônio Mascarenhas	Brazilian
Cachoeira Grande	Anônio Ferreira Alves da Silva	Brazilian
	João da Matta Teixeira	Brazilian
	Américo Teixeira Guimaraes	Brazilian
	Herculino França	Brazilian
Progresso Fabril	Carlos Vaz de Mello	Brazilian
Melancias	Jeronymo Francisco França	Brazilian
	João da Matta Teixeira	Brazilian
	Theophilo Marques Ferreira	Brazilian
São Domingos	Moreira Penna family	Brazilians
São João Nepomuceno	Daniel de Moraes Sarmento Junior	Brazilian
Jequitahy	Information not available	n.a.
Perpetua	Information not available	n.a.
Itinga	Information not available	n.a.

Note: (n.a.) information not available.

Sources: Compiled from M.A.G. Souza, *História de Itaúna*, I (Belo Horizonte, 1986), pp. 101–94; Versiani, *op.cit.*, pp. 128–243; G.M. Mascarenhas, *op.cit.*, p. 118; Tamm, *op.cit.*, p. 87; Companhia Industrial Pitanguense, 'Lista Nominativa dos Srs. Subscritores' (1894), in *Minas Gerais*, 5 January 1894, p. 7; Companhia Industrial Pitanguense, 'Estatutos' (1893) in *Minas Gerais*, 5 January 1894, pp. 7–8; Companhia Industrial Pitanguense, 'Ata da Assemblea Geral Institutiva' (1893) in *Minas Gerais*, 5 January 1894, p. 7; Companhia Progresso Fabril, 'Ata da Sessão da Assembléa Geral dos Accionistas para a Constituição da mesma Companhia' (1893), in *Minas Gerais*, 23 May 1893, pp. 6–8; Companhia Industrial São Domingos, 'Ata da Assembléa de Instalação' (1894), in *Minas Gerais*, 21 February 1894, p. 7; and Companhia Industrial São Domingos, 'Lista dos Acionistas' (1894), in *Minas Gerais*, 21 February 1894, p. 7.

São João Acima in 1891 by members of the Souza Moreira
family: Manoel José de Souza Moreira born in Bonfim, Minas

Gerais; his sons, Manoel Gonçalves de Souza Moreira and Augusto Gonçalves de Souza Moreira, born in Santana do São João Acima; and his son-in-law, Antônio Pereira de Mattos, born in Campos, Rio de Janeiro.[50] The São Joanense mill was established in 1891 by Antônio Moreira da Costa Rodrigues, of whom there is no information about his place of birth.[51] The Companhia Industrial Pitanguense which bought, enlarged and improved the Brumado mill was founded in 1893.[52] Its major shareholders were Luiz Augusto Vianna Barbosa, Francisco Bahia da Rocha, Sérgio Mascarenhas Barbosa and Antônio Mascarenhas Barbosa respectively.[53] Sérgio Mascarenhas Barbosa and Antônio Mascarenhas Barbosa were sons of Luiz Augusto Vianna Barbosa[54] and Custódia Mascarenhas, one of the sisters of the Mascarenhas brothers.[55] There is no information about the place of birth of Francisco Bahia da Rocha. However, one of his sons, who had the same name, was a minor shareholder in the CCC and had been manager of the São Vicente mill from 1894 to 1899.[56]

The Cachoeira Grande mill was established by Antônio Ferreira Alves da Silva, a farmer from Minas Gerais, associated with João da Matta Teixeira, Américo Teixeira Guimarães and Herculino França, all three shareholders of the CCM.[57] The promoter and major shareholder of the Companhia Progresso Fabril, established in 1893, was Carlos Vaz de Mello, a politician from Viçosa, Minas Gerais.[58] The Melancias mill was established by a group of *mineiro* investors who were already associated with other textile undertakings in Minas Gerais: Jeronymo Francisco França, João da Matta Teixeira – both of whom were directors of the CCM at the time of the establishment of the Melancias mill – and Theóphilo Marques Ferreira who was born in Lagoa Santa, Minas Gerais.[59] The São Domingos mill was founded in 1894 in Santa Bárbara by local people,[60] and four of the seven original shareholders belonged to the Moreira Penna family.[61] One of the members of the Moreira Penna family was Affonso Augusto Moreira Penna, who was one of the largest shareholders of the mill and Governor of Minas Gerais at this time.[62] The major shareholder of the Companhia de Tecidos Mineiros São João Nepomuceno, organized in 1894, was Daniel de Moraes Sarmento Junior, who also belonged to a local family, the Moraes Sarmentos.[63] There is no information available about the founders of the Itabira do Campo, the Jequitahy, the Perpetua and the Itinga mills.[64]

Hence, as evidence presented above has shown, most of the owners/shareholders of textile firms in nineteenth-century Minas Gerais were locals with strong ties of kinship and friendship. This is hardly surprising since, as Lydall has observed, in many societies families and associates are the main sources of entrepreneurial talents.[65]

Comparison between the nationality of the main promoters and shareholders of textile firms established in Rio de Janeiro and Minas Gerais illustrates very well the ethnic differences between the *mineiro* entrepreneur and his *carioca* counterpart. Most of the textile mills established during the period 1878–95 in the city of Rio de Janeiro were founded by foreigners. As shown in Table 2.5, the Fábrica de Tecidos São Lázaro (FTSL) was founded in 1877 by José Maria Teixeira de Azevedo, a Portuguese.[66] The Fábrica de Tecidos Pau Grande (FTPG) was founded in 1878 by Antônio Felício dos Santos born in Diamantina Minas Gerais, José Rodrigues Peixoto from Rio de Janeiro, and John Sherrington an Englishman.[67] The Fábrica de Tecidos do Rink (FTR) was founded in 1879 by Frederico Glette, a German.[68] The Fábrica de Fiação, Tecidos e Tinturaria Alliança (FFTTA) was founded in 1880 by José Augusto Laranja, Joaquim Carvalho de Oliveira e Silva, both of them Portuguese, and Henry Whittaker, an Englishman.[69] The Fábrica de Fiação, Tecidos e Tinturaria Bomfim (FFTTB) was probably founded in 1882 by Joaquim Marques da Costa, a Portuguese.[70]

The Fábrica de Fiação e Tecelagem Carioca (FFTC) was founded in 1884. The main promoters of the mill were three Englishmen Peter Steele, Henry Whittaker and George Holden.[71] The Fábrica de Tecidos São João (FTSJ) was probably founded in 1886 by Englishmen John Valentine Hall, James Grainger Bellamy and John Henry Lowndes.[72] The Fábrica de Tecidos de São Christóvão (FTSC) was founded in 1888 by two Brazilians, Frederico Pinheiro da Silva and José da Cunha Ferreira, and an Englishman John Henry Lowndes.[73] The Companhia de Fiação e Tecidos Confiança Industrial (CFTCI) was founded in 1885 by two Portuguese, Manoel Salgado Zenha and João José dos Reis, and Francisco Tavares Bastos, of whom there is no information about his

Table 2.5   The city of Rio de Janeiro: nationality of the main promoters of
the textile companies established in the period 1878–95

Company	Main Promoters	Nationality
FTSL	José Maria Teixeira de Azevedo	Portuguese
FTPG	Antônio Felício dos Santos	Brazilian
	José Rodrigues Peixoto	Brazilian
	John Sherrington	English
FTR	Frederico Glette	German
FFTTA	José Augusto Laranja	Portuguese
	Joaquim C. de Oliveira e Silva	Portuguese
	Henry Whittaker	English
FFTTB	Joaquim Marques da Costa	Portuguese
FFTC	Peter Steele	English
	Henry Whittaker	English
	George Holden	English
FTSJ	John Valentine Hall	English
	James Grainger Bellamy	English
	John Henry Lowndes	English
FTSC	Frederico Pinheiro da Silva	Brazilian
	John Henry Lowndes	English
	José da Cunha Ferreira	Brazilian
CFTCI	Manoel Salgado Zenha	Portuguese
	Francisco Tavares Bastos	n.a.
	João José dos Reis	Portuguese
CPIB	Banco Rural e Hypotecário	
	Banco Internacional do Brasil	
CFTC	Viscount of Figueiredo	Brazilian
	Cândido da Cunha Sotto Maior	Portuguese
CFTSF	Affonso de Lamare	n.a.

Notes: FTR – Fábrica de Tecidos do Rink; CFTC – Companhia de Fiação e
Tecidos Corcovado; CPIB – Companhia Progresso Industrial do Brasil;
FFTC – Fábrica de Fiação e Tecelagem Carioca; FTPG – Fábrica de Tecidos
Pau Grande; FTSC – Fábrica de Tecidos de São Christóvao; FTSJ – Fábrica
de Tecidos São João; FTSL – Fábrica de Tecidos São Lázaro; CFTCI –
Companhia de Fiação e Tecidos Confiança Industrial; CFTSF – Companhia
de Fiação e Tecidos São Félix; FFTTA – Fábrica de Fiação, Tecidos e
Tinturaria Alliança; FFTTB – Fábrica de Fiação, Tecidos e Tinturaria
Bomfim. (n.a.) information not available.

Source: A.M.F.C. Monteiro, 'Empreendedores e Investidores em Indústria
Têxtil no Rio de Janeiro: 1878–1895', Universidade Federal Fluminense,
unpublished M.Sc. thesis, Niterói, 1985, pp. 98–283.

nationality.[74] The Companhia Progresso Industrial do
Brasil (CPIB) was founded in 1889 by the Banco Rural e

Hypotecário and by the Banco Internacional do Brasil.[75] The Companhia de Fiação e Tecidos Corcovado (CFTC) was founded in 1889 by the Viscount of Figueiredo, a Brazilian, and Cândido da Cunha Sotto Maior, a Portuguese.[76] Finally, the Companhia de Fiação e Tecidos São Félix (CFTSF) was founded in 1891 by Affonso de Lamare, of whom there is no information about his nationality.[77]

A comparison between the nationality of the main promoters and shareholders of the *mineiro* and *carioca* textile industries reveals how different the *mineiro* entrepreneurial class was from that portrayed by the Brazilian economic historiography. Whereas a large number of *carioca* textile entrepreneurs were immigrants, their *mineiro* counterparts were mainly local entrepreneurs. The main reason accounting for this discrepancy was the larger concentration of foreigners in Rio de Janeiro. In the period 1872–1920, for example, foreigners represented no less than 20 per cent of the *carioca* population, while during the same period they represented less than 4 per cent of the *mineiro* population.[78] In addition, foreigners controlled the large sectors of commercial activities of the main urban centres. In the late 1850s, for example, they owned 62 per cent of wholesale textiles in Rio de Janeiro,[79] and they soon dominated the manufacturing activities closed linked to their commercial activities, a process already observed in São Paulo.[80]

The *mineiro* electricity generating industry of the turn of the century was also mostly established by local entrepreneurs. The Companhia Mineira de Eletricidade (CME) was founded by Bernardo Mascarenhas, who was born in Taboleiro Grande, Minas Gerais, as mentioned above. Further evidence that the CME was a family and local affair is found in the following letter written by Bernardo Mascarenhas:

> I am organizing the CME, with a capital of 150:000$000 [contos], divided into shares of 100$000 [miléreis] each – I will keep 500 shares for myself, another 500 will be offered to the inhabitants of the city [Juiz de Fora] and 500 will be distributed within our family to those who want them.[81]

Thus, among the 30 original shareholders, 12 belonged to the Mascarenhas family[82] and several others were prominent names of the local business community.[83] The Companhia

Força e Luz Cataguazes-Leopoldina (CFLCL), in its turn, was established by two Brazilians and one Portuguese: Norberto Custódio Ferreira born in Rio Novo, Rio de Janeiro;[84] José Monteiro Ribeiro Junqueira born in Leopoldina, Minas Gerais;[85] and João Duarte Ferreira born in Coimbra, Portugal, who came to Brazil in 1872.[86]

A review of the origin of entrepreneurs who established the electricity generating industry in the cities of São Paulo and Rio de Janeiro also reveals a sharp difference with Minas Gerais. In the cases of São Paulo and Rio de Janeiro, the first electricity generating companies established at the turn of the century were founded by foreigners. The São Paulo Tramway, Light and Power Company (SPTLPC) was promoted by Francesco Antonio Gualco an Italian businessman, and Frederick Pearson a US engineer and capitalist: the company was founded in 1899.[87] The Rio de Janeiro Tramway, Light and Power Company Ltd (RJTLPC) was promoted by Alexander Mackenzie, who was certainly a foreigner, and founded five years later by a group of Canadian capitalists.[88]

A further important aspect of the social origin of the *mineiro* entrepreneur is that the most prominent entrepreneurs of the nineteenth-century seem to have come from the ruling class and traditional families. Mariano Procópio Ferreira Lage, founder of the CUI, was born into a wealthy and prestigious family from Barbacena. His father, Mariano José Ferreira Armond, also born in Barbacena, was assigned a piece of land by the Portuguese government in 1794 and became an important farmer – the Fortaleza de Sant'Ana farm was huge and one of the most important farms in the Mata zone. In 1820, Mariano José was elected town councillor in Barbacena and later a provincial deputy.[89] Mariano José was as wealthy as prestigious. In 1861 he hosted the Emperor Dom Pedro II and his entourage, as he had done previously with the Emperor D. Pedro I.[90] Other close relatives of Mariano Procópio were wealthy and important. His sister, Maria José Ferreira Lage, married their cousin, Honório Augusto José Ferreira Armond, who was the second Baron of Pitanguy. Honório's father, Marcelino José Ferreira Armond – the first Baron of Pitangui – was Mariano José's stepbrother, an important political chieftain in Barbacena, and a wealthy farmer who had a fortune estimated at £400 000 in 1850.[91]

Like his father, Mariano Procópio Ferreira Lage was himself a man of power and influence. He was elected national deputy for Minas Gerais in 1861 and again in 1869, and was also the director of the Dom Pedro II railway (EFDPII) from 1869 until his death in 1872 and the director of the customs.[92] In 1849 he was nominated an official of the Order of the Rose by the Emperor D. Pedro II.[93] It also seems that he enjoyed some intimacy with the Royal family, as can be inferred from the following letter sent to him in 22 April 1871:

> The Minister and Secretary of the Affairs of the Empire informs the Illustrious Deputy Mariano Procópio Ferreira Lage that His Majesty the Emperor invites him to attend at the Royal chapel on the 26th of this month at 11 o'clock to the high mass, beginning on the 25th at 6 o'clock in the afternoon, which will be celebrated in memory of Her Highness the Princess D. Leopoldina, Duchess of Laxe.[94]

Mariano Procópio was very wealthy: when he died in 1872 he left a fortune of approximately 900 Contos (£93 600).[95]

Bernardo Mascarenhas – who founded several textile mills, a bank, an electricity generating company, and took part in several other enterprises – was also born into a wealthy and prestigious family. His father, Antônio Gonçalves da Silva Mascarenhas, started as a merchant in the central part of Minas Gerais and later became a farmer and financier. When Antônio died in 1884 he was certainly one of the richest men in Minas Gerais. As a wealthy landowner he enjoyed great political prestige, and although he never participated directly in political activity, some of his sons did.[96]

Antônio Gonçalves da Silva Mascarenhas had 13 children: Antônio Cândido, Antonino, José, Custódia, Escolástica, Francisca, Victor, Pacífico, Caetano, Bernardo, Maria Teodora, Sebastião and Francisco.[97] Most of them also became very wealthy and came to wield political influence. Antônio Cândido, Bernardo, Caetano, Victor, Pacífico and Francisco were partners in the Cedro and Cachoeira mills, and later in the CCC. Antonino, the second son, was a merchant, a muleteer and owned the Capim Branco farm in Sete Lagoas.[98] José, the third son, was established as merchant in Curvelo. Custódia married Luiz Augusto Vianna Barbosa, a farmer and an industrialist, as mentioned above. Escolástica was married to Quintiliano Soares Diniz, a farmer from Curvelo.[99] Morover, Pacífico – the eighth child – and Sebastião – the twelfth child – graduated in medicine and both became politicians. Pacífico was elected Vice-President of Minas Gerais in 1902 and Sebastião was several times elected national deputy for Minas Gerais.[100] The Mascarenhas family was and remained very wealthy, prestigious and politically powerful.

Francisco Baptista de Oliveira, a famous businessman in Juiz de Fora, was born in Entre-Rios de Minas on the Santa Cruz do Salto farm which belonged to his father. Francisco's paternal grandfather, Gervásio Joaquim de Souza, had been a prestigious merchant and farmer in Entre-Rios de Minas where he was also the leader of the Conservative Party. He had 14 children, among them João Baptista de Oliveira e Sousa, Francisco's father. João Baptista was also born in Entre-Rios and had been a merchant and cattle rancher. Francisco's maternal grandfather, Francisco Ribeiro da Silva, was a farmer, Lieutenant-Colonel of the National Guard, town councillor, district judge and leader of the Conservative Party in Entre-Rios de Minas. He was granted the title of Knight of the Order of the Rose by the Imperial government. He had 11 children, among whom was Maria da Natividade e Oliveira, João Baptista's cousin and Francisco Baptista de Oliveira's mother.[101]

The paternal grandfather of Américo Teixeira Guimarães, the promoter of the CCM, was Antônio Teixeira Guimaraes, owner of the Nova and the Paraiso farms. His father, João da Matta Teixeira, was the main shareholder of the CCM and an established capitalist. Furthermore, as João da Matta Teixeira was wealthy and owned land it is reasonable to conclude that he was also a farmer and that this must had been his main activity.[102]

José Monteiro Ribeiro Junqueira, one of the founders of the CFLCL, was the son of a farmer from Leopoldina, José Ribeiro Junqueira, and belonged to a traditional family from southern Minas Gerais. José Monteiro Ribeiro Junqueira himself had a long political career: after graduating in law he was elected state deputy and re-elected four years later; he was also elected Mayor of Leopoldina, federal deputy and senator, and in 1931 he became Secretary of Agriculture for the state of Minas Gerais.[103]

Norberto Custódio Ferreira, another founder of the CFLCL, was a public prosecutor in Ponte Nova and from 1895 to 1897 he was elected town councillor in Cataguazes.[104]

Francisco José de Andrade Botelho, founder of a textile mill in Brumado, Minas Gerais, came from an important *mineiro* family. His paternal great grandfather, Francisco Ignacio Botelho, was a prestigious and wealthy farmer from Lavras. According to the *Revista do Arquivo Público Mineiro* of 1911:

> Among the most traditional families of this town [Lavras] which still had representatives, are the Botelhos...The founder of the family Botelho was Francisco Ignacio Botelho, who died in this town on the 4th of August of 1796. He was the son of Francisco José Botelho and Thereza Maria Joanna, born in Carvilhan, Portugal.[105]

Furthermore, one of Francisco José de Andrade Botelho's brothers, Fidélis, was elected senator of the empire in 1888.[106]

João Antônio dos Santos, one of the founders of the Biribiry mill, was the bishop of Diamantina[107] and belonged to an important local family. One of his nephews, Antônio Felício dos Santos, was a doctor in the city of Rio de Janeiro, a Liberal Party deputy from 1867 to 1886, one of the founders and the first president of the Associação Industrial, and one of the founders of the Fábrica de Tecidos Pau Grande.[108]

Francisco Leite Ribeiro's grandfather, José Leite Ribeiro, was born in Portugal in 1723 and emigrated to Minas Gerais to wash for gold in partnership with another Portuguese. With the wealth José derived from mining he invested in land and raised cereals, cane and cattle. When he died in 1801 he was a wealthy man. Francisco's father added to the wealth of the family by trading between Rio de Janeiro and the family base in São João d'El Rey, Minas Gerais. Francisco Leite Ribeiro himself began in mining near São João d'El Rey. He moved to Barbacena in 1805 where he was briefly occupied in tax farming, and then moved to the border with Rio de Janeiro where he acquired 17 land grants after 1817. He devoted himself to the cultivation of coffee and by 1822 he was considered the largest farmer in Minas Gerais. When he died in 1845 he left a fortune of 1.087:000$000 contos

(£115 113), including 225 slaves. In the 1860s Francisco's son, Joaquim Vidal Leite Ribeiro, took part in banking in Juiz de Fora. In 1871, Joaquim moved to Rio de Janeiro where he died in 1883 leaving a fortune of over 2.000:000$000 contos (£179 600), largely in public debt bonds.[109]

Hence, biographical data reviewed above strongly supports the conclusion that most pioneer *mineiro* entrepreneurs came from the ruling class and traditional families: they and their relatives were wealthy and politically influential. This is in clear opposition to what is known about the social origins of the pioneer British entrepreneurial class, where only a relatively small proportion of the pioneer industrialists came from the upper or lower classes, with most coming from the middle ranks of society usually with mercantile connections.[110]

Finally, it is interesting to take a brief look at the intellectual formation of one of the most prominent and successful entrepreneurial families of nineteenth-century Minas Gerais: the Mascarenhas family. In several important respects, the family's intellectual formation conformed with the Protestant ethic described by Weber. As mentioned above, Antônio Gonçalves da Silva Mascarenhas (Bernardo Mascarenhas' father) had 13 children: nine sons and four daughters. Their formation began at home through an ascetic lifestyle based on religious principles and directed towards work as a mean to achieve self-fulfilment, emphasising discipline, sobriety and independence. Their father's success in business was an example to be followed.

Their entrepreneurial training also began at home, in their father's muletrain, retail store and farm, and in the daily contact with suppliers, customers and slaves, under the supervision of their father and elder brothers, in the case of the younger sons. Antônio Cândido, for example, began working in his father's retail store. Antonino began taking charge of his father's muletrain, while Caetano started overseeing the slaves of the São Sebastião farm. Furthermore, all 13 children studied in the best boarding schools of Minas Gerais, and after graduation, each son received a sum of 26 Contos as an anticipation of their inheritance in order to establish themselves as businessmen. Most of the sons followed their father becoming merchants, muleteers, financiers and farmers. Most of them also became industrialists. Furthermore, two of them – Pacífico and Sebastião – became doctors. Moreover, there is evidence to believe that this intellectual formation was not peculiar to the Mascarenhas family, since it met the spirit of the time and expressed very well the development of the Brazilian social and economic capitalist formation.[111]

This analysis of the social and ethnic background of the *mineiro* entrepreneur has shown that a large and important proportion of the *mineiro* entrepreneurial class does not conform with the description contained in the general Brazilian literature. There are important contrasts with the entrepreneurs of São Paulo and Rio de Janeiro, the most obvious being the smaller importance of immigrants and coffee planters in the formation of the *mineiro* entrepreneurial class as a whole. As Cammack stressed:

> some of the most successful families in Minas in the nineteenth-century, in economic terms, owed nothing... to coffee.[112]

Therefore, apart from a few prominent cases in the iron industry and apart from the Mata zone, where immigrants made up the largest proportion of the local industrial class, Brazilians born into the ruling and traditional families, usually not connected with coffee-growing activity, seem to have been the main source of entrepreneurs in nineteenth-century Minas Gerais. The social background of pioneer *mineiro* businessmen also differed from that of the pioneer British entrepreneurial class which was mainly recruited from the middle ranks of society. However, the peculiarities of the *mineiro* entrepreneurial class were not restricted to ethnic and social aspects, and it will be shown in the following section that there were important differences in the economic influences on the formation of the *mineiro* entrepreneurs. Finally, the analysis of the Mascarenhas family points to the existence of a 'spirit of capitalism' within the *mineiro* élite.

Economic Background

Here we examine the economic background of the *mineiro* entrepreneur and consider the main economic influences on the formation of the *mineiro* entrepreneurial class, the career pattern of *mineiro* businessmen and the activities which represented their main sources of capital.

As mentioned above, the Brazilian economic historiography has suggested – based mainly on the *paulista* experience – that the main sources of entrepreneurship and capital in nineteenth-century Brazil was either the trading house, mainly the export and import businesses,[113] or coffeegrowing, which was the basis for a process of economic development which spread to a wide range of other businesses.[114] Although trading and farming constituted the main sources of entrepreneurship and capital in nineteenth-century Minas Gerais, they were different owing to the particular nature of the *mineiro* economy. Firstly, Minas Gerais was landlocked, and trade was mainly oriented to local markets dealing with a limited number of basic items such as coffee, salt, bacon, cattle, tobacco, cereals, cotton and so forth. Import and export activities were concentrated in Rio de Janeiro, Santos and São Paulo. Secondly, coffee cultivation was confined to the southern parts of the province, the Mata and the South zones. Thirdly, in other regions of the province, especially the central and northern parts, a different range of activities were being undertaken ranging from gold-mining to cattle-raising and farming.[115] Thus, coffee growers and merchants dealing with export and import were not as important in the formation of the *mineiro* entrepreneurial class as they were in São Paulo.

Nevertheless, there is evidence suggesting that the coffee economy – directly or indirectly – provided part of the funds invested in the establishment of *mineiro* industry. *Mineiro* coffee growers were responsible, among others, for the establishment of the CUI in 1852.[116] As mentioned above, the company was organized by Mariano Procópio Ferreira Lage, who was a farmer himself, and several other coffee growers. Mariano Procópio's father, Mariano José Ferreira Armond, owned one of the most important farms in the Mata zone – the Fortaleza de Sant'Ana farm. The farm produced coffee and cereals, and raised cattle. Nevertheless, the lack of suitable means of transport for the production of the farm was one of the largest problems faced by Mariano José. This seems to have been the original motivation for the building of the União e Indústria turnpike, carried out by his son. Mariano Procópio started working in the Fortaleza de Sant'Ana farm and later established an import and cloth wholesaler firm (the partnership Ferreira Lage, Maia & Cunha) in Rio de Janeiro. Nevertheless, his career as merchant was short-lived and he soon went to Europe and to the USA in search of the new road-building technology invented by MacAdam. He also examined the systems of toll roads there, and on his return established the CUI.[117]

Moreover, coffee growers of the Mata zone itself financed the construction of several branches of the União e Indústria turnpike. The company report of 1861 stated that local farmers were paying the wages of the workers engaged in the construction of the branch to the town of Mar de Hespanha.[118] In a letter to the president of the province of Minas Gerais (Vicente Pires da Motta), the chairman of the CUI (Mariano Procópio Ferreira Lage) stated that:

> It is certain that the road built by the CUI (from Petropolis to Juiz de Fora), although rendering important services, needs to be complemented by branches which will facilitate the transport of goods of several centres of production to the stations of the company.
>
> There are in this situation several coffee-growing counties located between Juiz de Fora, Parahybuna, and Parahyba, which I will list – indicating the names of those farmers who are most interested and can, helped by the provincial government, supervise and contribute financially to the construction.[119]

It is interesting to point out that the process of funding the União e Indústria turnpike was similar to that of the first railways in São Paulo. According to Lewis, most of the first *paulista* railways were financed by direct local private investment, funds which were derived mainly from the rural sector, more specifically the coffee sector. As the *paulista* case suggests, the struggle of *mineiro* coffee growers to build the União e Indústria turnpike indicates a substantial degree of entrepreneurial initiative and the existence of funds available to be invested elsewhere.[120] Nevertheless, contrary to what happened in the case of the *paulista* railways, the União e Indústria turnpike was, shortly after the conclusion of its construction, taken over by the State.[121] State intervention in the CUI was not due to the technology gap – which in the case of turnpikes was certainly much less acute than in the case of railways – but to the diminishing interest on the part of the *mineiro* entrepreneurial class to invest more funds in the company after the construction of the Estrada de Ferro Dom Pedro II (EFDPII) railway. Moreover, State intervention reveals the difficulties that *mineiro* entrepreneurs had to fund more capital-intensive enterprises. This fact seems to corroborate Gerschenkron's view that depending on the degree of backwardness, and the supply of capital required, State action may be essential.[122]

Further evidence that the coffee economy provided part of the funds invested in the *mineiro* industry is the fact that although some industries – such as iron and textiles – were mostly concentrated in the central part of Minas Gerais, a large number of small factories started to emerge in the latter part of the nineteenth century in several coffee-growing counties. In 1861, Juiz de Fora – one of the most important *mineiro* coffee counties[123] – was already the third largest county in tax revenue, surpassed only by São João Del Rey and Ouro Preto in the Metalúrgica zone,[124] and one of the main industrial centres of the province. In 1870 there were 34 industrial establishments in Juiz de Fora, and seven years later 80.[125] Moreover, of the 20 largest *mineiro* counties in terms of industrial output in 1907, nine were located within the coffee-growing zones (7 in the Mata and 2 in the Sul) and 11 in the non-coffee-growing zones (10 in the Metalúrgica zone and 1 in the Oeste zone). The largest county in terms of industrial output was Juiz de Fora, followed by Sete Lagoas and Belo Horizonte, both located within the Metalúrgica zone.

In addition, 65 per cent of the *mineiro* industries in 1907 were established in coffee-growing regions, as opposed to only 30 per cent in non-coffee-growing regions, as shown in Table 2.6. However, of the total capital invested in *mineiro* industry only 44 per cent was invested in industries established in the coffee-growing regions, whereas more than 50 per cent was invested in industries established in non-coffee-growing regions. In terms of the number of workers employed, the industries established in the coffee-growing

Table 2.6   Distribution of *mineiro* industry between coffee-growing
and non-coffee-growing regions in 1907

Regions	Coffee	Non-coffee	Unknown	Total
Establishment				
Number	342	160	22	524
%	65.3	30.5	4.2	100.0
Capital				
Contos	11 774	13 568	1 172	26 515
%	44.4	51.2	4.4	100.0
Workers				
Number	3 751	5 162	508	9 421
%	39.8	54.8	5.4	100.0
Production				
Contos	17 815	12 891	1 537	32 244
%	55.2	40.0	4.8	100.0
Capital per establishment	34.42	84.80	53.27	50.60
Workers per establishment	10.96	32.26	23.09	17.97
Production per establishment	52.09	80.57	69.86	61.53

Source: J.H. Lima, *Café e Indústria em Minas Gerais (1870–1920)*
(Petrópolis, 1981), p. 89.

regions employed only 40 per cent of the total industrial
workforce, whereas those established in non-coffee-growing
regions employed nearly 55 per cent. Furthermore, industries established in the coffee-growing regions produced 50
per cent of the total industrial output, whereas those established in non-coffee-growing regions produced 40 per cent.
Thus, although the industries established in the coffee-
growing regions in 1907 were more numerous and productive, the industries established in non-coffee-growing
regions were more capital-intensive and employed more

workers per establishment. The fact that a large number of industries were established in the *mineiro* coffee-growing regions is undisputable evidence of the participation of the coffee economy in the establishment of the *mineiro* industry.

However, the coffee economy which developed in the southern parts of the province did not have a great impact on the rest of the *mineiro* economy.[126] In the Mata zone itself, one of the major coffee-growing regions of Minas Gerais, farmers were responsible for only 3 per cent of the industries established in Juiz de Fora (the most important industrial centre of the region) in the period 1858–1912. It was immigrants and Brazilians not connected with the coffee-growing activity who owned more than 90 per cent of the industries established in Juiz de Fora in the period 1858–1912.[127] The capital invested by Brazilians was originally accumulated in trading businesses or in their activities as professionals, or even in a combination of them.[128]

Immigrants (who were responsible for the establishment of more than 66 per cent of the industries founded in Juiz de Fora during this period) usually did not fit into the 'bourgeois immigrant' concept.[129] Most of them did not have capital and started working as labourers, craftsmen or even as farm workers.[130] Grieese, for example, was a German immigrant originally hired to work at the CUI, who in 1858 founded the first industry established in Juiz de Fora manufacturing carts and coaches.[131] During the same year, Wreied, a German brickmaker hired by the CUI, associated himself with a tanner to establish what became the largest tannery of the city.[132] Ten years later his stepson (Krambeck), himself an immigrant who was originally a carpenter and a farm worker, took control of the tannery and expanded the business successfully.[133] In 1865, Martin Kascher who also worked as a craftsman at the CUI established a workshop to make coaches.[134] Antônio Meurer, the son of immigrants, started as a salesman and representative of the breweries from Juiz de Fora, and later established a small shop and became a farm trader. In 1898, he established a mill to manufacture socks.[135]

In other parts of Minas Gerais domestic commercial activities and mixed farming (not connected with coffee-growing activity) were the starting point in the career of most entrepreneurs. For example, in the case of the iron industry which throughout the nineteenth century was concentrated in the central part of the province,[136] there is evidence that most of the foundries were established by farmers. According to Eschwege, by the time of his arrival in Minas Gerais in 1811 most of the foundries belonged to blacksmiths and large farmers.[137] Moreover, the capital invested in the setting-up of the Patriótica foundry, founded by Eschwege himself, was divided in 10 shares, each share representing 1000 cruzados of the initial capital. Eschwege subscribed two shares, the Conde de Palma (the governor of Minas Gerais) one, and a large and important *mineiro* family the remainder. Although there is no direct information about the activities of both the Conde de Palma and the family, there is evidence that they owned land:

> We had to choose the most appropriate place [to set-up the foundry]...
> The region of the Prata...was not as rich in woods. Nevertheless, there was the advantage that the administration of the future foundry would be under the close supervision of its most important shareholders, who had their properties in the neighbourhood.[138]

Moreover, it is reasonable to believe that at least part of the capital invested by Eschwege may have been accumulated in his activity as manager of iron foundries. As mentioned before, Eschwege worked in the Figueiró dos Vinhos foundry in Portugal before coming to Minas Gerais.[139] However, most of the capital invested in the establishment of the Patriótica foundry seems to have come from farming.

Further evidence that farmers established most of the *mineiro* foundries set up in the first three-quarters of the last century is provided by the fact that these foundries began as integral parts of farms. In 1886, for example, a newspaper advertised the sale of a foundry located in an estate in the Diamantina county which included, among other things, extensive grass for cattle, 30 head of cattle, a corn plantation and several fruit trees.[140] Even the São Miguel de Piracicaba mill, the most successful and one of the largest foundries of this period, was considered by its owner (Monlevade) as an integral part of his farm.[141] Therefore, as Libby suggests, it is reasonable to conclude that most of the small foundries established until the 1880s were also integral part of farms.[142]

One of the few foundries not to be established by farmers was the Morro do Pilar, which was financed by the Imperial government:

> Manuel Ferreira da Câmara decided to build, at the expenses of the King [of Portugal], a large iron foundry in Minas Gerais, for which purpose he lacked neither power nor money. He got both things from the government, who allowed him to use the former [power] and to withdraw the latter [money] from the cashier of the diamond mining business.[143]

The Morro do Pilar was the only foundry established in the first three-quarters of the nineteenth century to be financed by the State.

The larger foundries (the Esperança and Burnier) which were founded in the latter part of the century were not established by farmers. The Esperança was established by two engineers of the railway Central do Brasil (Amaro da Silveira and Henrique Hargreaves), a Swiss metallurgist (Alberto Gerspacher), and Carlos da Costa Wigg the main shareholder, of whom there is no information about his activities.[144] The Burnier foundry was established by Carlos da Costa Wigg and the son of Alberto Gerspacher (José Gerspacher), who had been the technical director of both the Esperança and the Burnier foundries.[145] These are examples of employees/managers who acquired skills (and capital) working for others and then set themselves up in business, and supports the view that one of the main sources of entrepreneurs are people who have been previously in employment.[146]

Thus, there is evidence that in the first three-quarters of the last century most of the iron foundries were established by farmers. This fact corroborates Lydall's view that a large proportion of the new industrial entrepreneurs who emerged in the early stages of industrialization came from the group made up by farmers. According to the author, this is explained by the fact that small manufacturing workshops could be established on farms,[147] as was the case of several *mineiro* foundries set up in the first part of the century. Moreover, it is interesting to point to the importance of managerial ability in Monlevade's success as an entrepreneur. The São Miguel de Piracicaba foundry was for more than 40 years managed by Monlevade, obtaining the best results among all the foundries in Minas Gerais. After Monlevade's death in 1872 his family assumed control of the foundry but the results were never the same and the foundry was finally sold to the Companhia Nacional de Forjas e Estaleiros (CNFE) at the beginning of the 1890s.[148] This seems to corroborate those authors who advocate management ability as one of the main characteristics of entrepreneurs.[149]

The textile industry, which was also concentrated in the central part of Minas Gerais, was established mostly by farmers (not connected with coffee-growing activity) and merchants. Among the founders of the Cedro mill, Antônio Cândido Mascarenhas was a farmer – he owned the Rasgão farm – a merchant and a capitalist, as shown in the following letter:

> I have, in partnership with two brothers, imported the machinery to establish a textile mill. By the time the mill will be set up it will cost us more than we have.... It is for this reason that I write to you, my cousin, to inform you that your debts, including interests to this date, amount to 1618 Contos. I also ask you from now on to pay what you owe me on a monthly basis.[150]

Caetano and Bernardo Mascarenhas started their entrepreneurial careers in a partnership fattening cattle for sale and trading in salt. The funds they used to start their partnership were drawn from a trust of 26 Contos which each son received from their father. With the change in the route of the muletrains and the decrease in their movement due to the Paraguay War, the salt trade became less attractive and the two brothers decided to change business, with the profits they had earned in the salt and cattle business (around 108 Contos) they established the Cedro mill. It seems that the idea to invest in a textile mill was mainly Bernardo's, because he was the intellectual organizer of the mill. The domestic cloth production of their father's farm (São Sebastião) was very profitable, even though the quality was poor and the process of production backward. Therefore cloth production was a familiar activity for both of them. Later, Caetano came to own the Nova Estância farm in Pirapora and Bernardo invested in an electricity generating company, a bank, another textile mill, and so on.[151]

The analysis of the establishment of the Cedro mill shows that its founders possessed several of the characteristics of the entrepreneur described in the literature.[152] It shows that the three Mascarenhas brothers were capitalists, that they possessed the foresight and willingness to act and to assume risk, and that they took advantage of changes in the business environment to act soundly and in an entrepreneurial way.

Among the founders of the Cachoeira mill, farmers and merchants were well represented, and funds for the establishment of the mill came from different sources. As happened to the founders of the Cedro mill, the three Mascarenhas brothers involved in this entrepreneurship also received a trust of 26 Contos from their father when they came of age.[153] Furthermore, before the establishment of the Cachoeira mill Victor Mascarenhas had been a merchant in Curvelo and manager of the São Sebastião farm. Later he became one of the owners of the São Sebastião textile mill and of the São Sebastião farm.[154] His brother Pacífico Mascarenhas was a local doctor, who later became a farmer. There is no information about Francisco de Paula Mascarenhas' activities before the establishment of the Cachoeira mill. However, he later became a farmer, a merchant, and took part in several other industrial undertakings. As a farmer he came to own the Periperi farm, and as a merchant he became partner in a retail store (Carvalho, Libano & Mascarenhas) in Rio de Janeiro at the beginning of the 1880s. As an industrialist, besides the Cachoeira mill he established the Periperi textile mill and was also partner in a hat factory (Machado & Mascarenhas) in Curvelo. Finally, he was shareholder and one of the founders of the CME and the Banco de Crédito Real de Minas Gerais, both enterprises organized by his brother Bernardo. Finally, Luiz Augusto Vianna Barbosa was the owner of the Cachoeira farm where the Cachoeira mill was set up.[155]

Later the founders of both the Cedro and the Cachoeira mills were joined by Theóphilo Marques Ferreira, a merchant, and Antônio Joaquim Barbosa da Silva, a lawyer, in the establishment of the CCC.[156] Thus, the funds invested in the Cedro mill the Cachoeira mill, and the CCC came mainly from trading businesses and farming (not connected with coffee-growing activity).

The Brumado mill was established in 1872 by capital accumulated in the trading business. Its founder, Francisco José de Andrade Botelho, was a *mineiro* who lived in Rio de Janeiro working as merchant in the partnership Botelho, Irmão & Andrade before founding the textile mill. The Botelho, Irmão & Andrade firm was a partnership with his uncle and one of his brothers. As was common among merchants of this time, Francisco travelled frequently to the hinterland of Minas Gerais as a representative of his firm, and he was already a wealthy man when he arrived in Pitangui, in western Minas Gerais, and met Francisca Alvares da Silva. Soon after they were married and Francisco decided to live in Pitangui. He quit the partnership in Rio de Janeiro, but Pitangui was too narrow a market for a retail store like the one he had possessed in Rio. Thus, he decided to establish a textile mill stimulated by the good results of the Cedro mill. The most suitable and available place to build the mill was found in the neighbouring district of Brumado.[157]

The main shareholder and founder of the SAIM, established in 1875, was Azarias de Souza Dias, who was also a farmer.[158] Among the remaining 23 shareholders of the mill mentioned by the *Almanach Sul Mineiro* in 1874, there is information about the activities of only 5 of them: Antônio Candido de Souza Dias, a farmer and a capitalist; Antônio Candido Teixeira, a district judge, a farmer and a capitalist; and Antônio Domingos de Souza, Marcos de Souza Dias and Gabriel Domingos, all of them farmers.[159] Thus, it is reasonable to conclude that the funds invested in this mill had been accumulated mainly in farming activities. However, it is important to point out that the mill was situated in a coffee-growing region (the Sul zone) and the farmers mentioned above might well have been coffee growers. Apart from the fact that one of the partners (João Antônio dos Santos) was the Bishop of Diamantina, there is no information about the activities of the other four partners prior to the establishment of the Biribiry mill in 1876. There is also no information about the activities of the founders of the União Itabirana mill established in 1876.[160]

Among the founders of the Filatório Montes Claros, Manoel and Donato Rodrigues who subscribed 53.3 per cent of the capital were both farmers from Grão Mogol, a county close to Montes Claros. Antônio Narciso Soares started his entrepreneurial career as a miner and diamond trader in Diamantina, and then moved to Montes Claros where he established himself as a local trader and later as a farmer. Gregório Velloso also started as a local trader and, subsequently, became a farmer. Finally, Angelo de Quadros Bittencourt had a farm in Campo Grande, in the county of Montes Claros.[161] Thus, the capital invested in the Filatório Montes Claros was accumulated in the trading business, farming and diamond mining.

Although there is no information about the activities of the founders of the Marzagão mill, it is telling that the mill was established on the Marzagão farm in the vicinity of Sabará.[162] There is no information about the activities of the founders of the Cassú, the Paulo Moreirense, the Industrial Ouro Preto, the Pedreira, the Bom Jardim, and the Viçosa mills.[163]

The São Sebastião mill was established by Antônio Gonçalves da Silva Mascarenhas, who was the youngest son of a Portuguese immigrant, Antônio Gonçalves Mascarenhas, who arrived in Brazil in 1778. Although the information about Antônio Gonçalves Mascarenhas is not very precise, it is said that he became a protégé of a prosperous muleteer with whom he started to work. Years later, Antônio Gonçalves Mascarenhas became his partner and, when the muleteer decided to retire, his heir. With his own muletrain and three slaves, Antônio Gonçalves Mascarenhas made frequent trips to the hinterlands of Minas Gerais, where he would sell salt and olive-oil and would bring back to Rio de Janeiro textiles, sugar and bacon. In 1792 he married an Indian brought up by his protector. They had four children, although only three survived: José, Caetano and Antônio Gonçalves da Silva Mascarenhas. When the youngest was almost seven years old his father decided to take the whole family with him on his trips. In 1811, Antônio Gonçalves Mascarenhas and his wife got ill and died in the middle of one of those trips.[164]

After the death of his parents, Antônio Gonçalves da Silva Mascarenhas was taken in by his godfather, José Teixeira da

Fonseca Vasconcelos, the Viscount of Caeté. Later, he became administrator of the Viscount's land and subsequently of other estates. In 1824, he established himself as a merchant in Taboleiro Grande, in the central part of the province, which was the main passage for all muletrains heading to the hinterlands of Minas Gerais. His business grew rapidly and at the age of 34 – by then a wealthy man – he bought the land which came to be known as the São Sebastião farm. He then sold the store and became a prosperous farmer and financier. In 1884 he established the São Sebastião mill on his farm.[165] Thus, although the fortune accumulated by Antônio Gonçalves da Silva Mascarenhas previously to the establishment of the São Sebastião mill originated from different sorts of activities, it is reasonable to conclude that the funds invested in the mill were mainly accumulated in trading and farming.

Very little is known about the activities of the founders of the São Vicente mill, which was established in 1885 and a few years later was acquired by the CCC.[166]

The main shareholders of the CCM were João da Matta Teixeira and Jeronymo Francisco França, who were local farmers. João da Matta Teixeira is also mentioned in the report of the meeting of shareholders for the establishment of the CCM as a capitalist.[167] Thus, the CCM was a farmers' enterprise.

Although there is no information about the activities of the founders of the União Lavrense mill, the first two directors of the mill were traders: Comendador José Duarte da Costa Negrão, a trader who lived in Rio de Janeiro at the time of the establishment of the mill, and Manoel Hermeto Corrêa da Costa, a local trader. Thus, it is reasonable to conclude that at least part of the capital invested in the União Lavrense mill originated in the trading business. However, it is not possible to say if the trading business of Comendador José Duarte da Costa Negrão, who lived in Rio de Janeiro, was or was not connected with the import and export trade.[168]

The Santa Bárbara mill was initially planned by João da Matta Machado, a diamond trader from Diamantina who also had a diamond-cutting workshop. After his death, his sons and sons-in-law, together with Antônio Moreira da Costa the Baron of Paraúna, set up a partnership to establish the mill.

Among João da Matta Machado's sons, one was a law student in São Paulo (Pedro da Matta Machado) and the other (Alvaro da Matta Machado) was a member of the Provincial Assembly at the time of the establishment of the mill in 1886. Among his sons-in-law, Francisco Ferreira Corrêa Rabelo worked as a lawyer, magistrate and teacher, and was also a politician. Pedro José Verciani was an engineer who lived in Rio de Janeiro at the time of the establishment of the mill, and João Antônio Lopes de Figueiredo was a local doctor in Diamantina. Finally, Antônio Moreira da Costa, the only partner outside the Matta Machado family, had been engaged all his life in the diamond business. Thus, as Versiani points out, although the capital invested in the establishment of the Santa Bárbara mill came from the different activities carried out by its owners, a significant part of it may have come from activities related to the diamond business.[169]

The São Roberto mill was promoted by Quintiliano Alves Ferreira, the Baron of São Roberto, who was engaged in a number of local businesses such as the manufacture of hats and earthenware, and diamond-cutting.[170]

The Tecelagem Mascarenhas mill was established by Bernardo Mascarenhas who started his entrepreneurial career in a partnership with his brother Caetano as mentioned above. Later, the two brothers decided to invest the money they had accumulated in a textile mill, but they did not have enough funds and needed a capitalist partner. Their father did not agree with the idea because they were very young (Bernardo was 20 and Caetano was 23 years old) and a textile mill was a complicated matter.[171] Their brothers were equally unsupportive, except Antônio Cândido who reluctantly agreed to join them but imposed the condition that the mill had to be established in Taboleiro Grande instead of Juiz de Fora as originally planned. The Cedro mill was thus set-up in Taboleiro Grande.[172] Some years later the Cedro mill was merged with the Cachoeira mill into the CCC. However, Bernardo was never happy with his life in Taboleiro Grande which was too small for his entrepreneurial talents, and with the death of his father in 1887 he decided to move to Juiz de Fora and set-up a textile mill there as he had previously intended. One year after his arrival in Juiz de Fora he established the Tecelagem Mascarenhas.[173] It is reasonable to conclude that the funds invested in this mill had originated partially from the capital made in the Cedro mill and in the CCC, and in part from what he had inherited from his father, funds accumulated in trading and farming.

The Industrial Mineira mill was established in Juiz de Fora by five Englishmen (Andrew Steele, John Steele, Peter Steele, William Moreth and Henry Whittaker). Most were traders living in the city of Rio de Janeiro, except William Moreth who lived in Petrópolis.[174]

Among the textile mills established during the 1890s, the CTS, also established in the central part of Minas Gerais, was founded by Manoel José de Souza Moreira, his sons Manoel Gonçalves de Souza Moreira and Augusto Gonçalves de Souza Moreira, and his son-in-law Antônio Pereira de Mattos. Manoel José de Souza Moreira, the main promoter and largest shareholder, was both a farmer and a local trader. He married one of the daughters of a wealthy local farmer (Manoel Gonçalves Cançado), from whom they inherited the Cachoeira farm where the CTS was later set up. He also owned a large merchant house, Moreira & Filhos, in Santana do São João Acima. Manoel Gonçalves de Souza Moreira, Manoel José de Souza Moreira's eldest son and the second largest shareholder of the CTS, was also a local trader working in partnership with his father in Moreira & Filhos. His brother, Augusto Gonçalves de Souza Moreira, was a doctor who at the time of the establishment of the mill was a member of the Constituent Assembly of the state of Minas Gerais.[175] Antônio Pereira de Mattos was a travelling salesman for large merchant houses from Rio de Janeiro, before getting married to one of Manoel José de Souza Moreira's daughters.[176]

There is little information about the activities of the promoter of the São Joanense mill, Antônio Moreira da Costa Rodrigues, or about the activities of the founders of the Itabira do Campo, the Jequitahy, the São João Nepomuceno, the Perpetua, and the Itinga mills.[177]

The Companhia Industrial Pitanguense was established by experienced industrialists. For example, Luiz Augusto Vianna Barbosa who was originally a farmer and one of the founders of the Cachoeira mill and the CCC. Furthermore, when he sold his shares of the CCC he invested the funds in the purchase of the Brumado mill.[178] There is no information about the activities of Antônio Mascarenhas Barbosa, one of Luiz Augusto Vianna Barbosa's sons. However, his other son, Sérgio Mascarenhas Barbosa, was an industrialist. There is also no information about the activities of the second largest shareholder, Francisco Bahia da Rocha. His two sons, Francisco and Américo Bahia da Rocha were an industrialist and a trader respectively. Together, Luiz Augusto Vianna Barbosa, Francisco Bahia da Rocha, and their sons held more than 80 per cent of the shares of the company. Among the other 10 shareholders of the company, three were clergymen, two were farmers, two were traders, one was a magistrate, and the activities of the remaining two are not known.[179] Here again it is possible to observe the presence of commercial and agricultural capital in the establishment of a textile mill, although a large proportion of the funds invested in this case came from the textile industry itself.

The Melancias mill was also established by experienced industrialists as the mill was set up by a group of investors who were already associated with other textile undertakings in Minas Gerais. Among the three largest shareholders, Jeronymo Francisco França and João da Matta Teixeira were both directors and two of the main shareholders of the CCM at the time of the establishment of the Melancias mill. The third, Theóphilo Marques Ferreira, had been one of the founders of the CCC and its general manager for several years.[180]

The promoter and major shareholder of the Companhia Progresso Fabril, Carlos Vaz de Mello, was a politician from Viçosa who at the time of the establishment of the mill was a member of the Constitutional Republican Party's executive committee. The first two directors of the mill, José Tinoco and Augusto Ferreira Brant, held 10 per cent and 12 per cent of the shares of the company respectively. The former was a farmer and a capitalist, whereas the latter was a local trader.[181]

The main promoter of the Cachoeira Grande mill was a farmer from the central part of Minas Gerais, Antônio Ferreira Alves da Silva. Anxious about the impact of the abolition of slavery on his agricultural operations he decided to establish a textile mill, but lacking experience in the textile business he associated himself with the founders of the CCM,

João da Matta Teixeira, Américo Teixeira Guimarães and Herculino França. Thus, the capital invested in the Cachoeira Grande mill came mainly from farming and the textile industry itself.[182]

Finally, the São Domingos mill was established by seven people, among them the members of the Moreira Penna family who were the main shareholders. Namely, Affonso Augusto Moreira Penna then Governor of Minas Gerais, and his brothers Domingos Moreira Teixeira Penna and José Moreira Teixeira Penna, both of whom were farmers.[183]

Thus, although on the whole coffee capital played a very minor role in the establishment of the *mineiro* textile industry, a substantial part of the capital invested in the industry was accumulated in farming. Trading was another important source of capital and several mills established in the county of Diamantina were financed mainly by capital accumulated in the diamond business. It is also important to point out that towards the end of the century several textile enterprises were being financed by capital accumulated in the industry itself.

Comparison between the origin of the funds invested in the establishment of the *mineiro* and the *carioca* textile industries reveals important similarities and differences. Most of the textile mills established in Rio de Janeiro during the period 1878–95 were also financed by merchants. However, while it seems that *mineiro* merchants were of a more generalist nature and engaged mainly in up-country trading, their *carioca* counterparts were more specialized, dealing mainly with cloth and engaged more specifically in the import–export trade. As shown in Table 2.7, the FTSL was founded in 1877 by a merchant, José Maria Teixeira de Azevedo, engaged in the import–export trade.[184] The FTPG was founded in 1878 by Antônio Felício dos Santos a doctor from Minas Gerais whose father and uncle established the Biribiry mill in Diamantina, José Rodrigues Peixoto a doctor and grocer from Rio de Janeiro, and John Sherrington.[185] The FTR was founded in 1879 by a merchant engaged in the import–export trade of cloth.

The FFTTA was founded in 1880 by José Augusto Laranja a merchant, Joaquim Carvalho de Oliveira e Silva a cloth wholesaler, and Henry Whittaker a technician.[186] The

Table 2.7 The city of Rio de Janeiro: activity of the main promoters
of the textile companies established in the period 1878–95

Company	Main Promoters	Activity
FTSL	José Maria Teixeira de Azevedo	Merchant
FTPG	Antônio Felício dos Santos	Doctor
	José Rodrigues Peixoto	Doctor
	John Sherrington	n.a.
FTR	Frederico Glette	Merchant
FFTTA	José Augusto Laranja	Merchant
	Joaquim C. de Oliveira e Silva	Merchant
	Henry Whittaker	Technician
FFTTB	Joaquim Marques da Costa	Merchant
FFTC	Peter Steele	Merchant
	Henry Whittaker	Technician
	George Holden	n.a.
FTSJ	John Valentine Hall	Merchant
	James Grainger Bellamy	Merchant
	John Henry Lowndes	Merchant
FTSC	Frederico Pinheiro da Silva	Merchant
	John Henry Lowndes	Merchant
	José da Cunha Ferreira	Doctor
CFTCI	Manoel Salgado Zenha	Merchant
	Francisco Tavares Bastos	n.a.
	João José dos Reis	Merchant
CPIB	Banco Rural e Hypotecário	Bank
	Banco Internacional do Brasil	Bank
CFTC	Viscount of Figueiredo	Banker and Merchant
	Cândido da Cunha Sotto Maior	Merchant
CFTSF	Affonso de Lamare	Merchant

Notes: FTR – Fábrica de Tecidos do Rink; CFTC – Companhia de Fiação e Tecidos Corcovado; CPIB – Companhia Progresso Industrial do Brasil; FFTC – Fábrica de Fiação e Tecelagem Carioca; FTPG – Fábrica de Tecidos Pau Grande; FTSC – Fábrica de Tecidos de São Christóvão; FTSJ – Fábrica de Tecidos São João; FTSL – Fábrica de Tecidos São Lázaro; CFTCI – Companhia de Fiação e Tecidos Confiança Industrial; CFTSF – Companhia de Fiação e Tecidos São Félix; FFTTA – Fábrica de Fiação, Tecidos e Tinturaria Alliança; FFTTB – Fábrica de Fiação, Tecidos e Tinturaria Bomfim.
Source: Monteiro, *op.cit.*, pp. 98–283.

FFTTB was founded by a merchant engaged in the cotton trade.[187] The main promoters of the FFTC were Peter Steele an Englishman living in Rio de Janeiro and engaged in the import–export trade of cloth, Henry Whittaker a technician who was also a partner in the FFTTA as mentioned above, and George Holden an Englishman.[188] The FTSJ was founded by three merchants engaged in the import– export trade of cloth, John Valentine Hall, James Grainger Bellamy and John Henry Lowndes.[189] The FTSC was founded in 1888 by Frederico Pinheiro da Silva a merchant, John Henry Lowndes an merchant who was one of the founders of the FTSJ, and José da Cunha Ferreira a doctor.[190] The CFTCI was founded in 1885 by Manoel Salgado Zenha a grocer, Francisco Tavares Bastos of whom there is no information about his activities previous to the establishment of the mill, and João José dos Reis one of the largest merchants established in the city of Rio de Janeiro in the second half of the last century.[191] The CPIB was founded by two banks: the Banco Rural e Hypotecário, and the Banco Internacional do Brasil.[192] The CFTC was founded in 1889 by the Viscount of Figueiredo a banker and merchant engaged in the import–export trade, and Cândido da Cunha Sotto Maior, a merchant engaged in the import–export trade of cloth.[193] Finally, the CFTSF was founded in 1891 by a merchant, Affonso de Lamare.[194]

Thus, comparison between the origin of the funds invested in the *mineiro*, the *carioca* and the *paulista* textile industries reveals important differences. In the first case, the capital invested originated in the generalist up-country trade business, in the diamond business and in farming (not connected with coffee-growing activities). In the second case, the main source of capital was the import–export trading business dealing mainly with cloth, whereas the capital invested in the *paulista* industry came mainly from coffee-growing activities.[195]

The electricity-generating industry established in the last decade of the nineteenth century was financed in a similar way; investors transferred capital from trade, farming, manufacturing, banking and so on. As already mentioned, the CME was organized in 1888 by Bernardo Mascarenhas who started in the trading business and then invested in the textile industry, only subsequently investing in the electricity-generating industry. The funds used in setting up the CME came from different sources, as in the case of the Tecelagem

Mascarenhas. Part of the funds came from the capital accumulated in the textile industry and part from what Bernardo inherited which had in turn been accumulated in trade and farming. Moreover, it is important to point out that Bernardo was the only one among the nine brothers who never came to own land. Bernardo later would take part in the establishment of the Companhia Construtora Mineira, the Sociedade de Imigração, the Banco de Crédito Real de Minas Gerais, the School of Commerce of Juiz de Fora, and the Companhia de Tecidos de Juta, a short-lived enterprise.[196]

Furthermore, among the 30 original shareholders in the CME, 12 belonged to the Mascarenhas family,[197] individuals who in one way or another had accumulated their funds in trade, manufacturing and farming.[198] Moreover, one of the main promoters, a shareholder, and one of the first directors of the CME, Francisco Baptista de Oliveira, began working with his father in his retail store in Entre-Rios. In 1882, he moved to Juiz de Fora where he founded a famous and well-known retail store in the Mata zone ('Casa da Barateza').[199] Oliveira met Bernardo Mascarenhas with whom he became a close friend and partner in several enterprises at the beginning of 1886. In 1887, he and the Baron of Santa Helena (who was also one of the original shareholders of the CME[200]) founded the first bank in Minas Gerais, the Banco Territorial e Mercantil de Minas.[201] Two years later, Oliveira was one of the founders of the Banco de Crédito Real de Minas Gerais. He was also a partner of Bernardo Mascarenhas in the Baptista, Mascarenhas, Bicalho & Companhia, a short-lived enterprise aimed at exploring gold mines in Sabará. He was also one of the founders and owners of a local newspaper from Juiz de Fora, *O Diário de Minas*. Finally, in 1891, again in a partnership with Bernardo Mascarenhas, he founded the School of Commerce of Juiz de Fora.[202]

Thus, the funds invested in the CME came from trade, manufacturing, banking, and farming. It is also reasonable to believe that coffee capital could also have featured in the company since the CME was established in one of the largest coffee-growing counties of Minas Gerais (Juiz de Fora).

The CFLCL was established in 1905 by Norberto Custódio Ferreira, José Monteiro Ribeiro Junqueira, and João Duarte Ferreira. In 1889, Norberto Custódio Ferreira established his law office in Cataguazes and in 1898 he was invited to open the first branch of the Banco de Crédito Real de Minas Gerais in the Mata zone in Cataguazes. In 1905 he was one of the founders of the CFLCL. In 1908 he was invited to establish and manage a branch of the Banco do Brasil in the city of Santos, the most important port in Brazil, and in the following year he was promoted director of the bank, a position that he maintained until his retirement in 1925. He also owned rich farms where he grew coffee and bred cattle.[203]

After attending schools in Barbacena, Petrópolis and Rio de Janeiro, José Monteiro Ribeiro Junqueira went to São Paulo where he also read law. He graduated in 1894 and returned to Leopoldina where, after working provisionally as a public prosecutor, he established his office. One year after graduating, he established with his partner in the law office the local newspaper, *Gazeta de Leopoldina*. In 1905 he co-founded the CFLCL, and in 1909 he established the Companhia Leiteira Leopoldinense which became the main milk supplier of the city of Rio de Janeiro. In 1912, together with his brother Custódio Junqueira and his brother-in-law Francisco de Andrade Botelho, he established the bank 'Ribeiro Junqueira, Irmao & Botelho'. In 1924, he established the São José sawmill. Two years later he established the Companhia Fiação e Tecidos Leopoldinense.[204]

João Duarte Ferreira was born in Coimbra, Portugal, and came to Brazil in 1872. He started working as an employee of the Leopoldina Railway and later he became partner in the Joaquim Estolano da Silveira firm. In 1891 he established the first coffee-mill of Cataguazes (one of the largest centres of coffee production at this time), which decisively boosted his wealth. In 1893 he established the Banco of Cataguazes and in 1905 he was one of the founders and the largest shareholder of the CFLCL and of the Companhia de Fiação e Tecelagem de Cataguazes. João Duarte Ferreira became one of the wealthiest men in Minas Gerais and his fortune included, among other things, coffee farms, coffee, sugar and rice mills, a sawmill, the Banco Construtor, and the Grande Hotel Villas.[205]

Thus, the establishment of the CFLCL was financed by capital accumulated in different activities – in manufacturing, banking and law practices. Furthermore, it is reasonable to conclude that at least part of the capital invested in the CFLCL originated in farming, as the father of one of the founders of the CFLCL, José Monteiro Ribeiro Junqueira, was a farmer in Leopoldina.[206] However, farming in this case probably means coffee-growing since Leopoldina was situated in one of the largest centres of coffee production of Minas Gerais.[207] It is also important to point out the importance of the coffee economy in the establishment of the CFLCL. Apart from the indirect contribution (the formation of a local consumer market, the funds for investment in infrastructure, and so on) that coffee-growing activity may have had to the establishment of the CFLCL, one of the founders' main sources of wealth previous to the establishment of the company was coffee milling.

A comparison of the process of funding of electricity-generating companies in the cities of São Paulo and Rio de Janeiro on the one hand, and in Minas Gerais on the other, reveals important differences. The STLPC and the RJTLPC were financed by Canadian capital[208] since the scale of the consumer market in the cities of São Paulo and Rio de Janeiro was such that the capital required could not be easily supplied locally without the intervention of the State. In the case of the *mineiro* electricity-generating companies, the respective consumer markets were smaller and local sources of capital were enough and available. In the end, the restricted dimension of the markets instead of working as a limitation imposed by the *mineiro* business environment, worked as the necessary condition for local investment in this particular industry. Furthermore, from the data presented above it is possible to observe that shareholders of both the CME and the CFLCL were either friends or members of the same family (or professions), further evidence of the local and personal nature of business affairs in Minas Gerais as late as the beginning of the twentieth century. In contrast, the *paulista* and *carioca* electricity-generating companies had a more depersonalized ownership structure.

This analysis of the main economic influences on the formation of the *mineiro* entrepreneurial class has revealed important differences with the *paulista* and *carioca* entrepreneurial classes. The participation of coffee planters, the so-called 'bourgeois immigrant', and merchants dealing with import–export trade was much smaller in Minas Gerias than in São Paulo and Rio de Janeiro. In the Mata zone – a major coffee-growing region – coffee planters only had a small participation in the establishment of local industrial enterprises. It was immigrants with very limited resources who thus cannot be classified as 'bourgeois immigrant', and Brazilians unconnected with coffee-growing who were responsible for the establishment of more than 90 per cent of the industries founded in Juiz de Fora during the period. Moreover, funds invested in the iron and textile industries concentrated in the central parts of Minas Gerais originated mainly in farming, again unrelated to coffee, in generalist up-country trade, and in the diamond business. The analysis of the *mineiro* electricity-generating industry has revealed that the funds came from a variety of sources – farming (included coffee-growing), manufacturing, banking and the professions. However, comparison with the funds invested in the *paulista* and *carioca* electricity generating companies has shown that, whereas the funds invested in the *mineiro* companies derived from local sources, those invested in the *paulista* and *carioca* companies derived from foreign sources.

CONCLUSION

Generally speaking, the study of the *mineiro* businessman has shown that he possessed most of the characteristics described in the economics literature. He was an employer of factors of production and a capitalist (or at least owned part of the capital invested); most of his life was devoted to the management of his businesses; and he was a leader and an innovator, as evidenced by the careers of men like Bernardo Mascarenhas and Mariano Procópio Ferreira Lage who pioneered several industries in Minas Gerais. Such businessmen were willing to assume risks. Furthermore, *mineiro* entrepreneurs introduced new goods such as electricity, or a new quality of a good such as a macadamized turnpike. They also introduced new methods of production as in the industrial production of cloth, and exploited new markets like the virtually unaccessible *mineiro* market for iron products. Moreover, they had an intellectual formation based on principles which were very close to the ethos of the first European entrepreneurs in several relevant respects. However, their businesses were restricted to the small-scale and/or light industry, and cautious attempts to invest in infrastructure ended with the intervention of the government, as in the case of the União e Indústria turnpike.

The analysis of the social background of the *mineiro* entrepreneur has shown that he had a different social and ethnic background to entrepreneurs from São Paulo and Rio de Janeiro. Immigrants were less important in the formation of the *mineiro* entrepreneurial class. Therefore, apart from the iron industry – where foreign entrepreneurs had a small but important participation in the establishment of the industry – and apart from the Mata zone – where immigrants were responsible for the establishment of the majority of the industries founded before 1900 – locals constituted the main source of entrepreneurs in nineteenth-century Minas Gerais. The CUI was organized by Mariano Procópio Ferreira Lage, who was born in Barbacena, and several local farmers. The *mineiro* textile industry was also established mainly by local entrepreneurs, in marked contrast to entrepreneurs who established the *carioca* textile industry. Even the first *mineiro* electricity-generating companies which were established in the Mata zone were also established by local entrepreneurs. The CME was founded by Bernardo Mascarenhas and other local businessmen, whereas the CFLCL was established by two Brazilians and one Portuguese. The case of the *mineiro* electricity generating companies also contrasts with that of the electricity generating companies established in the cities of São Paulo and Rio de Janeiro, where the first electricity-generating companies were founded and promoted by foreigners. Furthermore, several of the most prominent nineteenth-century *mineiro* entrepreneurs came from ruling traditional families.

The analysis of the main economic influences on the formation of the *mineiro* entrepreneurial class has shown that although trade and farming constituted the main sources of entrepreneurship and capital in Minas Gerais as in São Paulo, they were of a different nature owing to the peculiarities of the *mineiro* economy. Minas Gerais was landlocked, and import and export trade was concentrated in Rio de Janeiro,

Santos and São Paulo. Moreover, coffee cultivation was confined to the southern parts of the province and elsewhere a different range of activities were undertaken, notably gold mining, cattle-raising and the production of food staples. However, the *mineiro* coffee economy did provide – directly or indirectly – part of the funds invested in the *mineiro* industry. Coffee growers were directly responsible, among others, for the establishment of the CUI. The company was organized by Mariano Procópio Ferreira Lage, himself a farmer, and several coffee growers of the Mata zone who also financed the construction of several branches of the União e Indústria turnpike.

Nevertheless, farmers were responsible for only a small part of the industries established in the coffee-growing parts of Minas Gerais in the period 1858–1912, in a clear indication that coffee-growers were not as important in the formation of the *mineiro* entrepreneurial class as they were in São Paulo. It was immigrants and Brazilians unconnected with coffee who owned most of the industries established in the southern parts of Minas Gerais. Moreover, immigrants usually did not fit into the 'bourgeois immigrant' concept as most did not possess capital before arriving in Brazil.

In other parts of Minas Gerais, up-country trade of a more generalist nature and food production farming represented the starting point in the career of most entrepreneurs. In the case of the iron industry, for example, which throughout the nineteenth century was concentrated in the central part of the province, most of the foundries set-up in the first three-quarters of the century were established by farmers as an integral part of the rural economy. However, in the latter part of the century the larger ironworks (the Esperança and the Burnier foundries) were not established by farmers, but by professionals and established industrialists.

Yet the main sources of capital for the *mineiro* textile industry, also concentrated in the central part of Minas Gerais, were trade, ranching and agriculture, and the diamond business. Towards the end of the century several textile mills were financed by capital accumulated in the industry itself. The process of funding of the *mineiro* textile industry contrasts with Rio de Janeiro and São Paulo. In the case of Rio de Janeiro, most of the mills established during the 1878–95 period were financed by more specialized merchants engaged in the import-export trade dealing mainly with cloth. In the case of São Paulo, capital came mainly from the coffee sector.

Finally, the *mineiro* electricity-generating industry was financed by capital drawn from a number of different activities. Funds invested in the CME and the CFLCL came from trade, manufacturing, banking and farming. There is evidence that coffee capital could also have contributed to the funding of these companies as they were established in one of the largest coffee-growing counties of Minas Gerais (the Mata zone). Furthermore, part of the funds invested in the CFLCL derived directly from the coffee economy, as one of the founders' main source of wealth previous to the establishment of the company was coffee-milling. Comparison with the electricity-generating companies established in São Paulo and Rio de Janeiro has shown that they were financed by foreign, not local capital. Thus, the analysis of the *mineiro* entrepreneur has revealed the existence of a great deal of entrepreneurial initiative and the availability of local sources of capital. The general social attitude towards entrepreneurship seems to have been mostly positive as most entrepreneurs came from the local élite. The main restrictions to the development of a more dynamic and conductive business environment seems to have been of an economic nature, lack of direct access to international markets, inefficient means of transportation, and a scattered and diluted consumer market.

3 The Mineiro Firm

INTRODUCTION

One of the key indicators of the emergence of modern capitalism is the rise of large business enterprises operating many distinct units and managed by a hierarchy of salaried executives. This chapter examines different forms of organizational structures, their origins and implications. It also investigates the structure of several business enterprises in nineteenth-century Minas Gerais. This investigation assesses the degree of structural development of *mineiro* firms in the nineteenth century and relates it to the prevailing business environment.

A BRIEF REVIEW OF THE LITERATURE ON ORGANIZATION THEORY

Many authors have pointed out that one of the key indicators of the emergence of the modern stage of capitalism is the rise of modern corporate business enterprises. Weber, for example, identified three general types of organization based on how authority is exercised within them, each type being expressed in a particular administrative apparatus. The 'charismatic' type is where authority is exercised by one person only and is based on the personal qualities of the leader. The 'traditional' type is where authority and order are based on custom and precedent: selection and appointment is based on kinship rather than expertise. In the 'bureaucratic' type of organization authority is based on expertise. He presented them along an evolutionary scale: from the most personalized and least efficient (charismatic), to the most depersonalized and efficient type (bureaucratic). According to Weber, in modern society the bureaucratic type has become dominant because it is technically the most efficient form of organization possible.[1]

Chandler has advanced Weber's concepts by applying his analysis to capitalistic organizations of an economic nature. Chandler identified basically two types of organizations,

according to the complexity of their administrative structure
and to the scope of their activities: the traditional and the
modern business enterprises. In a traditional firm the administrative structure is embryonic or non-existent and owners
are responsible for all of its basic activities. The modern
business enterprise, by its turn, has a clearly defined administrative structure, employing a hierarchy of middle- and top-
salaried managers. This more developed administrative
structure is related to the larger scale of the operation of
these firms. They usually operate on a national basis and
have several units and divisions.[2]

Even a brief glance at the pattern of corporate development
in Minas Gerais during the last century reveals that most firms
were traditional and small family affairs. Their limited scale
never required the development of a more complex organization of the firm and *mineiro* entrepreneurs continued to manage their firms with old-century techniques and with the help
of a small number of people. The few exceptions which
emerged were due mostly to the nature of the industry rather
than the firm itself. Thus, this chapter analyses the organization
of the *mineiro* firm through an examination of the scope of the
activities and the administrative structure of several firms in
four different sectors: the iron industry; transport; the textile
industry; and the electricity supply industry.

THE SCOPE OF ACTIVITIES

To assess the scope of the activities of the business enterprises,
the analysis will first examine the size of the firms in terms of
the scale of production/operation, the number of workers, the
number of units operated and the economic functions fulfilled by the same company. The nature of their marketing
activities will then be assessed through the nature and size of
the consumer markets, the range of products offered and
channels of distribution.

The Size of the Firm

Owing to the fact that the firms investigated here vary
in nature, it is important to make some remarks before

beginning the analysis of the size of firms in nineteenth-century Minas Gerais. Concerning the number of units operated by each firm, it is important to point out that whereas industries like iron foundries, textile mills and hydroelectric power plants tend to concentrate their activities in only one site, road-construction and transport firms tend to have their activities spread over several sites. The implication of this is that a multi-site transport firm does not necessarily imply bigness owing to the nature of an individual firm, but to the nature of the industry itself. Therefore, this has implications for the organizational structure which has to be more institutionalized, bureaucratic (and less personalized). However, in other industries this can be a clear indication of the size of the firm. Furthermore, the size of the workforce employed by each company must be analysed in the light of the more or less labour-intensive nature of each particular industry.

Until the 1880s, the *mineiro* iron industry was dominated by a large number of very small firms. From then onwards a small number of larger firms began to emerge and predominate. Throughout the nineteenth century, iron firms were single-unit enterprises operating only one foundry. The only exception was the Companhia Nacional de Forjas e Estaleiros (CNFE), which in the early 1890s took over the São Miguel de Piracicaba, the Esperança and the Burnier foundries. However, the CNFE was based in Rio de Janeiro and a few years after having taken control of the above-mentioned foundries the company went bankrupt.[3] Furthermore, all the *mineiro* foundries during this period carried out a single economic function – the production of iron.

The scale of production of the iron firms during the first three-quarters of the last century was limited by the technology employed by them. Basically, there were three methods of production employed by the iron foundries: the '*cadinho*' method, the 'Italian' method and the 'Catalan' method. The first was the simplest and did not require a skilled workforce, and due to its simplicity it was the commonest method used by four-fifths of the *mineiro* foundries.[4] As shown in Table 3.1, output was very limited compared with that of the other two methods. To produce 100 kilos of pig iron by the *cadinho* method required three labourers working 27 days, 7 tons of

Table 3.1 Comparison of the methods of production of pig iron in nineteenth-century Minas Gerais

Method	Consumption of Charcoal (tons)	Consumption of ore (tons)	Number of working days	Production of pig iron (kilos)
Cadinho	7.0	1.0	27	100
Italian	5.5	1.0	18	120
Catalan	3.0	1.0	13	320

Source: J.A. Paula, 'Dois Ensaios sobre a Gênese da Industrialização em Minas Gerais: a Siderurgia e a Indústria Têxtil', in *Anais do II Seminário sobre a Economia Mineira* (Belo Horizonte, 1983), p. 34.

charcoal, and 1 ton of ore of high quality. Although the second method of production – the Italian – was used less, it was more efficient than the *cadinho* method, producing 120 kilos of pig iron, consuming 5.5 tons of charcoal and 1 ton of ore in 18 working days.[5] Nevertheless, it required a more skilled workforce since the process involved the operation of a blast-furnace which required more care in the regulation of the quantity of air to maintain the right temperature. Furthermore, it also required a regular series of successive heating and hammering operations to yield a good final product. Finally, the Catalan method was the most complex process. It required even more skill from the labourers for measuring the quantity of ore and charcoal as well as for making a perfect linkage of the heating and hammering operations. Furthermore, the employment of this method was only feasible if the work was supervised by a manager who had a good knowledge of metallurgy.[6] The Catalan method was the most productive: it yielded 320 kilos of pig iron, required only 3 tons of charcoal and 13 working days. Even so, its scale of production was very limited when compared with the more modern indirect process of production employed by the South Wales ironworks – then the most advanced in the world – using mineral fuel and steam power.[7] As shown in Table 3.2, the least productive ironwork in South Wales in 1812 produced a total of 35 tons per week per blast furnace.

Table 3.2   Output of pig iron from blast furnaces in South Wales
ironworks, 1812

Works	Total blast furnaces	Total output/ week (tons)	Average output/ week per furnace (tons)
Cyfarthfa & Ynysfach	6	340	57
Dowlais	5	200	40
Nantyglo	3	165	35
Plymouth	4	160	40
Penydarren	3	150	50
Ebbw Vale	3	135	45
Clydach	2	130	65
Aberdare	3	105	35
Beaufort	2	90	45
Sirhowy	2	80	40

Source: Adapted from M. Atkinson and C. Barber, *The Growth and Decline of the South Wales Iron Industry, 1760–1880* (Cardiff, 1987), p. 9.

Table 3.3 also provides a clear picture of the scale of production of the iron industry in Minas Gerais. In 1821, the estimated number of iron foundries in Minas Gerais was 31. There were almost three times that number in 1853, by 1864 the number of firms had almost doubled. From then onwards the number of companies started to decrease as railways reached the hinterlands of Minas Gerais, bringing with them foreign competition. In 1883, for example, there were only 80 foundries. For 1893 there are two estimates of the number of foundries: the first shows an increase to 100, and the second differentiates between small and large foundries but lists only 51 of the former. Nevertheless, the long-term tendency of the number of small foundries to decrease is clear, and they were to disappear almost entirely in the following decades.[8]

Although these are only rough estimates, they are useful for drawing a more precise picture of the scale of production of the *mineiro* iron firms. The annual average output per foundry in 1853 and 1880, for example, was about 27 tons. In 1893, according to the first estimate in Table 3.3, it was 20 tons. These average output figures are compatible with the

Table 3.3 Estimated number of iron foundries in nineteenth-century Minas Gerais, their annual output and their annual and weekly averages

Year	Number of works	Annual output (tons)	Average annual output	Average weekly output
1821	31	–	–	–
1853	84	2250	26.8	0.5
1855	105	–	–	–
1864	140	–	–	–
1880	110	3000	27.3	0.5
1881	120	–	–	–
1883	80	–	–	–
1893	100	2000	20.0	0.4
1893	51* 4**	–	–	–

* Number of small foundries.
** Number of large mills.

Source: Adapted from D.C. Libby, *Transformação e Trabalho em uma Economia Escravista: Minas Gerais no Século nineteen* (São Paulo, 1988), p. 154.

annual output of 29 tons forecast by Eschwege for the small foundries in Minas Gerais.[9] Comparison between Tables 3.2 and 3.3 shows clearly how limited the scale of production of the *mineiro* ironworks was. In 1812, the least productive South Wales foundry produced an average of 35 tons per week, but more than 40 years later *mineiro* foundries were producing an average of only 0.5 tons per week. In 1893, this average reduced even further to 0.4 tons. Furthermore, in 1880 the import of wrought iron into the port of Rio de Janeiro was more than 6000 tons,[10] more than double the combined output of all 110 *mineiro* foundries. In other words, to supply the market represented by the import of iron into Rio de Janeiro alone, it would have been necessary to double the existing number of foundries in 1880.

Comparison with the US iron industry is also revealing. In 1880 the US iron industry produced more than 4.2 million tons of iron as shown in Table 3.4. To produce the same quantity at least 154 000 foundries like the ones existing in

Table 3.4   Average net output of the US iron and steel industry,
1860–80

Year	Number of establishments*	Annual net output (tons)	Average output (tons)
1860	627	919 770	1466.9
1870	808	1 865 000	2308.2
1880	1005	4 295 414	4274.0

* The number of establishments includes blast furnaces, mills for the production of bar, sheet and railway iron, wire mills, forges and steel-plates mills.

Source: W.T. Hogan, *Economic History of the Iron and Steel Industry in the United States*, I (Lexington, 1971), pp. 14,91–3.

Minas Gerais in 1880 would have been required. Furthermore, average output per foundry in the US in 1880 was nearly 4300 tons, more than 159 times the annual average output of the *mineiro* iron foundry. Thus, only an industry dominated by large firms with complex administrative structures could have handled the enormous quantity of activities involved in the coordination, planning and appraisal of such production. Therefore, in terms of the scale of production, iron foundries in Minas Gerais in the first three-quarters of the nineteenth century were very small; compared with the South Wales and US works they were almost craft units.

An analysis of the scale of production of individual firms is also very illustrative. In the early 1880s, José Cândido da Costa Sena, an engineer from the Mining School of Ouro Preto, visited and described several foundries located in the Metalúrgica Zone between Ouro Preto and Serro. Altogether he surveyed 21 foundries producing from 694 to 803 tons of iron per year,[11] an average of 33 to 38 tons per year (or 0.6 to 0.7 tons per week) per foundry.

Among the largest foundries the São Miguel de Piracicaba foundry produced 450 kilos of iron per day in 1853; at that time it was the only foundry in Minas Gerais to use the Catalan method.[12] The Patriótica foundry had 4 small furnaces employing the *cadinho* method, and Table 3.5 shows its annual output from 1813 to 1820, the years of Eschwege's

Table 3.5   Annual output in kilos of the Patriótica and the Morro do Pilar foundries, 1813–21

Years	Patriotica	Morro do pilar
1813	14.6	n.a.
1814	14.7	n.a.
1815	18.8	5.8
1816	16.7	17.1
1817	13.5	11.7
1818	n.a.	13.8
1819	24.2	10.3
1820	18.1	37.3
1821	n.a.	5.0

Source: Adapted from W.L. von Eschwege, *Pluto Brasiliensis*, vol. II (Berlin, 1833; reprinted Belo Horizonte/São Paulo, 1979), pp. 212, 251 and 304.

administration. The highest level of output was 24.2 tons in 1819 – a figure which was two-thirds of the weekly output of the smallest South Wales foundry – and the lowest level was 13.5 tons in 1817. The figures for 1818 are not known. The average output for the whole period is 17.2 tons per year, less than one-third of the installed capacity of 58.8 tons.[13] At the Morro do Pilar foundry the story was not very much different. According to Eschwege, although the output of the Morro do Pilar was planned to be much higher, its actual output was scarcely higher than that of his own foundry.[14] Comparison between the two foundries presented in Table 3.5 shows that, apart from the years 1816 and 1820, the annual output of the Morro do Pilar was always less than that of the Patriótica. Furthermore, for the period 1815–21 the average output of the Morro do Pilar was 14.4 tons, 19 per cent less than the average output of Eschwege's foundry.

Thus, during the first three-quarters of the last century, iron firms in Minas Gerais were characterized by their low scale of production, both in terms of installed capacity and actual output. Compared with the South Wales and US ironworks, even the largest firms in Minas Gerais were very small in this respect.

Table 3.6   The Esperança foundry: annual output and variation in percentage year by year, 1899–1914

Year	Variation in % year by year	Annual output (tons)	Year	Variation in % year by year	Annual output (tons)
1899		80	1907	(+) 14.9	1901
1900	(+) 845.0	756	1908	(−) 1.7	1868
1901	(+) 9.3	826	1909	(+) 14.2	2134
1902	(+) 52.3	1258	1910	(+) 24.6	2658
1903	(+) 8.1	1360	1911	(+) 22.7	3262
1904	(+) 25.7	1710	1912	(+) 6.2	3463
1905	(−) 23.7	1304	1913	(+) 15.5	4000
1906	(+) 26.8	1654	1914	(−) 45.5	2181

Source: Adapted from C.M. Peláez, *História da Industrialização Brasileira: Crítica à Teoria Estruturalista no Brasil* (Rio de Janeiro, 1972), p. 146.

For the rest of the nineteenth century, the scale of production of the iron industry increased as larger works began to emerge, but, nevertheless, output continued to be small in comparative terms. The largest works existing during this period were the Esperança and the Burnier foundries. Until 1896 the Esperança had an installed capacity of 5 tons per day, or 1700 tons per year.[15] Although there is no more information about its installed capacity, figures of its annual output were not very impressive. As shown in Table 3.6, in 1899 its annual output totalled only 80 tons. This very low level of output seems to reflect the fact that the control of the foundry was passed to a group of banks after the bankruptcy of the CNFE. In the following year the foundry was sold to Joaquim Queiroz Júnior[16] and output increased considerably to 756 tons per year. In 1902 output increased by more than 50 per cent to 1258 tons. In 1909 output reached the 2000 tons per year mark and by the outbreak of the First World War stood at 4000 tons per year. Compared with the average output of individual US iron firms these figures are indeed not very impressive. In 1896 the installed capacity of the Esperança foundry was less than half of the average output of the US industry in 1880 (4274 tons per year). In 1900, output of the Esperança foundry was less than 18 per cent of the US average output in 1880. Finally, the 1880 US average output was still 7 per cent larger than the output of the Esperança foundry in 1913.

The Burnier foundry was no exception. Its initial installed capacity amounted to 5 tons per day, or around 1700 tons per year.[17] Unfortunately there is no information about its annual output. Nevertheless, the figures for both the Esperança and the Burnier foundries are indisputable evidence that the 'technology gap' was closing towards the end of the century. At the beginning of the nineteenth century *mineiro* ironworks were minute compared with the then world leader, South Wales. By the end of the century the Esperança capacity alone was half that of the US average. Thus, although the ironworks which emerged in the latter part of the nineteenth century represented an evolution in terms of the scale of production of this industry, in comparative terms iron firms were still only as large as the US ironworks had been three or more decades earlier, and as large as the smallest South Wales foundry of the first decade of the last century, as listed in Table 3.2.

Owing to the scarcity of information it is nearly impossible to state precisely the average number of workers employed by *mineiro* foundries before 1880. Nevertheless, from the scattered information available it is possible to say that very few foundries in this period employed more than 20 people. From 1831 to 1840, for example, there were 24 foundries spread across several districts of the Metalúrgica–Mantiqueira zones where the bulk of the industry was situated.[18] There is information about the workforce of only 22 foundries which, altogether, employed 168 slaves and 70 free workers,[19] an average of 10.7 workers per foundry. In 1864, from the 21 foundries established in Santa Bárbara a district within the Metalúrgica–Mantiqueira zones, 20 firms employed a total of 178 workers, each foundry employing between four and 16 people.[20]

The exceptions to this rule were the São Miguel de Piracicaba, the Morro do Pilar, the Girau and the Patriótica foundries which were the largest in terms of number of workers during this period. In 1840 the São Miguel de Piracicaba foundry employed 151 slaves. It seems that this number did not change very much in 1853 when, answering an inquiry about the iron industry in Minas Gerais organized by the president of the province, Monlevade mentioned that in his foundry there were 150 slaves.[21] In 1864 the foundry employed 103 workers.[22] The Morro do Pilar foundry was one of the first foundries established in Minas Gerais, but was short-lived: set up in 1808 it was shut down in 1831. In 1814 it employed a total of 34 workers and in 1821 137 workers.[23] The Girau foundry employed 25 workers in 1817, and in 1840 it employed 49 slaves and 1 manager. During the period 1831–40, only the Patriótica and the São Miguel de Piracicaba foundries were larger than the Girau in terms of the size of the workforce.[24] The Patriótica foundry was established by Eschwege a German engineer in 1811, and during his days, until 1821, the Patriótica employed a total of 24 people including Eschwege himself.[25] In 1831 the Patriótica was considered the largest foundry when it employed 55 slaves.[26]

Further evidence of the small size of *mineiro* iron firms emerges from the analysis of the number of workers required for the operation of the foundries which employed the widespread *cadinho* and the Italian methods of production. According to Ferrand, the *cadinho* process required at least three workers per furnace: one operating the *cadinhos* in the furnace, one working with the hammermill, and another as assistant. Although the preparation and procurement of charcoal and ore required the work of at least eight labourers, they could be acquired from a third-party. The Italian process also required very few people in its operation. It required at least four workers per furnace: one operating the furnace, one the hammermill, one as assistant, and another for carrying the ore. Thus, these small foundries using the *cadinho* and Italian methods required only three and four permanent workers on site respectively.[27] Unfortunately there is no information about the minimum number of workers required to operate a foundry using the Catalan process. Nevertheless, the Catalan was the least employed method of production in Minas Gerais and the foundries which employed this method were probably the least representative of the average *mineiro* foundry.

This brief analysis of the *mineiro* iron firms shows clearly how small the industry was, being made up of small foundries

Table 3.7 Average workforce in the US iron and steel industry for 1860–80

year	Number of establishments#	Number of workers*	Average
1860	627	40000	63.8
1870	808	77000	95.3
1880	1005	140000	139.3

* Estimated numbers.
# The figures include blast furnaces, mills for the production of bar, sheets and railway iron, wire mills, forges and steel plates.
Source: Hogan, *op.cit.*, pp. 91–3.

employing an average of 11 workers, with very few firms employing more than 20 workers and the largest employing at most 150 people. Around the 1860s, US firms had an average of approximately 64 workers as shown in Table 3.7. In 1870 the average number of workers employed by the US iron and steel industries increased to 95 and in 1880 to 139, when the US average was about the same as the largest foundries in Minas Gerais. Thus, the *mineiro* iron industry of the first three-quarters of the nineteenth century was small in every respect: economic functions, scale of production, number of workers employed, and the number of units operated.

By contrast, the Companhia União e Indústria (CUI) was certainly a large enterprise. Basically, it fulfilled two economic functions: the construction of roads and the transport of goods and passengers. The relevance of this fact to an organizational analysis of the CUI is that the construction of large transport undertaking in the USA, for example the Erie Canal, did not involve a lot of administrative coordination; it was more a technical than an administrative task. It was the operation of railways and canals which called for more administration, even though before the 1850s, due to their short length, the existing railways in the USA had little need for a systematic organizational structure.[28] Thus, the fact that the CUI not only built but also operated the União e Indústria turnpike indicates that it was an enterprise of considerable size in organizational terms.

Table 3.8   Length of the Brazilian railways in 1867

Railway	Length km
EFDPII	197.4
São Paulo	139.0
Bahia	123.5
Pernambuco	124.9
Cantagallo	49.1
Mauá	17.5
Total	651.4

EFDPII – Estrada de Ferro Dom Pedro II.

Source: Ministerio da Agricultura, Commercio e Obras Publicas, *Relatorio da Repartição dos Negocios da Agricultura, Commercio e Obras Publicas* (Rio de Janeiro, 1868), p. 84.

The scale of operation of the CUI was both large and unprecedented for nineteenth-century Minas Gerais. The establishment of the company and the construction of the turnpike predated any railway in the province, a time when the bulk of the transport of people and goods was made by muletrain, ox cart and horse. In 1853 the company was granted a franchise to operate a provincial road – the Paraibuna road – which extended from Barbacena to the Paraibuna river. From 1856 to 1861 the company built 144 kilometres of new carriageway linking the cities of Juiz de Fora, by the Paraibuna river in the province of Minas Gerais, and Petrópolis, in the province of Rio de Janeiro.[29] In 1867 the total length of roads operated by the company was approximately 380 kilometres.[30] To have an idea of what these figures represent, a comparison with railways in Brazil and the USA is revealing. In 1867, for example, the largest railway established in Brazil was the Estrada de Ferro Dom Pedro II (EFDPII), which was 197.4 kilometres in length as shown in Table 3.8. The smallest was the Mauá railway, which was 17.5 kilometres in length. Together, all the Brazilian railways in 1867 amounted to 651.4 kilometres in length; that is, less than double the length of roads operated by the CUI alone during the same year. A year later the EFDPII continued to be smaller with 216 kilometres.[31] Moreover, most

Table 3.9 Passenger and freight traffic, and percentage of goods exported on the União e Indústria turnpike, 1858–74

Years	Passengers	Total of goods transported (tons)	% of goods exported
1858*	5 499	10 974	68
1859	8 926	22 776	71
1860	10 093	26 970	75
1861	13 505	29 743	79
1862	14 291	20 695	59
1863	13 576	23 345	69
1864	13 962	23 802	64
1865	14 453	31 988	67
1866	14 902	32 627	65
1867	16 418	41 061	74
1868	21 969	36 641	73
1869	23 975	n.a.	–
1870	21 385	n.a.	–
1871	23 508	n.a.	–
1873	27 098	51 683	62
1874	27 682	55 861	63

* From April to December.

Source: Compiled from Companhia União e Indústria, *Relatório da Assembléia Geral dos Acionistas* (1864, 1865, 1872, 1875).

railways in the USA before the 1850s were rarely more than 160 kilometres in extent.[32] Thus, in terms of route mileage the Uniao e Indústria turnpike was larger than existing railways in both Brazil and the USA.

Nevertheless, the scale of the transport of passengers and goods operated by the company does not point to a considerable operation as Table 3.9 shows. From 1858 to 1860 the turnpike was not in full operation and this is reflected in the figures of the passenger traffic. The main section of the turnpike, between Juiz de Fora and Petrópolis, was inaugurated in June 1861, and in the following decade passenger traffic nearly doubled from 13 505 in 1861 to 23 508 in 1871. In 1874 traffic amounted to 27 682 passengers. Nevertheless, these numbers are very small if compared with the figures of the EFDPII. In 1869 the EFDPII transported a total of 778

543 people,[33] while the CUI handled only 23 975 passengers. In other words, the CUI transported 3 per cent of the number of passengers carried by the EFDPII in 1869.

Table 3.9 also presents the figures for freight carried by the CUI from 1858 to 1874. During this period the total weight of goods transported increased by a factor of five. However, compared with the tonage carried by the EFDPII, the total of freight carried by the CUI was also very small. In 1868, for example, the EFDPII carried a total of 104 530 tons of goods,[34] against the 36 641 tons carried by the CUI (that is, the road handled only 35 per cent of the freight carried by the EFDPII). Thus, although the CUI operated a large number of kilometres of roads, the scale of operation measured in terms of freight and passengers transported was not very large.

In terms of the size of its workforce, the CUI was certainly one of the largest employers in nineteenth-century Minas Gerais. In 1855, for example, the number of slaves employed by the company oscillated between 515 and 828. During that year the company also employed several skilled workers like engineers, architects, carpenters and so on, and the overall number of workers may have reached 1000 people.[35] In 1856 the company employed 1102 people, among them 900 slaves and 80 free labourers. The remainder was made up of architects, drivers, horse-masters, foremen, carpenters, bricklayers, coachmen, blacksmiths, engineers and so forth.[36] In 1857 the company employed 804 slaves and in the company report of that year the chairman of the board, Lage, indicated that the number of free workers had increased.[37] Thus, based on the figures of workers for the year 1856 when the company employed 1102 people, it is realistic to say that the total number employed in 1857 may have been around 1000. In 1858, according to a report by Lage to the president of the province of Minas Gerais, the company employed 2636 workers. In the section of the road between Juiz de Fora and Paraíba 1136 were employed – among them 800 slaves and 336 free workers. The other 1500 were employed in the section between Petrópolis and Paraíba do Sul. For this section of the road there is no breakdown of the number of workers between slave and free.[38]

In 1860, with new roads under construction, notably the section between Pedro do Rio and the Paraibuna river, the company employed 3500 workers. Again there is no information of how this workforce was constituted. There is no indication of the proportion of slaves, of skilled workers, of those employed directly by the company, or of those employed by contractors hired to build parts of the turnpike. Nevertheless, based on the figures of the previous years it is quite reasonable to say that the direct workforce for 1860 could have been well over 1000 people.[39] In 1861 the construction of the turnpike from Petrópolis to Juiz de Fora was completed and, as no other major construction work was undertaken, the number of workers fell steadily from then onwards. In 1866, for example, the company employed a total of 344 people.[40] By this time the company was in serious trouble and was taken over by the Imperial government, the road was being leased back to the CUI for 15 years.[41] In the following years, as the EFDPII advanced towards the hinterland of Minas Gerais, competition became extremely tough for the CUI. Ultimately, in 1869 the turnpike was absorbed by the EFDPII.[42] As a consequence investment decreased as shown in the company report of 1871, and it is reasonable to expect that the number of workers tended to stabilize as the demise of the company approached. For the period 1866 onwards, however, there is no information about the number of workers employed by the company.

Finally, in terms of capital the CUI could not be considered a large enterprise. The company was organized with a nominal capital of 5.000:000$000 contos, but the issued capital never exceeded 3.060:000$000 contos.[43] To appreciate the size of the capital of the CUI it is interesting to compare it with the capital of other Brazilian companies established during the same time. Of the 76 companies registered between 1850 and 1865 in the tribunal of commerce of Rio de Janeiro, only six had a capital larger than 10.000:000$000 contos, and were considered large enterprises in this respect. Furthermore, only five companies, with a capital between 5.000:000$000 and 10.000:000$000 contos, were considered medium-size enterprises. Of the remaining 65 companies, the capital of four was unknown and 61 were considered small companies with a capital smaller than 5.000:000$000 contos.[44] Thus, in terms of capitalization the CUI was considered a small enterprise.

The average *mineiro* textile mill of the last century could hardly be considered a large enterprise, even by Brazilian standards. Until the 1870s only two textile mills were established in Minas Gerais: the Companhia Industrial Mineira (CIM) founded in the late 1830s, and the Cana do Reino mill set up in the early 1840s. Both were small and short-lived enterprises. The only information about production at the CIM dates from the end of 1840, when the mill produced about 990 metres of cloth in 20 days of work, employing 21 workers and 16 spindles. The story of the Cana do Reino mill is better documented. Although it was shut down in the 1870s the mill was more successful than the CIM.[45] Nevertheless, it was a very small affair even when compared with other Brazilian textile mills of its time. Table 3.10 lists nine textile mills located in Bahia (BA), Rio de Janeiro (RJ), Alagoas (AL) and Minas Gerais (MG) in 1868. The sizes of these mills are measured in terms of the number of looms and workers employed, and the annual output. The largest was the Todos os Santos mill in Bahia employing 136 looms and 200 workers, with an output of 1 100 000 metres of cloth per year.

Table 3.10   Brazilian textile mills in 1868: number of looms, workers and annual output

Mills (province)	Looms	Annual output (in metres)	Worker
Todos os Santos (BA)	136	1 100 000	200
Santo Aleixo (RJ)	52	605 000	150
Nossa Senhora do Amparo (BA)	48	660 000	90
Sto. Antônio Queimados (BA)	30	352 000	90
Santa Theresa (RJ)	n.a.	n.a.	20
Modelo (BA)	39	550 000	110
Fernão Velho (AL)	40	160 600	33
Conceição (BA)	35	495 000	60
Cana do Reino (MG)	5	220 000	15
Average	48	517 825	85

Source: Adapted from Ministério da Agricultura, Commercio e Obras Publicas, *Relatorio da Repartição dos Negocios da Agricultura, Commercio e Obras Publicas* (Rio de Janeiro, 1868), p. 52.

The smallest was the Cana do Reino mill employing 5 looms and 15 workers, with an output of 220 000 metres of cloth per year. On average, the textile mills listed in Table 3.10 employed 48 looms, 85 workers and produced 517 825 metres of cloth per year. Thus, the Cana do Reino mill was considerably smaller than the average size of Brazilian textile mills in 1868.

It was only in the final three decades of the century that a number of larger and more successful textile mills emerged in Minas Gerais. Even so they were small or medium-sized firms, operating only one unit and fulfilling a single economic function – the manufacturing of cotton. In the 1870s six mills were established in Minas Gerais. The average initial capital was 150:000$000 contos (or £15 472) and the mills employed an average of 28 looms and 67 workers, as shown in Table 3.11. In the 1880s, investment in new mills boomed with 16 firms being established, and on average they were larger than the ones established a decade earlier. Nevertheless, they did not constitute large enterprises, and had an average initial capital of 237:000$000 contos (or £21 764) with an average of

Table 3.11 Minas Gerais: textile mills established in the 1870s

| Year | Mill | Capital | | No. of looms | No. of workers |
		Contos	£		
1872	Cedro	150	15 600	18	70
1872	Brumado	150	15 600	40	80
1875	Machadense	n.a.	–	10	n.a.
1876	BiriBiry	n.a.	–	20	n.a.
1877	Cachoeira	200	20 460	50	n.a.
1877	União Itabirana	100	10 230	28	50
Average (1870s)		150	15 472	28	67

Note: (n.a) information not available.

Sources: Compiled from A.M. Vaz, *Cia. Cedro e Cachoeira: História de uma Empresa Familiar, 1883–1987* (Belo Horizonte, 1990), p. 25; M.T.R.O. Versiani, 'The Cotton Textile Industry of Minas Gerais, Brazil: Beginnings and Early Development 1868–1906', University of London, unpublished Ph.D. thesis, 1991), pp. 70–111; Libby, *op.cit.*, pp. 227–30.

Table 3.12 Minas Gerais: textile mills established in the 1880s

Year	Mill	Capital Contos	£	No. of looms	No. of workers
1880	Marzagão	150	13 800	46	100
1880	Filatório Montes Claros	150	13 800	40	73
1881	Bom Jardim	233	21 250	50	140
1884	São Sebastião	189	16 273	40	75
1884	São Silvestre	200	17 220	50	60
1884	Industrial Mineira	240	20 664	73	200
1885	Cassú	150	11 610	28	60
1885	São Vicente	160	12 384	40	n.a.
1886	União Lavrense	200	15 560	176	n.a.
1886	Cachoeira dos Macacos	300	23 340	100	180
1886	Santa Bárbara	200	15 560	60	n.a.
1887	Paulo Moreirense	120	11 208	n.a.	n.a.
1888	Mascarenhas	600	63 120	30	n.a.
1888	Pedreira	200	21 040	65	n.a.
1888	São Roberto	500	52 600	60	n.a.
n.a.	Industrial Ouro Preto	200	18 800[#]	n.a.	n.a.
Average (1880s)		237	21 764	61	101

Notes: (n.a.) information not available.
[#] This figure was calculated based on the exchange rate for 1890.
Sources: Compiled from Vaz, *op.cit.*, p. 25; Versiani, op.cit., pp. 70–111; Libby, *op.cit.*, pp. 227–30.

61 looms and 101 workers employed, as shown in Table 3.12. In the 1890s 12 new mills were inaugurated in Minas Gerais which, in terms of capital, were smaller than the mills established in the 1870s and 1880s. It seems that in terms of the number of looms employed they were larger than the mills set up in the two previous decades, as shown in Table 3.13. However, it is important to point out that the average number of looms for the 1890s is biased towards the larger mills, since there is no information about the number of looms for several of the smaller mills founded during this period. Furthermore, there is no information about the size of the workforce employed by these mills. Thus, although in the long-run the *mineiro* textile mills tended to be larger, they did not

Table 3.13   Minas Gerais: textile mills established in the 1890s

Year	Mill	Capital		No. of looms	No. of workers
		Contos	£		
1891	Santanense	600	37 260	100	n.a.
1891	São Joanense	300	18 630	100	n.a.
1892	Itabira do Campo	360	18 036	100	n.a.
1893	Pitanguense	400	19 320	200	n.a.
1893	Cachoeira Grande	500	24 150	120	n.a.
1893	Progresso Fabril	150	7 245	n.a.	n.a.
1893	Melancias	100	4 830	38	n.a.
1894	São Domingos	150	6 300	n.a.	n.a.
1894	São João Nepomuceno	130	5 460	n.a.	n.a.
1895	Jequitahy	250	10 350	n.a.	n.a.
n.a.	Perpetua	n.a.	–	15	n.a.
n.a.	Itinga	n.a.	–	48	n.a.
Average (1890s)		294	15 158	90	–

Note: (n.a.) information not available.

Sources: Compiled from Vaz, op.cit., p. 25; Versiani, op.cit., pp. 70–111; Libby, op.cit., pp. 227–30.

constitute very large enterprises, at least not at the time of their establishment.

A comparison of *mineiro* and other Brazilian textile mills provides a better idea of the relative importance of firms in Minas Gerais. Table 3.14 lists eight textile mills located in Rio de Janeiro (RJ), São Paulo (SP), Bahia (BA) and Alagoas (AL) in 1881. The sizes of these mills are measured in terms of the number of looms and workers employed, and the annual output. They were considerably larger than any of the mills in Minas Gerais in the last three decades of the nineteenth century.

Even a comparison of the mills listed in Table 3.14 with the *mineiro* mills some years after their establishment yields the same result: *mineiro* textile mills continued to be smaller. Table 3.15 lists five of the six mills established in Minas Gerais in the 1870s. In 1881 and 1882 these five firms were certainly among the largest textile mills in Minas Gerais but, nevertheless, they were hardly half the average size of the eight

Table 3.14   Brazilian textile mills in 1881: number of looms,
workers and annual output

Year	Mill (province)	Looms	Annual output (metres)	Workers
1881	Santo Aleixo (BA)	110	1 000 000	180
1881	Petropolitana (RJ)	106	1 000 000	180
1881	Brasil Industrial (RJ)	450	3 200 000	400
1881	FFTTA (RJ)	100	2 000 000	210
1881	Fernão Velho (AL)	60	550 000	125
1881	FTR (RJ)	110	1 500 000	130
1881	FTPG (RJ)	60	500 000	110
1881	Santa Francisca (SP)	80	–	160
Average		216	1 393 000	187

FFTTA – Fábrica de Fiação, Tecidos e Tinturaria Alliançai; FTR –
Fábrica de Tecidos do Rink; FTPG – Fábrica de Tecidos Pau
Grande.
Source: Libby, *op.cit.*, p. 232.

textile mills listed in Table 3.14. Furthermore, the other
Brazilian mills listed in Table 3.14 had approximately five
times more looms, a workforce 45 per cent larger, and an
annual output five times larger than their *mineiro* counterparts in 1881–82: they were not only larger but also much
more efficient. By 1885, as shown in Table 3.16, things had
not changed very much as the *mineiro* textile mills were still
not half the size of the mills listed in Table 3.14, and it seems
that this pattern did not change very much during the rest of
the nineteenth century. In 1909 the 35 existing *mineiro* mills
on average produced 470 000 metres per year and employed
110 workers.[46]
    Thus, from the previous analysis it becomes clear that the
textile industry in nineteenth-century Minas Gerais was made
up of small and medium-sized mills, both in terms of
the number of looms and workers employed, and in terms of
the annual output. It is also clear that the *mineiro* textile mills
were more labour-intensive than their Brazilian counterparts.
    Although by 1920 Minas Gerais had the third largest
installed electricity-generating capacity (42 934 kW) and the

Table 3.15   Mineiro textile mills in 1881–2: number of looms, workers and annual output

Year	Mill	Looms	Annual output (metres)	Workers
1881	Cedro	40	220 532	130
1881	Cachoeira	60	401 323	130
1881	Brumado	20	–	80
1882	BiriBiry	40	–	130
1882	União Itabirana	28	–	42
Average		38	310 928	102

Sources: Compiled from Libby, op.cit., p. 232; Vaz, op.cit., pp. 62,77.

Table 3.16   Mineiro textile mills in 1885: number of looms, workers and annual output.

Mill	Looms	Annual output (in metres)	Workers
Cedro	56	369 136	132
Cachoeira	110	693 955	187
União Itabirana	28	–	64
Montes Claros	40	360 000	81
Cassú	24	200 000	58
São Sebastião	40	500 000	75
Marzagão	50	135 000	80
São Silvestre	50	400 000	60
Industrial Mineira	–	–	200
São Vicente	40	–	–
Average	49	379 727	104

Sources: Compiled from Libby, op.cit., p. 232; Vaz, op.cit., pp. 62, 77.

largest number of power companies (72) established in Brazil, the *mineiro* electricity-generating companies also could not be considered large enterprises. Most of them were small, fufilling only one economic function, working on a municipal basis, and operating power stations of a small scale.[47]

Table 3.17   Companhia Mineira de Eletricidade, 1889–1901: power production

Years	1889	1892	1896	1897	1901
Power production (kw)	250	375	600	600	600

Sources: Compiled from P. Oliveira, *Companhia Mineira de Eletricidade: Pioneira da Iluminação Hidrelétrica na América do Sul* (Juiz de Fora, 1969), pp. 24–44; Companhia Mineira de Eletricidade, 'Balanço e Relatório' reproduced in *O Pharol* (Juiz de Fora), 27 August 1897, p. 1.

Although the Companhia Mineira de Eletricidade (CME) was a multi-sector operation – the company first began producing electricity in 1889 and some years later, in 1893, it acquired the telephone service of Juiz de Fora[48] – the company could not be considered a large business enterprise. At the time of the inauguration of the lighting service, the company operated only one plant producing a total of 250 kW as shown in Table 3.17. In 1892 the company increased its generating capacity to 375 kW, and the construction of a second power plant increased the generating capacity to 600 kW in 1896. For the remainder of the century there was no further increase in the generating capacity.

Like the CME, the Companhia Força e Luz Cataguazes-Leopoldina (CFLCL) also could not be considered a large firm. It fulfilled only one economic function, that is the generation of hydroelectric power, and in 1908 the company inaugurated its first plant with a total generating capacity of 800 KW.[49]

Comparison of both companies with what came to be known as the Light System is very illustrative. The Light System was constituted by the São Paulo Tramway, Light and Power Company (SPTLPC) and the Rio de Janeiro Tramway, Light and Power Company Ltd (RJTLPC), which were foreign-owned companies. Both companies were constituted in Canada. The first in 1889 and the second in 1904. In 1901 the SPTLPC inaugurated its power plant with a generating capacity of 2000 kW, which was expanded to 3000 kW in February 1902, and to 4000 kW in March of the following year. In other words, in 1901 the SPTLPC had a generating capacity more than three times larger than that of the CME in 1896, and more than twice as large as that of the CFLCL in 1908. The RJTLPC, by its turn, inaugurated its first electrical power plant – considered the largest in Brazil and one of the largest in the world – in April of 1908 with a generating capacity of 12000 kW.[50] In other words, a generating capacity 20 times larger than that of the CME in 1896, and 15 times larger than that of the CFLCL in 1908.

In terms of the size of the workforce employed, *mineiro* electricity-generating companies of the turn of the century were also small. Although there is no information about the size of the workforce employed by the CME, the CFLCL in 1908 employed a total of 29 people,[51] which was a small workforce by any standard. The total number of workers employed by the company did not change considerably until the end of the 1910s, when it employed 30 people.[52]

The capital of both companies provides further evidence of their small size. The initial nominal capital of the CME amounted to 150:000$000 contos in 1888 (or £15 780). As mentioned above this is about the same amount as the initial capital of the Cedro mill in 1872 (£15 600), which was a small textile mill. In 1890 capital was increased to 300:000$000 contos (or £28 200), and in 1894 to 800:000$000 contos (or £33 600). Finally, in 1911, the capital of the company was increased to 1.400:000$000 contos[53] (or £94 780). The initial capital of the CFLCL in 1906 amounted to 500:000$000 contos[54] (or £32 800). A further comparison with the SPTLPC puts these figures into perspective. The SPTLPC was constituted in 1889 with an initial capital of US$ 6 000 000 (or £1 232 792[55]). Furthermore, the power plant built by the company, completed in 1901, alone cost 2.000:000$000 contos[56] (or £97 800), nearly three times the capital (in pounds) of the CFLCL in 1906 and about the same the capital of the CME in 1911.

Thus, the *mineiro* electricity generating companies of the turn of the century were small firms in every respect: scale of operation, number of workers employed, capital and range of activities.

To sum up, throughout the nineteenth century the *mineiro* iron industry was small in every respect. Firms were single-unit enterprises carrying on only one economic function – the production of iron. In the first three-quarters of the last century they employed very simple and primitive technology which imposed a strict limit to the scale of production. Towards the end of the century a few larger works emerged employing more complex technology. Nevertheless, the scale of production remained small. Finally, the number of workers was also small with very few foundries employing more than 20 people.

The data examined also reveals that the CUI was one of the largest enterprises in Minas Gerais in the nineteenth century. The company fulfilled more than one economic function: it constructed and operated the União e Indústria turnpike, and from the point of view of the length of the roads built and operated the company was a major concern even by the standards of the USA. The size of the workforce also indicates a substantial enterprise. Yet, the scale of operations measured in terms of freight and passenger transport could hardly be considered large when compared with that of the EFDPII. The size of its capital was also small when compared with that of the largest Brazilian companies established in the period 1850–65.

The analysis of the *mineiro* textile industry shows that the industry was made up of small and medium-sized firms, rarely operating more than one unit and fulfilling a single economic function – the manufacture of cotton. The scale of production of the largest *mineiro* textile firms proved to be only a third as large as that of the largest Brazilian textile firms. Finally, in terms of the size of the workforce, although the *mineiro* firms proved to be much more labour-intensive than their Brazilian counterparts, their workforce tended to be smaller in absolute terms.

Finally, the CME and the CFLCL were small enterprises in terms of the scale of their operations and the size of their capital, fulfilling no more than one economic function in the specific case of the CFLCL. Although there is no information about the size of the workforce employed by the CME, that of the CFLCL in 1908 points to a very small firm indeed.

The Market Structure

This part analyses the nature of the marketing activities of nineteenth-century *mineiro* firms through an examination of the nature and size of their consumer market, the range of products or services offered, and the channels of distribution used by them. Nevertheless, an analysis of the marketing of any firm must take into account the fact that, given the different nature of products and services, there are bound to be differences between companies producing tangible products – like iron foundries and textile mills – and those providing services – like transport and electricity-generating companies. Utilities often enjoy monopolies (although sometimes temporary monopolies), whereas physical commodities are more tradable and subject to distinct forms of external pressures as the parameters of a market shift. Thus, whereas channels of distribution may be a relevant aspect in the marketing strategy of those companies dealing with tangible products, for example, it may not be so relevant to companies providing services.

Nineteenth-century *mineiro* iron foundries were mostly restricted to local markets which were not very large and could absorb only a small quantity of products. Evidence of the limited size of the consumer market during this period is given by Eschwege, when he made the following remarks about the possibilities of setting up a large-scale ironworks in Brazil:

> The large factories which are setup in the interior of Brazil . . . would end up without finding a consumer market for their production. Although raw material and salaries there [in the interior of Brazil] are half the average price in the coastal regions, these large factories would have to face obstacles such as the lack of foreign technicians and suitable means of transport to the coast, rendering their products much more expensive than those imported from Europe.
>
> . . . And even in the interior, they [the large factories] would not be able to expand more than the local market could absorb.
>
> As competition among consumers is very small, because the population is scattered, the factories must be relatively small.[57]

Furthermore, when comparing the Patriótica foundry with the Morro de Pilar and the São João do Ipanema foundries, the latter located in São Paulo, Eschwege gives further evidence about the limited size of the *mineiro* consumer market for iron products:

> In what concerns my foundry... it produced iron in the same quantity and quality as that of the Swede's [the São João do Ipanema mill] and Câmara's foundries. The Patriótica foundry could produce more than 58 tons per year as long as it worked day and night without stopping. Nevertheless, it did not happen, first, because of the insufficient number of slaves to guarantee the production of the necessary quantity of charcoal; second, because it would not be possible to sell the whole output.[58]

And he concludes the description of his foundry by saying that:

> In Brazil it is still rewarding to establish a small foundry, with maximum annual output of 29 tons, because a larger quantity will not find a market.[59]

Further, he estimates the size of the market for iron in Minas Gerais:

> This province has a population of 500 000 people, spread over an area of 18 000 square leagues. Its five-year consumption... reached 36 699 arrobas [531 tons] of iron and 6 968 [101 tons] of steel, an annual average of 7 339 arrobas [106 tons] of iron and 1376 [20 tons] of steel.[60]

And he concludes by saying that it would be impossible to establish a large foundry in Minas Gerais intended to supply the province as a whole. Several small foundries were already in operation and it would be nearly impossible to hinder the importation from other places, especially from the coast. Even if the iron manufactured in Minas Gerais could be sold 50 per cent cheaper than that imported, merchants would not be able to sell it cheap to a consumer market more than 10 to 12 miles away from the foundry. The more distant consumer preferred to import iron from the coast which would come mixed with other goods, than to buy it directly from the foundries in which case it would be very expensive and would give him much more trouble to transport on the backs of mules.[61]

Mineiro iron foundries supplied mainly mining companies, farms and small towns. Needing replacement of components that were difficult to import, gold-mining companies became essential to the development of the foundries in Minas Gerais.[62] Mining companies had such a necessity for iron goods that some were led to try to produce them on site.[63] In his report to the president of the province in 1853, Monlevade provides further evidence of the importance of local demand, particularly by gold-mining companies, but also hints at the importance of the market for agricultural tools and equipment as a source of demand for iron.

In 1881, a study by Costa Sena concluded that the range of products produced by the *mineiro* iron industry included not only parts for mining machinery and agricultural tools, but also domestic appliances, horseshoes and a variety of other items for muletrains and carriages which constituted the transport system of that time.[64] Further evidence that the transport sector might have been a consumer of the iron produced in Minas Gerais is given by Esteves. He remarked that the CUI used in its workshops a great quantity of iron produced in Itabira, Minas Gerais.[65] Among the foundries located in the Metalúrgica zone in the early 1880s, which were primarily producing for the local market, Costa Sena mentions the following: João Carneiro's foundry, which produced 120 kilos of iron per day to be sold to other small foundries who transformed it into hoes, scythes, axes and so on; D. Ana's foundry, situated 3 kilometres from João Carneiro's, which produced 90 kilos of bar iron per day which was sold to smaller foundries; Captain Vicente Pessoa's foundry, situated 8 kilometres from São Miguel, which produced 90 kilos of iron per day transformed into hoes; the D. Luísa plant, located 11 kilometres from São Miguel, which produced 150 kilos of iron per day, also manufacturing hoes, sickles and axes; the Onça foundry, located around 7 kilometres from Itabira, which produced 135 kilos of iron per day used in the production of 20 hoes per day; Lieutenant João Martin's foundry, located in Lages and manufacturing hoes, scythes and ironware; Colonel Antônio Rodrigues' foundry, situated 3 kilometres from Morro do Gaspar Soares, producing horseshoes; Colonel Jorge's foundry, situated 3 kilometres from Morro do Gaspar Soares, producing horseshoes, hoes, horseshoe nails and so on; Capitão Modesto's plant, producing hoes; and Capitão Domingo's, manufacturing hoes. Monlevade's foundry manufactured not only parts for mining machinery and tools for agriculture, it also produced more delicate objects like clocks and even a sewing machine.[66] His hoes, for example, came to have a good reputation.[67] Thus, the evidence presented above shows that the iron industry as a whole supplied a number of different products to different customers, such as parts for mining machinery, agricultural tools, domestic appliances, horseshoes and so on, to very local markets. However, at the individual firm level, the range of products manufactured tended to be much narrower.

Until the arrival of the railways, distribution of the output was made by muletrains. Apart from duties, the lack of suitable means of transport explains why imports could not compete with local products; prices would increase in the same proportion as the costs of transport. Thus:

> In the greater part of the province of Minas, the price of [imported] iron has already increased 300%, since 100% is due to provincial taxes, 120% is absorbed by the costs of transport, and 80% by the merchants as profits.[68]

The outputs of the *mineiro* foundries were mainly commercialized by a large number small merchants spread all over the province, who, besides iron goods, sold a wide range of products. Thus, the industry did not use any specialized channel of distribution, which *per se* is strong evidence of how primitive were the local consumer markets for iron products and the distribution system as well.

The fate of the CUI was linked to the prosperity of one commodity, coffee, from a single region, the Mata zone. Freight was the most important source of revenue of the company as shown in Table 3.18. From 1858 to 1863, for example, the gross revenue provided by the transport service as a whole amounted to 4.091:521$880 contos. Passenger traffic contributed 13% of the total and freight with the remainder 87%. During the same period the net revenue amounted to 911:409$442 contos. Seventy-nine per cent of it came from freight and 21 per cent from passenger traffic.[69] The smaller importance of passenger traffic can also be

Table 3.18 Gross revenue provided by the transport of passengers and goods and their percentage contribution to the total gross revenue

Year	Passengers	%	Freight	%	Total revenue
1858*	27:051$000	11	217:242$595	89	244:293$595
1859	42:014$000	8	468:543$205	92	510:557$205
1860	50:319$200	8	616:654$454	92	666:973$654
1861	120:342$930	12	909:362$792	88	1.029:705$722
1862	154:640$800	18	687:449$522	82	842:090$322
1863	146:337$460	18	651:563$922	82	797:901$382
Total	540:705$390	13	3.550:816$490	87	4.091:521$880

* From April to December.
Source: Companhia União e Indústria, *Relatório da Assembléia Geral dos Acionistas* (1864), annexe 6,8,9.

observed in the case of the railway companies; the larger part of the revenue of the EFDPII, for example, also derived from freight. Although in the first six months of its operation freight revenue was just a fraction larger than passenger revenue, as soon as the railway started to reach the coffee-growing regions freight began to account for larger shares of the company's revenue. Thus, from 1859 onwards freight accounted for about 60 per cent of the revenue of the EFD-PII, and increased to 75 per cent in 1865.[70]

Freight consisted of a high proportion of exports – a one-way traffic which made for high operating costs –, mainly of coffee. As shown in Table 3.19, from 1858 to 1868 coffee accounted for over 70 per cent of goods transported by the CUI and more than 90 per cent of the goods exported. As freight provided nearly 90 per cent of gross revenue and as exports made up two-thirds of freight, and as coffee represented 90 per cent of the goods exported, company profits were linked to the fate of coffee. A slump in coffee exports in 1862, for example, caused a decrease of 31 per cent in the quantity of goods transported by the company during that year.[71]

Dependence on a single export (in most cases, coffee) seems also to have been the fate of the majority of the railways in Brazil. In the period 1873–1905 most of the Brazilian railways were located in the coffee-growing regions, as shown

Table 3.19   Coffee freight in the União e Indústria turnpike

Years	Total of goods transported (tons)	% of goods exported	Total of coffee transported (tons)	% of coffee over the total	% of coffee over export
1858*	10 974	68	7 400	67	97
1859	22 776	71	15 908	70	98
1860	26 970	75	20 024	74	99
1861	29 743	79	23 179	78	99
1862	20 695	59	11 342	55	93
1863	23 345	69	14 495	62	90
1864	23 802	64	13 042	55	85
1865	31 988	67	19 242	60	89
1866	32 627	65	19 504	60	92
1867	41 061	74	29 139	71	96
1868	36 641	73	24 602	67	92

* From April to December.

Source: Compiled from Companhia União e Indústria, *Relatório da Assembléia Geral dos Acionistas* (1868).

Table 3.20   Length of the Brazilian railway in the main coffee-growing provinces/states, 1873–1905

Province/State	Length of the railway network (kilometres)					
	1873	%	1883	%	1905	%
São Paulo	254	22	1457	26	3790	23
Minas Gerais	–		662	12	3843	23
Rio de Janeiro	510	45	1706	30	2661	16
Espírito Santo	–		–		336	2
Brazil	1129	100	5708	100	16782	100

Source: Adapted from H.P. Melo, *O Café e a Economia Fluminense: 1889/1920* (Rio de Janeiro, 1993), p. 11.

in Table 3.20. Thus, the dependence of the CUI on coffee for freight and profits was a feature that the company shared with other major Brazilian transport companies – all were characterised by a limited market.

The *mineiro* textile industry in the nineteenth century also operated on a local basis; most firms supplied mainly their immediate neighbourhood, with a few supplying larger sub-regional markets. However, the industry as a whole was restricted to those markets that could not be supplied from overseas or by producers based in Rio de Janeiro and São Paulo. Nevertheless, if the lack of adequate means of transport constituted a barrier to the penetration of foreign competition, at the same time it limited the size of the market of the *mineiro* mills.

The output of the Brumado mill, for example, was consumed in Pitangui (the town where it was located) and in the neighbouring towns of the western part of the province. The Biribiry mill located in Diamantina, and the Cassú mill located in Uberaba, also sold their output in the immediate vicinity.[72] The Companhia Cachoeira de Macacos (CCM) commercialized its output in both the immediate locality and in the neighbouring north-eastern part of the province.[73] The sales of the Cedro and the Cachoeira mills were also restricted to the province of Minas Gerais.[74] Nevertheless, they did not supply the whole province, as the Triângulo and the Southern zones were supplied by the mills located in São Paulo, and the Mata zone was supplied by the local production and by the mills located in Rio de Janeiro.[75] These regions already enjoyed reasonably good communications with neighbouring provinces.

As output increased after the constitution of the CCC the company tried to expand its market by penetrating other areas, such as the Triângulo zone and the province of Goyas.[76] The company also tried unsuccessfully to penetrate Rio de Janeiro, then the most important market in Brazil. The reasons for the failure do not seem to have been restricted simply to costs and freight charges, but also to the quality and design of the textiles produced by the company. In 1887 Rodolpho Alves, a textile merchant from Rio de Janeiro, stated that after examining and comparing the products of the company with those produced by the mills from Rio de Janeiro he did not believe that they could be sold there.[77] In 1889, Theóphilo Marques Ferreira, then general manager of the company, outlined his marketing strategy and provided further evidence of the limits of the market supplied by the company. According to him most customers made their purchases directly at the mills, in a clear indication of the range of the market of the company.

Moreover, it seems that the company did not employ a sales staff and production was sold to a small circle of warehouses and merchants, evidence of the primitive nature of the channels of distribution. Nevertheless, as a consequence of the commercial crisis that the company was facing, the company had to open several of its own warehouses and branches throughout the province. Once again, as in the merger of the Cedro and Cachoeira mills and the purchase of the São Vicente mill, innovation was driven by crisis rather than as part of a planned strategy. The change in the marketing strategy of the CCC represented an integration of functions (production and distribution) within the company, a move similar to that made by US companies in the nineteenth century.[78] However, such strategy does not seem to have worked as planned, as all the warehouses and branches were closed down a few years later.[79]

Furthermore, Ferreira decided to send to the provinces of Paraná and Santa Catarina the manager of the branch in Ouro Preto:

> ...who expects to sell a large amount of our products there. Also, acknowledging that Rio de Janeiro is the largest market, I sent some samples of our products to the evaluation of some of the most respected merchants from that city...[80]

Ferreira expected to sell at least one-third of the output of the company in Rio de Janeiro,[81] but he did not succeed for the reasons suggested by Rodolpho Alves: high costs and unsuitable quality. As the São Vicente mill began to operate in 1894, the traditional markets of the company proved to be not large enough to absorb the increased output,[82] and the company tried once again to penetrate the market of Rio de Janeiro. In 1895 Rodolpho, Irmão & Mattos, a textile merchant from Rio de Janeiro, acknowledged the receipt of samples of the products of the São Vicente mill.[83] Some months later Eugenio de Azevedo & Companhia, another textile merchant from Rio de Janeiro, explained that:

It seems that it is going to be very difficult for this company [the CCC] to sell its products in this market, since the several mills located here have stock enough for the necessities of the market. Furthermore, the prices are not competitive.[84]

The company was not to succeed in penetrating the Rio de Janeiro market until 1918, when it managed to establish contracts with the large merchants and warehouses in Rio. In the meantime, the company developed a marketing policy to preserve and expand its traditional markets, which were made up of a large number of towns located mainly in the northern part of Minas Gerais.[85]

Therefore, throughout the last century the *mineiro* textile industry was restricted to local markets. The CCC, for example, tried to supply a larger market but it did not succeed; the company had neither suitable products nor competitive prices to compete and operate on a national basis. The company, like most of the *mineiro* textile industries, was therefore restricted to those markets inaccessible to foreign competition and the products of the larger mills in São Paulo and Rio de Janeiro.

But the *mineiro* textile mills were not only restricted to the local markets: they were also restricted to the poorest niche of the market. They produced a limited range of products of low quality, mainly cloth for the labour force, either slave or free, and sackcloth for packing. As Stein observed, the production of these products did not require skilled workers, the machinery was simple to operate and the market relatively secure. Furthermore, the wealthiest classes of Brazilian society continued to consume imported cloths made of cotton, linen, silk and wool.[86]

The case of the CCC is illustrative in this particular respect. As the company was made up of mills which were established in rural areas, its consumer market was constituted of slaves and free people on low incomes. Thus, the company specialized in a type of product destined to this market: cheap and low-quality textiles.[87] There is evidence that the consumer market of the CCM was made up of the poorest stratum of the population, as the company sold its products in the north-eastern part of Minas Gerais, one of the poorest areas of the province.[88]

Furthermore, it seems that the mining companies constituted another important customer of the *mineiro* textile mills.
In 1889, for example, the St John del Rey Mining Company
(SJDRMC) ordered cloth from the CCC to be used as gauze
for filtering mine slurry in the production of gold.[89] During
the same year the SJDRMC was also purchasing cloth for the
same purpose from the CCM.[90] Two years later the store-
keeper of the SJDRMC, M.J. Clemence, complained about
the quality of the cloth supplied by the CCC, indication of the
regular supply for the mining companies and of the poor
quality of the product manufactured by the CCC.[91] A
month later he notified the CCC of payment for the cloth
supplied.[92] Finally, in 1899 the SJDRMC ordered scraps of
cotton to be used in the cleaning of the machinery.[93] Thus,
during the last century the *mineiro* textile mills produced low-
quality products, like cloth for the low-income stratum of the
population and sackcloth for packing. Furthermore, the mills
which were located in the mining areas found in the mining
companies what may have been an important niche of the
market.

Furthermore, as the markets supplied by the *mineiro* textile
companies were scattered over a wide area and of difficult
access, the main channels of distribution were the muletrains,
either belonging to the textile companies themselves or to
independent merchants. At the beginning, the output of the
CCM was sold by salesmen travelling with muletrains to
farms, villages and hamlets spread along their routes. Later,
with the extension of the railways, these salesmen would go
by train until Corinto where they would rent muletrains and
head for Montes Claros.[94] In further evidence of the integration of both production and distribution within the company,
the CCC had its own muletrain as Francisco Bahia da Rocha,
manager of the São Vicente mill, showed in his report in
1895.[95] More evidence of the integrated nature of the business is found in the correspondence of the general manager
of the CCC. In 1898, Manoel Pimenta Figueiredo, a merchant from Capelinha, wrote offering a boy to look for the
muletrain of the São Vicente mill.[96] However, the company
also relied on its customers' muletrains to distribute production or consignments. Independent merchants, like Cassimiro
Teixeira Collares, loaded their muletrains with cloth at the

mills and travelled around the province selling it.[97] Mill managers also sold directly on orders. Dealings between the CCM, the CCC and the SJDRMC are shown clearly, as the following letter written by Américo Teixeira Guimarães, the general manager of the CCM, also shows:

> Concerning the 12 packs of striped material you ordered in your letter of yesterday, I am sorry to tell you that I cannot provide it. I have a customer here loading 80 packs and after that I have to provide another customer with 120 packs. Furthermore, I have several other orders received a long time ago which are already late.[98]

Another important channel of distribution used by the CCC was the company's own warehouses, as mentioned above, and when the commercial situation became increasingly difficult after 1886 the company reluctantly decided to establish several warehouses in an attempt to boost sales.[99] Warehouses were established in the most important consumer markets, with their own team of salesmen,[100] and the company continued to distribute through its own warehouses until the beginning of this century when they were replaced by local merchants who acted as representatives.[101] Hence, from the evidence presented above it is reasonable to conclude that *mineiro* textile mills relied on a diverse and somewhat sophisticated marketing structure, developed throughout the years by several crises. The development of such a strategy was an attempt to replace the 'invisible hand' of the market – which in the case of nineteenth-century Minas Gerais was very precarious – by the 'visible hands' of the managers.

The *mineiro* electricity-generating companies of the turn of the century supplied very small markets, even taking into account that markets for utilities such as electricity are different from those of tangible products like iron and textiles. Throughout the nineteenth century the CME supplied only the city of Juiz de Fora, which was not a large market, both for the supply of electricity and for the provision of a telephone service. Although demand was continuously increasing, the market for lighting in Juiz de Fora was not very large as shown in Table 3.21. In 1889 the company began supplying electricity to 40 street lamps; there is no information

Table 3.21   Number of street and domestic lamps powered by the
Companhia Mineira de Eletricidade, 1889–1901

Years	No. of street lamps	No. of domestic lamps
1889	40	–
1892	185	700
1896	–	–
1897	304	2470
1901	337	–

Sources: Oliveira, *Companhia Mineira de Eletricidade, op. cit.*, pp. 24–
44; Companhia Mineira de Eletricidade, 'Balanço e Relatório'
reproduced in *O Pharol* (Juiz de Fora), 27 August 1897, p. 1.

about the number of domestic connexions. Nevertheless,
Bernardo Mascarenhas gives an idea of it in the plan that
he drew in specifying equipment ordered from the Westinghouse Electric Company (WEC) in 1888. According to Mascarenhas' plans, the power plant would have a capacity to
supply energy to 500 domestic lamps.[102] In 1892, according
to the company report, that number increased to 185 street
lamps and 700 domestic lamps. In 1897 the company
reported powering 304 street lamps and 2470 domestic
lamps in 225 houses. Finally, in 1901 the company supplied
electricity to 337 street lamps but there is no information
about the figures for domestic customers. Even so the company struggled to keep pace with demand, as shown in the
company report of 1892.[103]

Juiz de Fora also did not constitute a large market for
power, and its supply only began after the inauguration of
the second plant in 1896. The first two electric engines began
to operate only two years later, one of them at Bernardo
Mascarenhas' textile mill – which was a separate enterprise
from the CME – and the other at the Pantaleone Arcuri &
Timponi establishment.[104]

Finally, even though there is no information about the
number of telephone lines supplied by the company, there
is evidence that the market was not large. A report of the
American Telephone & Telegraph Company (AT&T) of 1919
attested the precariousness of the telephone service in Juiz de
Fora at the time when the CME acquired the concession.[105]

In 1901 a company report stated that the revenue provided by the telephone service had decreased,[106] further evidence of the precarious nature of the market in Juiz de Fora.

At the beginning, the CFLCL supplied electricity to four different towns – Cataguazes, Leopoldina, São João Nepomuceno and Rio Novo – all of them located within the Mata zone. Even so, taking into account the original generating capacity of the CFLCL of 800 KW,[107] it is reasonable to conclude that these markets were very limited in size. As mentioned above, the generating capacity of the CME in 1901, which supplied only the city of Juiz de Fora, was 600 kW. Further evidence of the limited size of the markets supplied by the CFLCL is found in the company report of 1909, which stated that in 1908 the company powered a total of eight engines and lit 512 houses.[108] Unfortunately there is no information about the number of street lamps lit by the company for that year. Nevertheless, evidence presented above leaves no doubt about the small size of the markets explored by the CFLCL. In addition, those markets were also precarious; as Ivan Botelho who became president of the company in 1963 observed:

> [at the beginning] It was not enough to light the houses. First, the company had to convince the owner of the house that the supply of light was useful. Then, the company had to do everything – to install the cables, to give the lamps – to make the people used to having electricity at home. The people were used to live in the dark and did not have any idea of progress.[109]

Although this was hardly a peculiarity of the markets supplied by the CFLCL, it is undisputable evidence of their precarious and backward nature.

Comparison of both the CME and the CFLCL with the Light System is once more very illustrative. As the names of the companies which constituted the Light System suggest – the São Paulo Tramway, Light and Power Company and the Rio de Janeiro Tramway, Light and Power Company Limited – they supplied the two largest Brazilian consumer markets, that is the cities of São Paulo and Rio de Janeiro.[110] Thus, the *mineiro* electricity-generating companies were restricted to much smaller markets when compared with their *paulista* and *carioca* counterparts.

To conclude, for most of the last century the *mineiro* iron industry operated on a local basis supplying mining industries, farms and small towns. It manufactured parts for mining machinery, agricultural tools, domestic appliances, horseshoes and horsenails. Nevertheless, individual firms produced a narrow range of products. The distribution of output was undertaken by a large number of small generalist merchants spread all over the province and by muletrains until the arrival of the railway.

The analysis of the marketing activities of the CUI revealed that, as happened with the majority of the Brazilian railways, a larger proportion of its revenue came from freight which was heavily dependent on one product – coffee. Furthermore, the company did not operate on a national or provincial basis. It was limited to the Paraíba Valley in the province of Rio de Janeiro and the Mata zone in Minas Gerais, a coffee-growing region.

Most of textile firms in nineteenth-century Minas Gerais sold their products in local and sub-regional markets, and were limited to the least sophisticated end of the market. Furthermore, the most common channels of distribution were muletrains and travelling salesmen, either independent merchants or employees of the mills themselves. In the last decade of the century the CCC resorted to the opening of a number of warehouses in an attempt to boost the distribution of its increasing output. The development of a diverse and sophisticated marketing structure was an attempt to overcome the limitations imposed by the market mechanisms.

Finally, in providing new and technologically advanced services – the generation of hydroelectricity and the provision of telephone services – the *mineiro* electricity-generating companies were restricted to small and precarious markets.

THE ADMINISTRATIVE STRUCTURE

As most firms in nineteenth-century Minas Gerais operated on a small scale and supplied small and local markets, very few of them had even an embryonic administrative structure. Often they had no administrative structure whatsoever. They were managed personally by their owners, who made long-term and day-to-day decisions assisted by one or two managers. They were usually owned by a small number of people, often members of the same family. Consequently, appointment, especially for managerial positions, was more often based on kinship than on expertise.

The iron industry shows this clearly. Iron foundries in the first three-quarters of the last century were mainly family affairs, even the largest ones like the Patriótica and the São Miguel de Piracicaba. The only exception was the Morro do Pilar which was financed by the Imperial government and organized by Manuel Ferreira da Câmara. Even so the foundry was personally controlled by Câmara throughout its existence.[111] The Patriótica was founded by Eschwege. In setting-up the foundry he had the help of the president of the province of Minas Gerais, Conde de Palma, who:

> Enjoyed the confidence of several important people and, mainly, of a large and important family which was courted in the whole province. He had a great influence in the ministry and soon he succeeded in getting the interest of this family to the business.

Thus, the ownership was divided in 10 shares, each representing 1000 cruzados[112] of the initial capital. Eschwege subscribed to two shares, the governor one, and the large and important family the remainder.[113] The São Miguel de Piracicaba foundry was established by Monlevade and Captain Luiz Soares de Gouveia in 1827. After Monlevade's death in 1872, his family assumed the control of the foundry until it was sold to the Companhia de Forjas e Estaleiros at the beginning of the 1890s.[114]

In the latter part of the nineteenth century, although the size of iron firms grew they continued to be owned by very few people. The Esperança foundry, set up in 1888, was established by Amaro da Silveira (an engineer of the EFDPII), Alberto Gerspacher (a metallurgist), Henrique Hargeaves (chief of the extension works of the EFDPII) and Carlos G. da Costa Wigg. The latter was the main shareholder, owning 70 per cent of the initial capital. The Burnier foundry, built a few years later after the sale of the Esperança foundry, was established by José Gerspacher, Alberto's son, and Carlos G. da Costa Wigg who owned 80 per cent of the capital.[115] Thus, throughout the last century iron foundries were owned by a small number of people and were very often family affairs. Furthermore, short and long-term administration was carried out by the owners themselves. Câmara, for example, personally handled all the basic activities of the firm. He supervised the production,[116] planned long-term investments such as the building of a large road with the purpose of exporting iron, and also controlled and personally disciplined the workers.[117] Finally, appointment at the Morro do Pilar mill was clearly based on kinship, as observed by Schoenewolf a German foundry master.[118] Like Câmara, Eschwege also personally handled all the basic activities of the firm, like the construction of the mill.[119] and the supervision of production.[120] Like Câmara and Eschwege, Monlevade was deeply involved in every aspect of his business; he personally drew up the plans for the construction of his foundry.[121] and was also involved in its daily activities, especially in the supervision of the workers.[122]

Even in the larger ironworks which emerged in the last quarter of the century, owners continued to be involved in the daily management of their firms. At the Esperança foundry, for example, management was entrusted to Alberto Gerspacher, who was its technical director and one of the owners. Soon, the initial capital proved to be insufficient for further developments and the foundry was sold to the CNFE.[123] The CNFE tried to constitute an iron trust in Brazil but went bankrupt,[124] and the Esperança foundry was then sold to the firm Queiroz Júnior e Leandro whose partner, the engineer Queiroz Júnior, served as manager for several years.[125]

Hence, throughout the century iron foundries in Minas Gerais were owner-managed, irrespective of their size. However, the production of iron was not the only economic activity of foundry owners or even of their workers. Usually the foundries, especially the smaller ones, were part of a farm and work in the foundry was combined with the activities of the farm. Monlevade, for example, described to the president of the province what he called the 'Monlevade farm', which included the famous São Miguel de Piracicaba foundry and plantations.[126] Furthermore, the death of the owner in many occasions meant the end of the activities of the foundry. Costa

Sena, for example, mentions the existence of a well-established foundry close to Conceição, in the Metalúrgica zone, which was abandoned because of the death of its owner, Eduardo Félix. He further refers to the Cubas foundry which was also abandoned as a consequence of the death of its owner.[127] When Monlevade died in 1872 his son took control of the São Miguel de Piracicaba foundry, but as he could not find any one technically competent to operate the Catalan method he hired a master who transformed it into an Italian foundry.[128] The case of the São Miguel de Piracicaba foundry shows clearly how bad was the problem of shortage of skills in nineteenth-century Minas Gerais.

The lack of administrative structure was generalized among the iron firms in Minas Gerais. In 1814 the Morro do Pilar foundry, for example, employed a total of 34 workers; among them 15 smelters, eight blacksmiths, six carpenters, two blacks, two apprentices and one foreman. Thus, it had no administrative personnel apart from Câmara himself. In 1821 it employed one manager, one foundry master, six foremen, one master-blacksmith and one blacksmith, two master-carpenters, 28 workers for furnace and hammermill, 17 apprentices for furnace and hammermill, and 70 slaves for the coal-bunkers.[129] Although the number of workers had increased from 34 in 1814, to 127 in 1820, it still employed very few managerial staff for an enterprise of its size. There was also no administrative structure in the Patriótica foundry. Until 1821 the foundry employed 20 slaves, two free Brazilians, occasionally one German foundry master, and Eschwege himself.[130]

The CUI, in its turn, was organized on a larger basis. The nominal capital of the company was divided into 10 000 shares, although the issued capital never exceeded 6120 shares. As the chairman of the company, Mariano Procópio Ferreira Lage was certainly one of the largest shareholders. In his will, written before a trip to Europe in 1867, Lage declared a holding of 805 shares (or 13 per cent of the issued capital).[131] However, although ownership of the CUI was spread among a larger number of people, control was firmly in the hands of its founder. Until his death in 1872 Lage had a great influence on the company as its president and main executive. Furthermore, some of his relatives like José

Antônio da Silva Pinto and Lino José Ferreira Armond were shareholders who had made important contributions to the company.[132] Thus, because ownership of the CUI was diffused, Lage was able to control the company with a relative small share participation.

Furthermore, as chairman of the company Lage's activities were not only concerned with long-term decisions but also with short-term decisions, like personnel management.[133] He was also directly involved with activities like the engagement of foreign engineers and the recruitment of workers.[134] Thus, the involvement of the founder of the company in its top administration constitutes evidence that if the CUI was a modern enterprise, in Chandlerian terms, it should be considered a modern entrepreneurial – and not managerial – firm.

Nevertheless, both the construction and operation of the turnpike União e Indústria required a wide range of professionals. From 1853 to 1860 the company payroll included engineers, architects, geometricians, drivers, foremen, bookkeepers and so on.[135] In 1865, for each one of the 10 stations located along the turnpike the company employed one manager in what might have constituted a layer of management.[136] In 1866 the administrative structure of the technical staff of the company was clearly organized in a hierarchical way. It was divided into seven categories, each with a distinct status which was translated into higher and lower salaries. At the head was the chief engineer, assisted by a deputy called the first engineer. The chief engineer earned 12:000$000 contos and his deputy 8:400$000 contos per year. Then there were four section heads, who were engineers as well, earning 6:000$000 contos. They were assisted by six first-class assistants and five second-class assistants. The former received 4:800$000 contos and the latter 3:600$000 contos per year. Then, came six first-class drivers earning 3:000$000 contos, and nine second-class drivers earning 2:400$000 contos. There was also a general traffic inspector and a chief of the workshops, both engineers: there is no information about their salaries.[137] Thus, the existence of a clearly defined administrative structure of the technical body of the CUI is beyond any doubt.

However, the existence of this somewhat more complex administrative structure of the technical body was due to the nature of the industry rather than the CUI itself. In 1864, for example, the EFDPII was divided into several different departments: headquarters, warehouse, traffic, telegraph, construction, rolling-stock and stations. Apart from the headquarters, which was a small department employing a total of seven people, the others were strictly technical departments. Each was organized in a hierarchical way with posts being divided according to seniority with different status and salaries. At the head of the traffic department, for example, was the general traffic inspector assisted by a deputy called the resident engineer. The general traffic inspector earned 14:000$000 contos and his deputy 6:000$000 contos per year. Then there was the chief of traction earning 5:000$000 contos, the chief of the traffic department accountancy earning 3:600$000 contos, and the secretary earning 3:000$000 contos per year. Finally there were five employees without clearly defined occupations, earning at most 2:200$000 contos per year.[138] The existence of a clearly defined administrative structure of the technical body of the EFDPII and the CUI derives from the nature of their operations.

Nevertheless, the structure of the top administration of the CUI indicates that its administrative structure was in an embryonic stage, as a study of the merger of the company and the EFDPII suggests:

> It seemed to me that the administration of such important roads as the EFDPII and the União e Indústria turnpike required a larger board of directors than the existing one at the CUI, constituted of only three members...[139]

Further evidence of the embryonic nature of the structure of the top management of the company is confirmed in the reports of 1865, 1869, 1870 and 1875. They were all signed by the board of directors, invariably constituted by three members: the president, the secretary and the treasurer.[140] Finally, it is interesting to point out that the structure of the top administration of the CUI was very similar to that of the textile companies, which were neither complex nor large firms as seen above. The board of directors of the CCC, for example, was also constituted by three members, who ought to hold at least 50 shares of the company.[141]

Table 3.22   Companhia Cedro e Cachoeira in 1883: individual share participation, occupation and family connections of the founders

Name (family connection)	Occupation	Number of shares	% of the total
Antônio Cândido Mascarenhas (brother)	Capitalist	658	13.16
Bernardo Mascarenhas (brother)	Merchant	658	13.16
Caetano Mascarenhas (brother)	Farmer	658	13.16
Francisco Mascarenhas (brother)	Merchant	658	13.16
Pacífico Mascarenhas (brother)	Doctor	658	13.16
Víctor Mascarenhas (brother)	Capitalist	658	13.16
Luíz Augusto Vianna Barbosa (brother-in-law)	Merchant	658	13.16
Theóphilo Marques Ferreira (married to a Mascarenhas)	Merchant	353	7.06
Antônio J. Barbosa da Silva (no connexion)	Lawyer	41	0.82

Sources: Compiled from Mascarenhas, *Centenário da Fábrica do Cedro*, p. 118; D.M. Mascarenhas, *Genealogia da Família Mascarenhas, 1824–1989* (Belo Horizonte, 1990), p.183.

The *mineiro* textile industry was no exception in its lack of complexity of administrative structure. The textile companies were family affairs, owned by a small number of people and managed exclusively by the founders and their relatives. The CCC, for example, was the result of the merger between the Cedro and the Cachoeira mills, both of them belonging to members of the Mascarenhas family. Although organized as a joint stock company, the CCC was actually family run. As shown in Table 3.22, of the nine founders of the CCC six were brothers, one (Luíz Augusto Vianna Barbosa) was a brother-in-law,[142] and another (Theóphilo Marques Ferreira) was married to a niece of the Mascarenhas brothers.[143]

Table 3.23 Companhia Cedro e Cachoeira, 1883–1900: individual
share participation of the nine founders

Years	Number of shares	Number of shareholders	Percentage of the founders
1883	5 000	9	100
1884	5 000	17	94
1885	5 000	17	93
1890	5 500	49	68
1891	7 500	64	65
1895	10 000	118	51
1900	10 000	139	44

Source: Adapted from Vaz, *op.cit.*, p. 150.

Apart from Antônio Joaquim Barbosa da Silva, who left the
company in 1884,[144] the group formed by the founders concentrated in their hands the ownership of the company
throughout the last century. As shown in Table 3.23, although
the number of shareholders jumped from nine in 1883 to 49
in 1890, the founders still held 68 per cent of the total shares
of the company. In 1900 the number of shareholders
increased to 139, and the remaining seven founders (Bernardo Mascarenhas died in 1898.[145]) still possessed 44 per
cent of the total number of shares.

Nevertheless, these figures still do not tell the whole story
about the concentration of the ownership of the CCC in the
hands of the Mascarenhas family. The share participation of
the family as whole, including that of the founders, their
brothers and sisters, their parents and their direct descendants
is shown in Table 3.24. In 1883, for example, the family owned
92 per cent of the shares of the company. Family share ownership came to just over 90 per cent in 1884 and 82 per cent in
1888, and was 62 per cent and 56 per cent in 1893 and 1899
respectively. At the beginning of this century, family ownership
was less than 50 per cent but they were still firmly in control.

Thus, although the CCC was one of the first companies in
Minas Gerais to be formally organised as a joint stock com-
pany, in reality it was run as a private, family-owned affair.
One of the consequences of this was that throughout the last

Table 3.24   Share participation percentages of the founders of the
Companhia Cedro e Cachoeira – their brothers and sisters, parents
and their direct descendants, 1883–1902

Shareholders	1883	1884	1888	1893	1899	1902
Antônio Cândido Mascarenhas	13.16	10.00	8.70	8.00	6.85	7.22
Luís Augusto Vianna Barbosa*	13.16	12.66	12.72	–	–	0.05
Víctor Mascarenhas	13.16	12.66	9.96	10.97	10.44	9.21
Pacífico Mascarenhas	13.16	12.40	12.78	8.01	10.50	11.23
Caetano Mascarenhas	13.16	13.16	12.00	10.86	8.54	8.95
Bernardo Mascarenhas	13.16	12.66	10.54	8.22	5.17	–
Francisco Mascarenhas	13.16	12.90	9.12	9.04	5.19	5.34
José Mascarenhas	–	0.60	–	–	–	0.26
Escolástica Mascarenhas	–	–	–	–	0.31	0.37
Francisca Mascarenhas	–	0.60	1.41	1.46	2.02	3.00
Maria Teodora Mascarenhas	–	2.74	2.72	2.76	3.10	4.04
Sebastião Mascarenhas	–	–	0.03	–	–	–
Policena Mascarenhas**	–	–	2.54	2.77	4.27	0.01
Antônio Gonçalves Mascarenhas**	–	0.02	0.01	–	–	–
Total	92.12	90.40	82.53	62.09	56.39	49.68

* brother-in-law; ** parents.
Source: Adapted from Vaz, *op.cit.*, p. 274.

century the top administration of the company and managerial posts were filled by members of the Mascarenhas family
only. As shown in Table 3.25, during the period 1883–1901
all members of the board of directors of the CCC belonged to
the Mascarenhas family, either as brothers, brothers-in-law or
as nephews, a trend which continued until the 1970s.[146]

Appointment of managers reflected the real nature of ownership – the requirement being kinship rather than merit or
expertise. As Vaz pointed out, at the CCC the appointment of
managers represented more a compromise to maintain equi-
librium between the main branches of shareholders than anything else.[147] As shown in Table 3.25, all the general
managers of the CCC during the period 1883–1901 belonged
to the Mascarenhas family. Bernardo Mascarenhas was the
first general manager of the company from 1883 to 1887. He
was replaced by Theóphilo Marques Ferreira in 1888. His

Table 3.25 List of the members of the board of directors and general managers of the Companhia Cedro e Cachoeira, 1883–1901

Period	Members of the board	Period	General manager
1883–88	Antônio Cândido Mascarenhas Bernardo Mascarenhas Pacífico Mascarenhas	1883–87	Bernardo Mascarenhas
1888–89	Antônio Cândido Mascarenhas Pacífico Mascarenhas Theóphilo Marques Ferreira	1887–93	Theóphilo Marques Ferreira
1889–92	Antônio Cândido Mascarenhas Pacífico Mascarenhas Aristides José Mascarenhas Antônio Diniz Mascarenhas		
1892–95	Antônio Cândido Mascarenhas Aristides Mascarenhas Antônio Diniz Mascarenhas	1893–95	Francisco de Paula Mascarenhas
1895–99	Antônio Cândido Mascarenhas Aristides José Mascarenhas Viriato Diniz Mascarenhas Caetano Mascarenhas	1895–1901	Aristides José Mascarenhas
1899–1901	Aristides José Mascarenhas Viriato Diniz Mascarenhas Caetano Mascarenhas		

Source: Mascarenhas, *Centenário da Fábrica do Cedro*, pp. 245–7.

successor was Francisco de Paula Mascarenhas, who in turn was succeeded by Aristides José Mascarenhas, a nephew of the original group of shareholders, for the remainder of the period.[148]

The same phenomenon can be observed for the remaining managerial posts of the CCC. As shown in Table 3.26, the Cedro mill was managed by Bernardo Mascarenhas,

Table 3.26   Companhia Cedro e Cachoeira, 1883–99: list of factory
managers

	Cedro	Cachoeira	S. Vicente
1883	Bernardo Mascarenhas	Francisco de P. Mascarenhas	
1887	Theóphilo Marques Ferreira		
1891			Caetano Mascarenhas
1892		Dario Diniz Mascarenhas	Francisco de P. Mascarenhas
1893	Francisco de P. Mascarenhas		
1894			Francisco Bahia da Rocha
1895	Aristides José Mascarenhas		
1899			Caetano Mascarenhas

Source: Mascarenhas, *Centenário da Fábrica do Cedro*, pp. 247–8.

Theóphilo Marques Ferreira, Francisco de Paula Mascarenhas and Aristides José Mascarenhas. The Cachoeira mill had only two managers during the century: Francisco de Paula Mascarenhas, and Dario Diniz Mascarenhas another nephew of the original shareholders. Finally, the São Vicente mill was managed by Caetano Mascarenhas, Francisco de Paula Mascarenhas and Francisco Bahia da Rocha, who was married to a niece of the original shareholders.[149]

During the nineteenth-century the roles of shareholders, directors, managers and relatives were synonyms at the CCC. Although the company was formally established as a joint stock company, ownership and managership never reflected that. On the contrary, ownership of the company was always safely in the hands of the founders and all managerial positions were filled by members of the Mascarenhas family, without exception.

The scope of the activities performed by managers reflects the stage of organizational development of the CCC and gives further evidence about the complexity of the business environment in Minas Gerais in the last century. As in the iron sector, managers were involved in every aspect of the life of the company from long-term investment decisions to daily operations: all managerial tasks were concentrated in their hands.[150] Therefore, there was no trace of any departmentalization or specialization of any sort. Managers, assisted by one or two persons, were responsible for several tasks – like marketing, industrial relations, finance, production, and even legal affairs – which in modern firms are the subject of specific departments. In 1884, for example, Francisco Mascarenhas, then manager of the Cachoeira mill, established the conditions of sales of the output of the mill.[151] He also administered sales made in markets closer to the mill.[152] Furthermore, it is possible to find the manager of the Cachoeira mill in 1895 – Dario Diniz Mascarenhas – administering the accounts of customers, as he reported to the general manager Francisco Mascarenhas.[153] Each mill manager was also responsible for the management of his workforce. Francisco Mascarenhas directly recruited and hired workers while he was at the Cachoeira mill; in June 1884 he wrote to his brother Bernardo that he could not find anybody who could write well and correctly and who could count regularly, and he decided to look elsewhere.[154] In the same year he wrote again to Bernardo complaining that it was hard to obtain workers since it was the time of clearing the land.[155] On another occasion Francisco explained to his brother his industrial relations policy:

> It does not matter how hard you try, the result will always be the same: more people will not come. A better way to hold people has been studied by me and applied since the beginning – if one works from 30 to 40 days, he will earn 660, from 50 to 60 days, 680, and from 85 to 90 days, 700. The rewards will be paid for the days worked, when the job is finished. In this way, I have managed to hold a great number of people whose interest in the rewards have kept them here until the end.[156]

Furthermore, he was also responsible for controlling the workforce.[157] Also, as already mentioned, each mill manager was responsible for the finance of his mill, and Francisco Mascarenhas again provides a good example. In January 1885 he wrote to Bernardo reporting that the balance sheet of the Cachoeira mill was ready showing a result of 68:757$391 contos.[158] In 1895, Dario Diniz Mascarenhas reported to Francisco Mascarenhas that:

> It seems that the balance sheet was done correctly, but as I cannot rely on my expertise on this matter, I ask you to take a look at it and make all the necessary corrections until the 1st of January to avoid further changes in the balance sheet.[159]

Dario's letter also indicates a lack of professional skills. Mill managers were also deeply involved in minute and different aspects of the production, from raw materials supply to sources of energy. On two different occasions in 1885, Francisco Mascarenhas wrote about the problem concerning the cotton supply of the Cachoeira mill: in February he complained about increasing raw cotton prices due to the activities of speculators, and two months later he signed a contract to supply the mill.[160] In 1900, Caetano Mascarenhas, then manager at São Vicente, also looked for a supply of raw cotton.[161] The maintenance of the machinery was another concern of mill managers, as Dario Diniz Mascarenhas in 1904 informed Caetano Mascarenhas:

> New looms – at the beginning the machinery worked with locally manufactured belts, but these often broke. New belts were then ordered from England. These also broke but not so often, probably due to their greater width. Hence, I am now ordering wider English belts.[162]

A recurrent problem throughout the nineteenth century was the question of power for the mills; the supply of water was very irregular and steam also had its own problems. Managers were therefore always busy trying to resolve the problem of energy, as Francisco Mascarenhas wrote in 1885.[163] Finally, mill managers also dealt with legal affairs whenever the situation required: in 1885, for example, Francisco asks Bernardo for a letter of attorney in order to:

> Defend the rights of the CCC in the civil and criminal court of justice in Curvello. People are destroying our woods and I can do nothing to prevent it.[164]

This analysis of the administrative structure of the CCC shows that there was little trace of any sort of departmentalization or specialization, an organizational process already underway in firms in the most developed countries at that time. In other words, management reflected the degree of development and complexity of the business context.

Nevertheless, as a result of the fact that the CCC was a multi-site company, an embryonic administrative structure can be identified with at least two layers of managers: the general manager and the managers of the mills. The latter reported to the general manager, who in his turn reported to the board of directors, although he himself was usually one of the members of the board. Furthermore, in the case of the Cedro mill the general manager also served as the manager. Bernardo Mascasenhas filled both posts from 1883 to 1887, followed by Theóphilo Marques Ferreira from 1887 to 1893, Francisco de Paula Mascarenhas from 1893 to 1895, and Aristides José Mascarenhas from 1895 to 1901.[165] This accumulation of posts is another clear indication that the business environment in the nineteenth century was not very complex even for one of the largest textile companies in Minas Gerais.

The CCM was also constituted as a joint stock company. The company was founded by João da Matta Teixeira, who subscribed 79 per cent of the initial capital, and he was elected director of the company in 1886 and held the position until 1923, when he died. His son, Américo Teixeira Guimarães, was the only general manager of the company throughout the last century, following his election on 15 July 1887.[166] It was Américo Teixeira Guimarães who actually managed the company from its inception, and he chose, ordered and supervised the installation of machinery at the mill.[167] He managed every aspect of the life of the company, from the purchase of raw material[168] to relations with other companies.[169]

The Companhia de Tecidos Santanense (CTS) followed the same pattern of administrative structure observed in both the CCC and the CCM. The CTS was typically a family affair, although again established as a joint stock company. It was founded on 23 October 1891 by members of the Souza Moreira family: Manoel José de Souza Moreira, his sons Manoel Gonçalves de Souza Moreira and Augusto Gonçalves de Souza Moreira, and his son-in-law Antônio Pereira de Mattos.[170]

Table 3.27   Companhia de Tecidos Santanense: share participation
of the founders and their relatives

Names	Number of shares
Manoel José de Souza Moreira	600
Manoel Gonçalves de Souza Moreira	400
Augusto Gonçalves de Souza Moreira	150
Antônio Pereira de Mattos	150
Members of the family Gonçalves de Souza Moreira*	515
Total number of shares	3000

*The identified relatives of the four founders of the company are:
Orozimbo Gonçalves de Souza, 100 shares; Arthur Pereira de Mat-
tos, 20 shares; Vicente Gonçalves de Souza, 150 shares; Josias
Gonçalves de Souza, 20 shares; Francisco Gonçalves de Souza
Junior, 5 shares; Mardocheu Gonçalves de Souza, 5 shares; Virgilio
Gonçalves de Souza Moreira, 10 shares; Francisco Gonçalves de
Souza, 200 shares; and Jovino Gonçalves de Souza, 5 shares.

Source: M.A.G. Souza, *História de Itaúna*, I (Belo Horizonte, 1986),
pp. 124–6.

Together they held 43 per cent of the shares of the company,
and, furthermore, among the original shareholders the relatives of the founders held another 17 per cent of the shares as
shown in Table 3.27.

Further evidence that the CTS was a family affair is provided
by the fact that the company was not only owned but also
administered by members of the Souza Moreira family. According to the statutes, the company was to be administered by the
board of directors, whose members were elected every four
years by the general meeting of the shareholders. Furthermore,
each member of the board was to hold at least 50 shares of the
company.[171] In practical terms this meant that only a small
group of people were eligible for the board. Among the 56
shareholders of the company in 1895, for example, only 15
held at least 50 shares, and 10 of those 15 belonged to the
Souza Moreira family.[172] Therefore, throughout the century
the posts on the board of directors were filled by members of the
Souza Moreira family as indicated in Table 3.28.

Table 3.28   Members of the board of directors of the Companhia de
Tecidos Santanense, 1891–9

Year (month)	Name	Post
1891 (Sept.)	Manoel José de Souza Moreira	Chairman
	Manoel Gonçalves de Souza Moreira	Treasurer
	Augusto Gonçalves de Souza Moreira	Secretary
	Antônio Pereira de Mattos	Manager
1891 (Dec.)	José Gonçalves de Souza	Chairman
	Manoel Gonçalves de Souza Moreira	Treasurer
1893	Manoel José de Souza Moreira	Chairman
	Manoel Gonçalves de Souza Moreira	Treasurer
1894	Augusto Gonçalves de Souza Moreira	Chairman
	Manoel José de Souza Moreira	Treasurer
1899	José Gonçalves de Souza Moreira	Chairman
	Manoel Gonçalves de Souza Moreira	Treasurer

Sources: Compiled from Souza, *op.cit.*, pp. 124–6; Companhia de
Tecidos Santanense, *Ata da Primeira Assembléia Geral Extraordinária
dos Acionistas* (Itaúna, 19 December 1891); Companhia de Tecidos
Santanense, *Ata da Assembléia Ordinária dos Acionistas* (1893, 1894,
1899).

The appointment of managers also reflected the control of
the Souza Moreira family over the company. The first manager was Antônio Pereira de Mattos, one of the founders of
the company and Manoel José de Souza Moreira's son-in-law,
and he was also a member of the board of directors in 1891.
He was succeeded by Manoel Gonçalves de Souza Moreira,
Manoel José de Souza Moreira and, finally, by João Cerqueira
de Lima who was also Manoel José de Souza Moreira's son-
in-law[173] and shareholder of the company.[174]
   The CME, conceived and organized by Bernardo Mascarenhas, was also a family-owned and local affair. According to
Mascarenhas, the CME was organized with a capital of
150:000$000 contos divided into 1500 shares: 500 shares he
kept for himself, 500 were offered to the inhabitants of Juiz
de Fora, and 500 were distributed within his family.[175]
Although the firm was founded on 7 January 1888 as a joint
stock company, Mascarenhas and his family concentrated
ownership of the company in their hands until 1911, when

a group of capitalists bought the company.[176] Among the 30 original shareholders, 12 belonged to the Mascarenhas family.[177] and together they held 833 of the total 1500 shares, or 56 per cent. Bernardo Mascarenhas himself held nearly 27 per cent of the shares of the company.[178]

Even though the company pioneered the production of hydroelectricity in South America and could be considered modern in some respects, the structure of its top administration followed the traditional pattern of nineteenth-century Minas Gerais. The board of directors consisted of only three members: the chairman, the secretary and the treasurer. Furthermore, throughout the last century all these positions were filled by shareholders. The board elected in 1888 consisted of Bernardo Mascarenhas as chairman, Francisco Baptista de Oliveira as secretary, and Francisco Eugênio de Rezende as treasurer.[179] Francisco Baptista de Oliveira and Francisco Eugênio de Rezende were both among the largest shareholders, holding 5 per cent and 6 per cent of the shares of the company respectively.[180] The only changes to the board during the last century occurred in 1897 when Francisco Baptista de Oliveira resigned and in the following year when Bernardo Mascarenhas died. Francisco Eugênio de Rezende covered the position previously held by Francisco Baptista de Oliveira until the next election for the board in 1900. Bernardo Mascarenhas was succeeded by Azarias Monteiro de Andrade, who was also one of the original shareholders and two years later became Mascarenhas' son-in-law.[181]

Furthermore, Bernardo Mascarenhas was himself involved in every aspect of the life of the company; for example he drew up the specifications for the equipment to be ordered[182] and personally supervised the assembly of the plant.[183]

Thus, during the nineteenth century, the CME was owned by a small number of people, mainly local and members of the Mascarenhas family. Furthermore, at least at the beginning, the main shareholders of the company were deeply involved in its day- to-day management. However, apart from the board of directors there is no information about the administrative structure of the company.

Although there is no detailed information about the ownership of the CFLCL, there is evidence that the company was owned by a small number of people, who also controlled its administration. Although the CFLCL was established in the twentieth century, the structure of its top administration was similar to that of companies established in nineteenth-century Minas Gerais. The company was founded by José Monteiro Ribeiro Junqueira, Norberto Custódio Ferreira and João Duarte Ferreira, who were also the directors of the company from its inception in 1905. José Monteiro Ribeiro Junqueira was the chairman, Norberto Custódio Ferreira the treasurer, and João Duarte Ferreira the secretary.[184] The latter was the main shareholder of the company,[185] and in 1909 he resigned[186] to dedicate to his political career.[187] Further evidence that ownership and control of the company continued firmly in the hands of the founders and their families is the fact that in 1982 the chairman of the company was Ivan Botelho, José Monteiro Ribeiro Junqueira's grand-nephew.[188]

The administrative structure of the CFLCL was composed of the headquarters, the power-station, five local offices, and the distribution department. The headquarters was headed by a manager who reported to the board of directors.[189] Moreover, on 9 June 1910 the board of directors authorized the manager to increase the salaries of the employees by 10 per cent.[190] The manager was assisted by an engineer, a bookkeeper, and senior and junior assistants. The manager and the engineer earned 550$000 mil-réis per month, the bookkeeper 250$000 mil-réis, and the assistants 90$000 and 40$000 mil-réis per month respectively. The power-station was headed by a manager who earned 400$000 mil-réis per month, assisted by a technician in charge of the turbines, three senior and a junior assistants who earned 150$000, 90$000 and 60$000 mil-réis per month respectively. The local offices in each one of the five towns supplied by the company in 1910 (Cataguazes, Leopoldina, São João Nepomuceno, Rio Novo and Providencia) were headed by a manager who was aided by a senior and a junior assistant. The salaries of the managers of the local offices varied from 130$000 to 150$000 mil-réis, and that of their assistants from 50$000 to 110$000 mil-réis per month. Furthermore, there were three workers in charge of the transmission cables, each earning 70$000 mil-réis per month.[191]

The analysis of the CFLCL has revealed that the company was controlled by a small number of people. Although the structure of the top administration was similar to the pattern adopted by most *mineiro* firms in the nineteenth century, the company had a fairly developed administrative structure with at least two layers of managers. As in the case of the CUI, this seems to be related with the nature of the industry rather than with the complexity of the company *per se*.

Thus, in the last century the *mineiro* iron industry was owned by a small number of people, usually drawn from one family. Foundries were managed by their owners, irrespectively of their size, without the assistance of any kind of administrative staff. In addition, the foundries rarely constituted the sole occupation of owners and workers.

Although ownership of the CUI was not restricted to a small number of people, control over the company was in the hands of a small number of shareholders. Furthermore, the company employed a wide range of professionals and workers, organized in an extensive administrative structure. In this structure it is possible to identify a layer of managers who operated the several stations along the turnpike and a technical body organized on a hierarchical basis. However, this somewhat more complex administrative structure was due to the nature of the business rather than to the peculiar complexity of the company itself. Because transport companies were physically different – with workers spread around several distinct locations – when compared, for example, with textile mills and iron foundries – which usually employed all workers on a single site – a different and more complex structure had to be devised. Therefore, structural differences were industry-specific and not due to different managerial approaches. This is evidenced by the structure of the top administration of the CUI, which was very similar to that of the textile mills.

The administrative structure of some of the largest textile firms shows that they were invariably family affairs, even though organized as joint stock companies. The board and managerial positions were filled by members of the controlling families in a clear indication that kinship was one of the basic requirements for appointment. The most extensive administrative structure consisted of no more than two layers of managers. Managers were responsible for a wide range of activities, from short to long-term decisions – further evidence of the lack of complexity of the business life.

Finally, the electricity-generating companies were also owned by a small number of people, usually locals. Due to the nature of the industry, these companies had a more developed administrative and technical structure. Nevertheless, administrative personnel were very limited in number and the structure of the top administration, which did not differ from that of the other industries examined here, reflected the embryonic stage of their organizational structure.

CONCLUSION

This chapter has examined the organization of *mineiro* firms in the nineteenth century by analysing the scope of their activities, measured in terms of the size of the firms, the structure of their markets, and their administrative organization. The analysis shows that, generally speaking, they were traditional business enterprises. They were small, single-unit firms carrying on only one economic function, producing a limited range of products and restricted to local markets. Furthermore, most of them applied traditional methods and sources of energy – such as wood, wind and water, man and beast – in the production and distribution of daily output.

The iron industry in the first three-quarters of the last century was dominated by a large number of small foundries employing a very simple and primitive technology which imposed a strict limit on the scale of production. In the latter part of the century a few larger mills emerged employing more complex technology, although the scale of production remained small. The size of the workforce was also small, with very few foundries employing more than 20 people in the first three-quarters of the nineteenth century. Furthermore, they operated on a regional basis supplying mining companies, farms and local towns. The *mineiro* iron industry manufactured parts for mining machinery, agricultural tools, domestic appliances and horseshoes. Nevertheless, individual firms produced only a narrow range of products. The distribution of the output was made by a large number of small generalist merchants spread across the province and by muletrains.

The CUI was certainly an exception in some respects. From the point of view of the length of the roads built and operated, the company was certainly a large business. The size of its workforce also points to a large enterprise. Nevertheless, in terms of the scale of the operation measured by freight and passenger transport, the company could hardly be considered large. Furthermore, the company operated on a local basis, being limited to the market consisting of the Paraíba Valley in the province of Rio de Janeiro and the Mata zone in Minas Gerais, and highly dependent on the transport of only one product – coffee.

The *mineiro* textile industry was made up of small and medium-sized firms, rarely operating more than one unit. Their scale of production was very limited compared with that of the largest Brazilian textile firms. In terms of the size of the workforce, although the *mineiro* firms proved to be much more labour-intensive than their Brazilian counterparts, their workforce tended to be smaller in absolute terms. They were restricted to local markets and to the less sophisticated niche of the market. Their output was distributed by muletrains and travelling salesmen, although in the last decade of the century the CCC resorted to the opening of warehouses accross the province.

Finally, although the electricity-generating companies established at the turn of the century provided technologically advanced services (the generation of hydroelectricity and, in the case of the CME the provision of telephone services), they also could hardly be considered large firms. They fulfilled only one economic function, they were small both in the scale of their operation and the size of their capital, and they were restricted to small and local markets.

Furthermore, the analysis of the administrative structure of the *mineiro* firms has shown that, in this respect, they were even more traditional and less complex than the analysis of their activities may have suggested. They were usually owned by a small number of people, managed by their owners, and very often they had no administrative structure whatsoever. Iron companies were rarely owned by more than a handful of people, and they were managed by their owners, irrespective of their size, without the assistance of any kind of administrative structure. Although the ownership of the CUI was not restricted to a small number of persons, control was in the hands of a small number of shareholders. The company's administrative structure consisted of a few layers of managers and a technical body organized on a hierarchical basis. Nevertheless, the top administration was very small, in a clear indication that the CUI was still in an embryonic stage of administrative development. Textile firms were invariably family affairs, even though organized as joint stock companies. The board of directors and the managerial positions were filled by members of the controlling families in a clear indication that appointment was based on kinship rather than expertise. The most extensive administrative structure consisted of no more than two layers of managers. Managers' responsibilities included a wide range activities, in further evidence of no departmentalization or specialization of any sort. The electricity-generating companies were also owned by a small number of people, mainly locals. Although these companies had a clear administrative structure for their technical bodies, organized on a hierarchical basis with a few layers of managers, the main shareholders had a tight control of the daily life of these companies and the structure for the top administration once more revealed the embryonic stage of the organizational development of these firms.

Finally, the organizational analysis of *mineiro* firms has revealed that towards the end of the century firms tended to become more and more bureaucratic, as they grew in size or were replaced by larger firms. Nevertheless, the *mineiro* economy continued to be dominated by traditional firms which became more numerous and specialized towards the end of the century. These are the phenomena which preceded the emergence of the large and modern business enterprises and of the managerial capitalism in the USA, Great Britain and Germany. Therefore, it is reasonable to conclude that from the organizational point of view the business environment in nineteenth-century Minas Gerais was characteristic of the first stage of capitalist development – traditional and personal capitalism.

4 Technology

INTRODUCTION

The prime influence behind the more or less rapid rates of economic growth of the Western European economies during the last 200 years has been technological progress,[1] a necessary element of economic development. Capital goods, the means of production in which much of technology has been embodied, have enormously increased productivity. In the absence of technological progress, the process of growth by capital accumulation and division of labour as proposed by Adam Smith would eventually have encountered diminishing returns. The process of economic development is not only a matter of the increase of capital goods of the same type.[2] As Schumpeter has pointed out, economic development consists primarily in the employment of different resources in a different way, in doing different things with them. Different methods of employment of economic resources, and not savings and the increase in the availability of labour, has changed the face of the world.[3] Furthermore, over the years one of the key indicators of the formation of a positive business environment is the capacity of an economy to absorb and refine imported technology.

Thus, this chapter reviews the literature on technological progress and discusses the dependence of various *mineiro* firms on foreign technical knowledge and the limits to the development of an indigenous technology during this period. It also discusses how *mineiro* entrepreneurs managed to absorb these technologies, from selection to operation, adaptation and modification.

A BRIEF REVIEW OF THE TECHNOLOGICAL PROGRESS LITERATURE

Technological progress may be defined as changes in the ways of doing things – manufacturing goods, organizing production and distribution, transporting goods and people, and

128

providing services to consumers. It consists of the introduction of new machines, products and systems.[4] There are basically two views about the nature of technological progress, which, rather than being contradictory are complementary. The first, represented chiefly by Schumpeter, stresses discontinuity: technological progress is seen as a series of major 'breakthroughs' which have a great impact upon the pace and direction of economic development. The second view emphasizes the continuous, cumulative and piecemeal nature of technological progress: there are small sequential steps spread over long periods of time before full technological potential is achieved. The process is one of 'learning by doing' and 'learning by using'.[5]

Moreover, three different stages can be identified in the process of technological progress: invention, innovation, and diffusion or adoption. Invention may be defined as conceiving an idea for some change and demonstrating its feasibility. Innovation is the incorporation of an invention into the production process.[6] Innovation is closely linked to the inventive process and constitutes the beginning of the diffusion process. The diffusion process is dependent upon a series of improvements in the performance of an innovation, its progressive modification and adaptation to suit the requirements of various submarkets, and the availability and introduction of other complementary inputs which decisively widen the economic usefulness of an original innovation.[7] Thus, the diffusion process relates to the spread in the use of an already-established technological innovation.[8] It also includes the transfer of technology both from one industry to another and from one country to another.[9] Therefore, the processes of diffusion and technology transfer form a continuum with no clear dividing line.[10]

The international transfer of technology is widely recognised as the principal means for relieving world poverty, technology being crucial not only for growth, but also for the capacity to grow.[11] Although the international transfer of technology has been going on for a long time, its scale and impact has vastly accelerated since the Industrial Revolution when the introduction of a number of new technologies brought immense improvements to productivity. Although the Industrial Revolution began in England, new technologies spread and were adopted elsewhere when circumstances and conditions were propitious. British technologies provided the basis for industrial development in several Western European countries, the USA and other countries where conditions were positive. Countries receiving foreign technology were in a favourable position. They could industrialize through the mere transfer of existing technologies without having to reinvent them.[12] The classic example in the nineteenth century was the USA[13] and in the twentieth century Japan.[14]

Furthermore, as Gerschenkron has correctly pointed out, the opportunities for rapid industrialization through technology-borrowing was one of the few advantages of backward countries. Their prospects of industrialization were more promising the greater the accumulation of technological innovations at their disposal in more advanced countries. Borrowed technology was one of the primary factors assuring a rapid development in a backward country.[15] However, the importance of this advantage should not be exaggerated. The successful transfer of technology is not just a matter of transporting a piece of hardware from one geographical location to another. The transfer of technology and its diffusion through the recipient economy has never been a simple, easy or effortless task. To begin with, the import of foreign technologies requires some minimum level of technological skills, not only to modify and adapt the foreign technology, but also to provide the basis for an intelligent selection among the wide range of potential foreign suppliers. The nineteenth-century experiences suggest that the successful transfer of technology depends greatly upon the specific domestic circumstances in the recipient country.[16]

Technological change in Latin American countries has relied mainly on foreign sources of technical knowledge and information, as the case of nineteenth-century Minas Gerais illustrates very well. Although foreign technological knowledge has often come embodied in imported machinery and equipment, it has also come in the form of blueprints, patents, instruction manuals and other technical documents. However, rather than being exogenously given and freely and instantaneously accessible to everybody, technical knowledge and information has to be sought systematically. This obviously implies time and cost. Firms seeking new technologies need to engage in various tasks. Furthermore, a package of technical information is almost never absolutely precise, rarely perfectly understood or easily replicable.

An important aspect of the transfer of technology to less-developed countries is the structural differences between them and the developed countries. Less-developed countries such as Brazil are characterized by smaller domestic markets, higher degrees of tariff protection, shortage of skills, acute market imperfections, distortions in technical information, a higher business concentration, a weaker competitive atmosphere, a lack of basic infrastructure, and so on. The size of the domestic market is one of the most important differences between developed and less-developed countries, and it is certainly one which greatly influences the choice of technology. With very few exceptions, industrial firms operating in less-developed countries are much smaller than their counterparts in developed nations. These differences in size influence the selection of appropriate technology. Thus, manufacturing firms established in less-developed countries usually settle for a technology involving a method of production of a more discontinuous nature, and for a much lower degree of automation. This has a major impact upon plant lay-out, type and cost of equipment and machinery, the overall organization of production including, for example, the degree and patterns of subcontracting, the number of workers and so forth. Such choices will also affect the size of economies of scale which can eventually be captured by the firm.

The technology originally chosen by manufacturing firms in less-developed countries also differs from that employed by industrial enterprises in developed nations in terms of the degree of vertical integration. Manufacturing firms in less-developed countries usually make much less use of subcontracting than do their contemporary counterparts in developed countries, as the study of *mineiro* firms shows clearly. The degree of subcontracting may increase over time but not at a very rapid rate. The slow rate at which the division of labour and the development of a sufficiently vast network of subcontractors seem to proceed in less-developed countries has at least two different explanations: the size of the market and the shortage of skills.

Size of market affects the likelihood of attaining economies of scale and specialization, and therefore the relative cost of external as opposed to internal production. Availability of technical skills and entrepreneurship is associated with quality standards and reliability and these are certainly two major aspects taken into account by firms considering subcontracting decisions. A high degree of vertical integration usually means in-house provision of goods and services which are technologically dissimilar to the company's major activity, as in the case of the Companhia União e Indústria (CUI), for example. A high degree of technological dissimilarity necessarily means lower technical specialization, underutilization of equipment, and many difficulties concerning production planning and industrial organization.[17]

As the following section will show in detail, the above-mentioned peculiarities of the transfer and absorption of borrowed technology to Latin American countries were, to different degrees, present in the *mineiro* experiences of the nineteenth century. Structural differences between nineteenth-century Minas Gerais and the more advanced economies of that time were certainly large and had an immense impact on the whole process of technology absorption.

THE PROCESS OF TRANSFER OF TECHNOLOGY

Here we examine the transfer of technology in nineteenth-century Minas Gerais. As local production of technical knowledge was virtually non-existent, most industries relied on foreign technology. Thus, we shall first examine the limits on the development of indigenous technology and the reliance of most *mineiro* industries on foreign technologies. Of the industries investigated here only the iron foundries established in the first three-quarters of the last century employed indigenous technology. The other three – textile, electricity-generating, and transport and road-construction – relied exclusively on foreign technology. This will be followed by on investigation of the several stages in the process of handling a technology, from equipment selection to its adaptation to the local environment.

However, technologies of different natures presented distinct problems. The selection of an intangible technology, for example, was primarily determined by the availability of skilled workers, whereas in the case of tangible technologies, price and technicalities were more relevant. Thus, the industries investigated are divided into two groups according to the nature of the technology adopted by them. The first group is constituted by those industries which employed a highly intangible technology and where production or operation relied heavily on the technical expertise of workers and managers/entrepreneurs. These were the iron and transport industries. The second group is composed of those industries which employed a technology much more 'embodied' in machinery and equipment, that is the textile and electricity-generating industries. Production in these cases required comparatively less skill from the workforce, where the pace of work was primarily determined by the machinery/equipment itself.

Reliance on Foreign Technologies and the Limits of Indigenous Technology

The experience of successfully industrialized countries in the nineteenth century indicates that the existence of a capital-goods industry was of critical importance for the development of indigenous technology. The crucial learning process involved in machinery production was a vital source of technological dynamism, flexibility and vitality. Reliance on foreign technology perpetuates a posture of dependency, depriving a country of the development of a domestic capital-goods industry properly adapted to its own needs.[18] Thus, firms established in countries lacking a capital-goods industry were forced to resort to foreign technologies and faced all the problems that this dependence involved. The example of nineteenth-century *mineiro* business enterprises are in this sense very illustrative.

This section examines the main sources of technology of *mineiro* firms during the last century, and the nature of the technological dependence of each industry investigated in this book. As mentioned above, among the industries investigated three – the textile, electricity-generating and transport industries – relied exclusively on foreign technology. Consequently, they also relied upon foreign sources for the supply of materials, components, parts, equipment and machinery. The only industry in nineteenth-century Minas Gerais to employ an indigenous technology was the iron industry, although a few foundries employed foreign methods of iron production. Therefore, iron foundries relied even less upon foreign suppliers. Nevertheless, their development was limited by the deficiencies of such indigenous technology and by the limited ability of the local business environment to develop technical knowledge.

The terms of the dependence of each industry upon foreign suppliers depended on the nature of the technology employed by them. Industries employing a more tangible technology used more specialized equipment and machinery usually supplied by specialized suppliers. Therefore, the dependence of such industries on their suppliers was more critical. Industries employing a more intangible technology used more universal equipment, which tended to be more easily replicated locally and manufactured by generalist suppliers. Thus, among the industries examined in this book the dependence on foreign suppliers was much greater for the textile and electricity-generating industries, due to the nature, complexity and age of the technologies employed by them. These technologies were more tangible, embodied in complex machinery and equipment which could not be found locally. Furthermore, these technologies were recent developments when compared with those employed by the transport and the *mineiro* iron industries.

The technologies employed in road construction and in the transport of goods and passengers were of a more intangible nature, technical knowledge being carried by experts. Therefore reliance was upon people rather than upon equipment. Moreover, the technologies for road construction and the building of wheeled vehicles drawn by animals were century-old and well-established by the middle of the nineteenth century. Nevertheless, although several components and materials employed in the construction and operation of roads were not produced internally and *mineiro* road-building and transport companies had to resort to foreign suppliers, equipment and operational methods were soon replicated locally.

Finally, the technology employed by the iron industry was also of a more intangible nature and the reliance was also upon people rather than equipment. Furthermore, methods of iron production employed by the *mineiro* foundries in the first three-quarters of the nineteenth century were also centuries-old and well-established technologies by the middle of the last century. On the other hand, although only a small number of foundries employed foreign technology and the equipment used in iron production was of a more universal nature, a few foundries very occasionally imported part of the equipment which could not be produced on-site. Nevertheless, the iron industry was the least dependent on foreign suppliers.

Table 4.1   Estimated geographic distribution of Brazilian textile mills, 1866, 1875, 1885

Provinces	1866	1875	1885
Maranhão		1	1
Pernambuco		1	1
Alagoas	1	1	1
Bahia	5	1	12
Rio de Janeiro*	2	5	11
São Paulo		6	9
Minas Gerais	1	5	13
Total	9	30	48

* The city and the province of Rio de Janeiro.
Source: S.J. Stein, *Origens e Evolução da Indústria Têxtil no Brasil, 1850–1950* (Rio de Janeiro, 1950), p. 36.

The textile industry was not only the first industrial sector to emerge in Brazil, but also the most important until the late 1930s. In the second half of the last century several textile mills were established in the country, being favoured by a number of factors: the availability of raw materials, the increasing domestic demand for textiles, the availability of cheap labour, and protection against foreign competition.[19] As shown in Table 4.1, the number of textile mills established in 1866 was nine. In 1875 there were 30 textile mills in Brazil, and ten years later the estimated number in the whole country amounted to 48. Yet no indigenous textile technology emerged in Brazil during this period, and textile entrepreneurs had to look for machinery and equipment abroad. The most obvious sources of textile machinery and equipment during the last century were Great Britain and the USA. The textile industry was at the heart of the Industrial Revolution in late eighteenth-century England. Until the beginning of the twentieth century, the British textile industry was the most important in the world and British equipment was the most modern available.[20] Furthermore, technological transfer between Great Britain and the USA in the early part of the last century was relatively quick and effective. Both countries were closely related culturally; they shared a common language, legal and economic systems, and enjoyed a common technical heritage. The technological synergy between the two meant that by the end of the eighteenth century machinists building all kinds of textile machines could be found in the USA. British immigrant machine-makers played a major role in the diffusion of new textile technology in the USA, and as early as the beginning of the last century the USA was already an important producer of textile equipment.[21] Moreover, at the beginning of the twentieth century the US textile industry was the second largest in the world[22] and the leadership in output and invention was passing to the USA.[23] Rapid textile technology transfer between Britain and the USA also demonstrates the mobility and adaptability of the textile technology 'package' – that is, equipment and personnel.

Thus, for obvious reasons, *mineiro* mill owners relied mainly on British and US suppliers of technology. When the Cedro mill was established in the early 1870s, the mill machinery was bought from Guilherme Van Vlick Lidgerwood, a representative in Rio de Janeiro of the US manufacturer, Author Danfort Paterson of New Jersey.[24] Nearly a decade later, and with 48 mills already established in Brazil, the Cedro mill continued to rely exclusively on foreign suppliers, especially British and US, clear evidence of the inability of Brazilians to replicate internally textile technology. Replying to an inquiry from the president of the Sete Lagoas city council in Minas Gerais in 1882, the proprietors of the Cedro mill stated that the machinery employed in the mill was partly US and partly English.[25]

The original machinery of the Cachoeira mill was also acquired in Britain and the USA. As Bernardo Mascarenhas had already had the experience of setting up a mill (the Cedro), he was appointed by his family to organize the establishment of the Cachoeira factory. As shown in his correspondence, Bernardo decided to go to the USA and Europe to select and purchase machinery. In April 1874 he wrote from Manchester that he had visited the main English manufacturers, including Platt Brothers & Co., and that he was about to leave for New York to inspect US machines.[26] In December of the same year he wrote to his brothers from New York saying that he had decided to return to England after buying three Tenk spinning machines in the USA.[27] It is interesting to point out that Bernardo decided to buy machines of different origins, a decision which had long-run consequences as will be discussed in greater detail below.

In 1883, after the constitution of the Companhia Cedro e Cachoeira (CCC), the company decided to expand productive capacity and another 50 new looms for the Cachoeira mill and 16 for the Cedro mill were ordered from England.[28] Further evidence that the CCC continued to be supplied by British and US manufacturers throughout the nineteenth century can be found in the extensive correspondence of the company with its suppliers and agents. In 1884, a year after the merger of the Cedro and the Cachoeira mills into the CCC, Max Nothmann, an agent in Rio de Janeiro, was expecting to soon dispach a turbine from New York.[29] In 1887 the CCC ordered machine parts from the USA through the same agent.[30] Four years later Robert L. Kerr, an engineer and machinery agent from Manchester, wrote informing the company that the English manufacturers of hydro-extractors wanted to supply the machine assembled and not in parts.[31] In 1893 the same agent wrote saying that he expected to deliver a steam engine and boiler ordered by the company as soon as possible.[32] In 1895 James Leffel & Co., manufacturers of steam engines and steel boilers based in New York, wrote saying that they had received an order and specifications for the construction of a turbine.[33] In 1899 the company ordered machinery from England for both the Cedro and the Cachoeira mills.[34] Finally, in 1901 Kerr stated in his letter of 27 November that he was sending the estimate and specifications of a spinning machine as had been requested.[35]

As this correspondence indicates, the CCC's reliance on foreign suppliers was not restricted to textile machinery. The company purchased capital equipment such as turbines, boilers and steam engines and inputs such as lubricants, yarns, dyes, chemicals and so on. In 1899 Victor Uslaender, an agent in Rio de Janeiro, informed the CCC that a shipment of oil (apparently bought in England) to him was larger than he had expected, and consequently he was dispatching two barrels of oil instead of the one ordered by the company.[36] In 1883 Max Nothmann wrote that he had already sent the company's order for yarn to England.[37] On yet another occasion, Blum & Co. (another agent in Rio de Janeiro) wrote charging the company for part of the dye and chemicals shipment cleared from customs and already dispatched.[38]

There is no reason to believe that other textile mills in nineteenth-century Minas Gerais were not equally reliant on foreign suppliers. On the contrary, evidence from other *mineiro* mills suggests that the entire industry not only relied on foreign suppliers, but that it was also mainly supplied by British and US manufacturers. The Tecelagem Mascarenhas was equipped with machinery supplied by Hogson and Robert Hall & Sons of Manchester, England.[39] The machinery of the Companhia Cachoeira de Macacos (CCM) was purchased in England[40] as was that of the Companhia de Tecidos Santanense (CTS), with the exception of the turbine and the spinning machine which was purchased in New York.[41]

The machinery of the Sociedade Anônima Industrial Machadense (SAIM) – a textile mill established in Machado, southern Minas Gerais, in 1872 – seems to have been purchased from a firm named 'Lidgerwood', the name reported as being on the machinery. Coincidentally, as mentioned above, the machinery of the Cedro mill was purchased from a representative called Guilherme Van Vlick Lidgerwood from Rio de Janeiro.[42] Moreover, a local almanac of 1874 reported that the machinery of the SAIM had come from England.[43] Further evidence indicates that some of the machinery was English and some US,[44] a pattern already observed in the case of the CCC. The União Itabirana also bought its machinery from both the USA and England: in 1883 the company observed that some of their machines were English and some US.[45]

It is interesting to note that the heterogeneity of the origin of the machinery (the result of the lack of a native capital-goods industry) employed by the *mineiro* textile mills must have created and aggravated a number of problems. It most probably complicated the servicing and the operation of different machinery, created incompatibilities in the production line, and increased the costs of procuring replacement parts.

Thus, as the evidence presented above suggests, the *mineiro* textile industry relied on foreign suppliers for parts, machinery, equipment, components and all sorts of material such as lubricants, dyes and yarn. This was the result not only of the absence of an indigenous capital-goods industry, but also of the total absence of a domestic network of suppliers of any kind. As Katz has suggested, the absence of a network of independent and domestic suppliers in Latin America is due to the limited size of the markets, shortage of skills and entrepreneurship.[46] Although there was a sufficient supply of entrepreneurship for the emergence of new industrial sectors, the *mineiro* business environment was not conducive to the generation of the whole range of enterprises required by a complex and advanced economy. Furthermore, in several cases the same mill was supplied by both British and US manufacturers adding to the already long list of problems (caused by cultural and economic differences and by the geographic distance between users and suppliers) *mineiro* textile entrepreneurs had to face in relying on foreign technology.

Such reliance was not restricted to the textile industry. Any industrial sector which employed more sophisticated and mechanized equipment depended heavily on foreign technology, as was the case of the *mineiro* electricity-generating industry. However, due to the difference in the nature of electricity and textile technologies (the former was a 'breakthrough' scientific development and the latter a piecemeal development of traditional crafts), the terms of the dependence of the electricity-generating industry were somewhat different from those of the textile industry. Owing to its scientific complexity, electricity technology was under the firm control of a few specialized firms in the world and was less feasible to be replicated locally, with less opportunities for adaptations. Furthermore, as electrical equipment was even more specialized than textile machinery, there were less opportunities for the use of equipment of different manufacturers without major consequences.

Electricity in the last century was a new technology even in the most advanced countries. Its first practical use was in telegraphy, invented in the USA and Britain during the 1840s. After the 1880s, telephone and electrical power were developed in both the USA and Germany. As the progress of electrical technology in the USA and Germany was particularly rapid with the introduction of successive innovations (a classic example of a Schumpeterian major technological 'breakthrough'), the transfer of electrical technology was by no means easier than that of older technologies such as steam engines, mechanical spinning and iron smelting with coke. Electricity was a development of nineteenth-century physical science, in contrast to the mechanical and metallurgical technologies of the eighteenth century which were developed from empirical skills in traditional crafts. Thus, the transfer of electrical technology at the end of the nineteenth century assumed an unusual character.

Since there were essential differences between the utilization of electricity and the manufacture of equipment, the spread of electrical utilities (including communication and power supply) within less-developed countries was only possible when machinery was imported. As a public utility, the electricity-generating industry supplied a service which was instantly consumed. Most firms were located close to their markets and, given the nature of the 'commodity', were immune from foreign competition, unlike textile firms. Indeed, like all public utilities, the electricity-supply industry enjoyed a natural monopoly, capital start-up costs precluded the entry of new firms into the industry once a successful operator had been established. Moreover, machinery embodied the most up-to-date advances in electrical technology – as was also the case of textile machinery – so any country could make use of these innovations and the utility industries could emulate progress in power and communication technologies in the advanced countries.[47] This was a classic example of backward countries taking advantage of technological innovations available in more advanced countries, as pointed out by Gerschenkron.[48]

In contrast, electrical equipment was hardware which could be transported long distances and preserved over time. Furthermore, electrical machinery was an international good and their consumers – utilization industries – had the choice of buying either domestic or imported equipment, as was also the case for textile equipment. Nevertheless, most electrical machinery was made in Britain, Germany or the USA, and in particular by the big five manufacturers: Western Electric, General Electric and Westinghouse Electric Company (WEC) of the USA, and Siemens and AGE of Germany. These firms were not only the world's largest producers of electrical machinery, but also the main innovators in electrical technology.[49] At the beginning there were favourable conditions for entry into the heavy electrical industry. In the 1880s electrical equipment was still in its infancy and could easily be copied by domestic mechanics with poor tools and little skill, as the case of Japan illustrates very well. However, by the end of the century the products of the big US and German firms had improved in capacity as well as in quality, embodying the most recent achievements in electrical technology. Thus, the technological gap in the production of electrical equipment became so great that technology transfer could never be realized without the will of the big US and European electrical manufacturers.[50]

Therefore, electricity-generating companies established in Minas Gerais at the turn of the century had to rely on foreign suppliers of electrical equipment and most of them relied on US suppliers. A month after the foundation of the Companhia Mineira de Eletricidade (CME) in 1888, Bernardo Mascarenhas ordered power station equipment through a representative in Rio de Janeiro, Max Nothmann & Cia. The order was then passed to the WEC which supplied equipment for the transmission of electricity.[51] For the remainder of the century, the CME continued to be supplied by WEC. In 1891 the company ordered new machines as the old ones had been damaged and the lighting service had been suspended.[52] In 1896 the new plant, the Marmelos-1, was also equipped with machinery supplied by the WEC.[53] The equipment employed by the Companhia Força e Luz Cataguazes-Leopoldina (CFLCL) was acquired in the USA and Europe. The turbine of the Maurício power plant, inaugurated in 1908,[54] was purchased from Escher Wyss, a Swiss manufacturer, whereas the rest of its equipment was acquired from WEC.[55]

The CUI also employed foreign technology, although its reliance upon foreign suppliers was very limited compared to that of the textile and electricity-generating industries. The reason seems to have been due to the nature of the technologies employed in the construction of roads and in the transport of goods and people at that time. The technology for constructing roads was more intangible. In other words, road building in the nineteenth century relied mostly on technical knowledge carried by experts: the equipment used was of a very simple nature and universally available and reproducible. Furthermore, by the middle of the nineteenth century the prevailing technology was a century old and accessible. The transport of goods and people employed technology embodied in wheeled vehicles drawn by animals, and the technology to build carts, waggons and coaches dated to ancient times and was not very complex. This meant that local production of these vehicles was feasible. The most modern methods of road construction in the nineteenth century evolved from the French methods of construction developed in the preceding century. From the beginning of the eighteenth century French roads were admired, and to some extent imitated, by the rest of Europe.[56]

In Britain, Turnpike Trusts operating their own toll-gate-enclosed sections of roads created a better road system and became the characteristic English highway by the middle of the nineteenth century.[57] They made regular coach services possible and, furthermore, had better road surfaces which were created by engineers like Telford and McAdam. The Telford and McAdam technology reduced the camber of road surfaces, thereby improving drainage, safety and speed. By 1834, for example, while English coaches were driven at an average of 9–10 miles per hour, the French *malle-poste* averaged only 6 miles per hour.[58]

John L. McAdam wrote several books about road building which were translated into various languages, thus popularizing the McAdam system abroad. In the course of the nineteenth century, the terms 'metalled' and 'macadamized' (roads using broken stones in their construction) became almost synonymous in descriptions of roads. McAdam's system had such an impact in Europe that by the end of the last century some 90 per cent of the main highways were macadamized. Slowly the macadam road penetrated beyond Europe. US road engineers studied his method of road construction and in 1832 the first US national road east of the Ohio river was given a macadamized surface.[59] In Minas Gerais the first macadamized road was built in the late 1850s. The União e Indústria turnpike was 144 kilometres long, linking Juiz de Fora in the Mata zone to Petrópolis in the province of Rio de Janeiro.[60]

Furthermore, until the beginning of the nineteenth century the equipment used in the building of roads consisted of simple tools such as hammers, sieves, spades, wheelbarrows, rammers and pickaxes. Machines for compaction, such as rollers, had been used by the ancients. However, it was only in the 1830s that horse-drawn rollers were gradually introduced in Europe. The first steam-driven roller was invented in 1859, but despite its manifest advantages it gained ground only gradually. Moreover, in McAdam's days stones were broken by hand and continued to be so until as late as 1900, although the first stone-crusher was invented in 1858.[61] Thus, until the late nineteenth century, road building preserved its craft nature involving very little sophisticated equipment. The basic requirement was technical knowledge carried by craftsmen and trained road engineers.

The construction of the União e Indústria turnpike, for example, involved the work of several experts. The construction of the road began in 1856 under the supervision of foreign engineers and architects with a large experience of road construction in Europe. The company also employed European surveyors and a number of foreign craftsmen, such as bricklayers, blacksmiths, locksmiths, painters, carpenters, belt makers, and so on.[62]

In the case of the road system, the technology employed in the manufacture of wheeled vehicles also required little equipment and was largely embodied in skilled personnel. Light-wheeled chariots were used even before the ancient

Greeks and the Romans who used two and four-wheeled chariots for the transport of goods more than passengers. From the seventeenth century onwards, several developments in coach design and building were introduced such as sprung suspension, dished wheels, one-piece iron tyres, and better brake systems. Individually these developments amounted to little, but collectively they transformed the primitive vehicle – which was little more than a box on wheels – into comparatively speedy and luxurious coaches. From the 1780s onwards goods vehicles changed little, but many new and improved passenger vehicles of European origin appeared.[63]

Thus, the technology for building wheeled vehicles drawn by animals had been basically the same for nearly a century when the CUI started the construction and operation of its turnpike in the late 1850s. Therefore the company was able to build the vehicles used in the transport of goods and passengers locally. Evidence of this fact is the existence of several workshops established at the Juiz de Fora station. Among them were the carpenters' workshops for the construction of all kinds of vehicles (carts, coaches and carriages).[64] Furthermore, a Parliamentary Decree of 7 August 1852, mentioned in the company report of 1856, exempted the company from customs duties for 12 years on purchases of machines, instruments and any other objects destined for the construction of roads and vehicles of the company.

Nevertheless, due to the lack of a domestic network of suppliers the CUI also had to rely on foreign suppliers and manufacturers for a wide range of materials. In 1856, for example, based on the Parliamentary Decree of 7 August 1852 mentioned above, the company purchased several commodities in Europe (from stationery to screws for bridges, carts and carriages).[65]

To sum up, the technologies employed by the CUI in the construction of the turnpike and in the transport of goods and people were also foreign. However, they were century-old technologies, of more or less common knowledge. Even so, owing to the total absence of a network of suppliers of any kind, the company had to rely on foreign suppliers for the supply of various components and materials. However, the CUI's reliance was much smaller when compared to that of both the electricity-generating and textile industries. Materials, components and equipment used by the CUI were relatively simple and were soon replicated locally, and the simplicity and universal nature of the technology employed meant that backward linkages were more easily created, as the workshops of the company indicate.

In contrast with the textile, the electricity-generating and the transport industries, the *mineiro* iron industry established during the first three-quarters of the last century was the only industry to employ an indigenous technology. However, a few foundries did rely on foreign technologies which were primitive when compared with those being employed at the same time in more developed countries. Although a few foundries resorted to foreign suppliers of equipment on a few occasions, the intangible nature of iron technology meant that the industry relied much more upon the technical expertise of people rather than upon equipment. Furthermore, due to the universal nature of the equipment used in iron production they were also more easily reproduced locally.

The production of iron in Minas Gerais was introduced by African slaves at the beginning of the last century.[66] Initially, foundries were essential components of agricultural enterprises, with scores of slaves specialized in the domestic production of iron for farm use. Gradually iron-making emerged as the main activity of some estates.[67] Until the first decade of the nineteenth century, several farmers and blacksmiths produced iron solely for their own consumption, not only because until the arrival of the Portuguese Royal family in 1808 the commercial production of iron was prohibited, but also because they did not have the technical knowledge for large-scale production.[68] Later, Eschwege, the founder of the Patriótica mill – the first foundry to produce iron on an industrial scale in Minas Gerais.[69] – and other foreign technicians introduced modifications to this local process, resulting in what became known as the *cadinho* method. These modifications were based on the Swedish method of production called *stückofen*. The name *cadinho* derived from the shape of the cavities in the walls of the furnace which facilitated the introduction of ore and charcoal as well as the withdrawal of pig iron. There was also a small opening for the introduction of air by hydraulical bellows. The pig iron was taken to the hydraulical hammermill, where the slag was separated, and when the separation was completed the pig iron was resmelted for transformation into cast iron. The *cadinho* method was very simple, requiring neither complex facilities nor skilled workers. It required only proximity to stands of timber and deposits of iron ore, and an abundance of water. Due to its simplicity, this method of iron-making was widely used in Minas Gerais in the first three-quarters of the nineteenth century.[70] However, output was very limited compared with that of the two foreign methods employed by some of the *mineiro* foundries during this period, namely the Italian and the Catalan methods.[71]

Among the four largest foundries established in Minas Gerais in the first three-quarters of the nineteenth century, three – the Patriótica, Morro do Pilar,[72] and Girau[73] – employed the *cadinho* technology. Furthermore, in his survey of the foundries located in the Metalúrgica zone, Costa Sena found 17 foundries employing the *cadinho* technology,[74] clear evidence of the widespread employment of the *cadinho* method in Minas Gerais. However, there were a few occasions in which even those foundries had to resort to foreign manufacturers for the supply of materials and equipment, because of the total lack of conditions to produce them on site. When Eschwege set up his foundry in 1811 he imported the hammermills from England because it was very difficult to find someone who could produce them manually in Brazil.[75] In 1815 Schoenewolf informed Eschwege that Câmara had requested from the government refractory material from England.[76] These two cases suggest that, at least in the first decades of the nineteenth century, the local conditions for the manufacture of any kind of equipment were inadequate despite the existence of an indigenous technology.

Hence, for the first three-quarters of the nineteenth century the large majority of the *mineiro* iron foundries relied on the indigenous *cadinho* method, but this did not prevent ironmasters from resorting to foreign suppliers, although their dependence was most probably much less intense than that observed for the textile, electricity-generating and transport industries. On the other hand, the employment of the *cadinho* method imposed strict limits to the development of the iron industry. The demise of small foundries in the last quarter of the century is undisputable evidence of this fact. Once the natural barriers against foreign competition were lifted, the limits of the indigenous technology employed by the large majority of the *mineiro* iron-masters became evident.[77] As an engineer of the Mining School of Ouro Preto observed:

> In the period between 1881 and 1888, the iron industry began to realize that it was not possible to develop against foreign competition brought with the arrival of the railway in the hinterland of Minas Gerais. The national industry was not prepared to compete against foreign products, since it did not apply scientific industrial techniques.[78]

Despite the simplicity and popularity of the *cadinho* technology, a few *mineiro* foundries established in the first three-quarters of the last century employed foreign methods of iron production, namely the Italian and the Catalan. However, all three methods produced iron through the so-called direct process,[79] where wrought iron is produced directly from the ore. Nevertheless, from the 1750s onwards this process was gradually replaced by the indirect process, which was more productive and rapidly superseded the direct process as the major producing system in Great Britain.[80] Hence, the Italian and the Catalan technologies were obsolete when compared with those being employed at the same time in more developed countries such as Britain.[81]

From the middle of the eighteenth century to the First World War, Great Britain led the world in developing new technologies for the production of pig and wrought iron, and steel. In 1709 Abraham Darby successfully used coke instead of charcoal in blast furnaces to produce pig iron, and by the end of the eighteenth century coke had displaced charcoal in smelting. In the early 1740s Benjamin Huntsman developed the crucible process for making high-quality steel, which remained the dominant technique worldwide for more than a century. From the 1760s onwards British ironmasters developed new technologies to replace charcoal with coke in the production of wrought iron. In 1784 Henry Cort developed the 'puddling and rolling process', a method of making wrought iron from cast iron with mineral fuel which freed ironmakers from their last dependence on charcoal. By the end of the Napoleonic Wars, Cort's techniques had come to dominate the refining stage of production.

In the 1850s Henry Bessemer introduced a new revolutionary process for manufacturing steel, and shortly after, William Siemens, a German who spent most of his life in Britain, together with two Frenchmen, Pierre and Emile Martin, developed the Siemens–Martin process, an open-hearth method for making steel. Until the First World War British industry continued to lead the world steel industry in the introduction of technological improvements.[82] By the middle of the last century, although Britain was the world's leading producer of iron and in many respects was almost alone, other countries also developed important iron and steel industries. Based on the English model there were important ironworks in Belgium and France. Germany had some works of note and US ironmaking was growing as well. The Swedish iron industry was in a special position, since the country's very pure iron ore enabled its industry to produce iron of very high quality.[83]

However, metallurgical processes of production differ from more purely mechanical technologies in some important respects, and the international transfer of such technologies require further consideration. Metallurgical processes are intimately related to the qualities of the natural resource inputs. For example, the successful introduction of mineral fuel into the blast furnace in the last century depended upon the use of coal which had a chemical composition appropriate for smelting. However, until the latter part of the nineteenth century such relations between particular processes and the qualities of natural resources were not understood in any serious scientific sense. Hence, metallurgy during this period was essentially an empirical activity and variations in resource inputs affected the success of the productive process in ways which could not be understood or predicted.[84]

Thus, the transfer of technology for the production of iron was a most complex process – sometimes even impossible – and *mineiro* foundries which employed foreign technology were restricted to the use of more backward processes such as the Italian and the Catalan. The Italian method was constituted by a furnace, bellows and hammermill: it employed blast furnaces which varied from 3 to 2 feet deep, 5 to 3 feet long, and 3 to 2 feet wide, and required more care in the regulation of air for the maintenance of the temperature of the fire than the *cadinho* technology.[85] Moreover, this process required a regular series of successive heating and hammering operations. The Italian method was more productive and economical than the *cadinho*, and the quality of the final product was higher. However, this method was a simplified version of the Catalan process, the most productive and economical method used in Minas Gerais during the first three-quarters of the nineteenth century. The Catalan process was a complex method of production, requiring even more skill from the workers for measuring the quantity of ore and charcoal as well as for ensuring a perfect linkage of the heating and hammering operations. Furthermore, local experience indicated that the use of this process of production was only feasible if supervised by someone with a good knowledge of metallurgy.[86]

Among the four largest foundries established in Minas Gerais in the first three-quarters of the nineteenth century, only the São Miguel de Piracicaba foundry employed the Catalan method of production. Even so, in the early 1870s, at the time of the death of its owner and founder, Monlevade, the ironwork was transformed into an Italian foundry.[87] Furthermore, among the 24 foundries surveyed by Costa Sena in the Metalúrgica zone, seven employed the Italian method of production, including the São Miguel de Piracicaba.[88] However, due to the empirical and intangible nature of metallurgical technology, and confirming what has already been said about the technology employed by the road-construction and transport industry, foundries which employed foreign technology did not rely heavily upon foreign suppliers. The only known case of the import of equipment is that of the São Miguel de Piracicaba foundry. When Monlevade established the foundry he imported more than 7 tons of equipment from England.[89]

Hence, for the first three-quarters of the nineteenth century only a small number of the *mineiro* foundries employed foreign technologies, which were outdated compared with the technology employed in more developed countries. The large majority of the iron foundries in Minas Gerais relied on the indigenous *cadinho* method which freed ironmasters from dependence on foreign sources of supply experienced by the textile, electricity-generating and, to a lesser extent, the transport industries. However, the widespread employment of this indigenous technology imposed strict limits to the development of the iron industry. Without access – and, most important, without the economic and technical conditions to have access – to the more modern foreign technology, the *mineiro* industry was doomed to lag and perish. In the late nineteenth century a few larger iron works emerged employing the more modern and productive indirect method of production. Nevertheless, until the end of the 1930s the Brazilian iron industry was mostly made up of small-scale industries still using charcoal. A large-scale iron and steel industry would only emerge as a result of the intervention of the federal government in the 1940s with the establishment of the CSN (Volta Redonda) in the state of Rio de Janeiro.[90] Minas Gerais had to wait until the late 1950s for the emergence of its first integrated iron and steel industry based on coal and on Japanese technology, the USIMINAS.[91]

To conclude, since the Industrial Revolution the international transfer of technology has become crucial to latecomer economies, not only for initial growth, but also for their capacity to sustain development. Most nineteenth-century *mineiro* industries relied on foreign technology and foreign manufacturers of equipment, machinery, parts, components and materials. During this period, apart from the most elementary tools, sophisticated equipment could only be found abroad, mainly in Britain and the USA. However, such dependence differed according to the nature of the technology employed. Industries employing more tangible technology and specialized equipment depended more intensely on foreign sources than those employing more intangible technology and universal equipment and machinery. The *mineiro* textile industry imported a range of materials from machinery to yarn and dyes, and the electricity-generating industry also relied heavily on foreign equipment, material and components.

Although the CUI also relied on foreign technologies, it did not rely on foreign plants because the equipment used in road construction and in the transport of goods and passengers was simple, more universal and could be produced locally. Furthermore, as the technologies used by the company were of a more intangible nature the company relied more on the expertise of people than on equipment. Nevertheless, the company did rely on foreign manufacturers to supply components and materials of every sort. This reflects the absence not only of a domestic capital-goods industry, but also the absence of a domestic network of suppliers. The only industry in nineteenth-century Minas Gerais to employ an indigenous technology was the iron industry, although a few foundries also employed outdated foreign technologies. Most of the foundries established in the first three-quarters of the last century employed the *cadinho* technology, an indigenous method of production. Although this method was very simple the results were poor, and consequently the domestic industry perished when it had to face foreign competition.

THE HANDLING OF THE TECHNOLOGIES

The handling of any technology is a process which begins with the selection of equipment or a process, and involves a range of services which are essential to the continued operation of the technology. These include the ability to diagnose correctly the causes of mechanical breakdown or other sources of poor equipment performance, the availability of facilities and skilled labour to perform repair work and provide routine maintenance, and the provision of spare parts.[92] However, when technologies are carried to points remote and culturally different from where they emerged, they need to be adapted to local conditions. Therefore, the handling of foreign technology poses special problems which require particular attention, often requiring different approaches for each stage. The selection of tangible technologies, for example, depends less on the availability of experts than does the selection of an intangible technology where their presence might be a critical factor. Consequently, this part of the chapter investigates several of the stages of the handling process of technologies employed in nineteenth-century Minas Gerais. It examines the process of selection of different technologies, the relationship between users and foreign suppliers, and the adaptation and eventual modification of the technologies adopted.

The Process of Selection

Technologies are generally selected on the basis of highly imperfect information. First of all, in most sectors the degree of choice is often so overwhelming that no single businessman can be aware of the full range of feasible alternatives. Although in most cases decision-makers could benefit from a much greater flow of information, this may be expensive and require a considerable time for the accumulation of knowledge. Furthermore, businessmen with a wide range of responsibilities do not generally know where suitable information is to be found. Thus, entrepreneurs rely on a range of imperfect mechanisms for identifying the most suitable sources of supply and/or the most suitable sets of equipment; for example, word-of-mouth recommendations, well-known brand-names, occasional advertisements, or firms with whom they have dealt in the past. These criteria for choice are not likely to lead to a reliable determination of technological choice, as the experience of many firms in industrially advanced and developing countries alike have shown. The costs of this form of ignorance can indeed be very large.[93]

In nineteenth-century Minas Gerais, the criteria for the selection of equipment were not very reliable. Entrepreneurs resorted mainly to acquaintances, imported books and specialized magazines, foreigners living in the country, and even business trips abroad. However, different technologies required distinct evaluation criteria. Because intangible technologies are carried by people – and not by machinery which might perform most of the process of production with minimum human intervention – their selection is highly dependent on the availability of those experts. In this sense, metallurgy and road-building during the last century are illustrative.

Metallurgy for most of the nineteenth century was still essentially an empirical activity, so that the selection of a method of production of iron depended largely on the technical knowledge of workers and/or entrepreneurs/managers. Success in the productive process was affected by variations in resource inputs in ways that could not be predicted or understood, and the best mix of resource inputs was found by trial and error.[94] Therefore, not surprisingly, the most successful *mineiro* foundries in the first three-quarters of the century were set up by foreigners with extensive knowledge of metallurgy.

Eschwege, for example, had a wide knowledge of natural sciences and wrote extensively on the subject, and, furthermore, he came to Brazil after having worked in the Figueiró dos Vinhos foundry in Portugal.[95] However, one reason why he used the *cadinho* method at his foundry was his lack of knowledge of a more complex method of production.[96] Monlevade, founder of the São Miguel de Piracicaba foundry, also had an extensive knowledge of metallurgy. Between 1809 and 1812 he studied mining engineering in the Polytechnic of Paris,[97] and his foundry was the only one to employ the Catalan method in Minas Gerais during this period. For more than 40 years the foundry obtained good results because of Monlevade's technical knowledge.[98] Nevertheless, when Monlevade died in 1872 his family had to hire an Italian master, who switched from the Catalan to the Italian method, because they could not find anyone who could operate the Catalan system.[99] This shows clearly that intangible technologies were selected on the basis of the availability of skilled labour. Once Monlevade was dead, the choice of a method of production was determined by the availability of people able to operate the plant, even if this meant going back to a simpler and less productive process.

Further evidence of the crucial role played by the technical competence of entrepreneurs in the successful selection of a method of production of iron is provided by the appalling results of the Morro do Pilar foundry. The foundry failed mainly because of poorly conceived plans and the incompetence of its manager.[100] According to Eschwege, Manuel Ferreira da Câmara, founder of the ironwork, made several mistakes in the establishment of the Morro do Pilar foundry. To begin with, insufficient wood was available at the site for the three blast furnaces planned,[101] and Câmara made so many mistakes in the construction of the buildings and furnaces that he started production only in 1814, two years later than initially planned.[102] After trying unsuccessfully for some time to produce iron, Câmara finally hired a German foundry master who spent six months demolishing and reconstructing all the installations of the foundry.[103]

The history of the Patriótica, São Miguel de Piracicaba and Morro do Pilar foundries illustrate well three different degrees of success in the selection of an intangible technology such as metallurgy. They also illustrate the importance of the technical competence of entrepreneurs. Eschwege's choice of a method of iron production was determined by his own technical knowledge rather than abstract appraisals of available technology. For this reason the Patriótica was the first successful foundry in Minas Gerais. Monlevade got the best results for more than 40 years due to his technical competence on the chosen method of production, but as soon as he died his achievements in the São Miguel de Piracicaba foundry vanished owing to the lack of an expert to replace him. Câmara is the exemplar case of a complete failure for mistakes committed from the very beginning, that is, the process of selection.

The case of the União e Indústria turnpike is also illustrative of the process of the selection of an intangible technology. It took Mariano Procópio Ferreira Lage several months after a trip to the USA and Europe, where he spent some time studying science and technology, to decide what type of road to build and which method of construction to employ.[104] This was certainly a lengthy and expensive process of selection if one bears in mind that this happened in the first half of the nineteenth century – a time when a trip to Europe or the USA was very long and expensive – and that all the effort was only to enable him to choose the technology. In the construction work of the turnpike and the operation of the transport service, Lage employed a number of foreign engineers, architects, surveyors, drivers, craftsmen and so on,[105] who together carried the appropriate technologies for these activities. Thus, the analysis of the process of selection of intangible technologies, such as that employed by the iron and transport industry in nineteenth-century Minas Gerais, has shown that the availability of skilled labour was a crucial factor.

The selection of technologies of a more tangible nature was much less dependent on the local availability of expertise, mainly because this kind of technical knowledge is found embodied in machinery and equipment. Moreover, there are usually a larger number of producers of capital goods competing against each other. Machine manufacturers therefore have a more aggressive marketing approach – producing catalogues, appointing representatives and so on – which in the end facilitates the process of selection. Nevertheless, the selection of tangible technologies in the last century was also a lengthy and sometimes very expensive process. In order to acquire detailed practical knowledge of the capabilities and operating technique of machinery, early entrepreneurs resorted to different strategies. They sought to establish direct contacts with overseas producers of machinery or with their representatives in Brazil; they asked for the help of foreigners established in the province; or they read technical literature and travelled abroad.

When the Cedro mill was founded, Bernardo Mascarenhas was appointed to select and purchase the machinery. He first went to Rio de Janeiro and São Paulo where he visited the Santo Aleixo and the São Luís mills respectively. There, he obtained information about the construction of the buildings and the costs involved in the establishment of a textile mill.[106] He then went to the USA where he stayed for a year and a half. During this period he inspected various makes and types of machinery, and visited several textile mills in order to acquire knowledge about the techniques of cloth production, the lay-out of the factory, and the performance of equipment.[107]

Some years later, with the establishment of the Cachoeira mill, Bernardo Mascarenhas sent his brother Francisco to talk to J.N. Gordon, chairman of the St John del Rey Mining Company (SJDRMC), a British gold-mining company which was exploiting the Morro Velho mine in Minas Gerais, in order to obtain information about English machinery. The information obtained from Gordon was not very precise or helpful and Bernardo decided to select the machinery himself. He then went to the USA and Europe, as mentioned above, where he spent some time inspecting and comparing the various makes and types of machinery and learning how to assemble and operate them.[108]

Further evidence of the way in which *mineiro* entrepreneurs selected technology can be found in a letter from Kerr in 1884:

Knowing that you are interested in bleaching and desirous of being made acquainted with all the latest improvements I have pleasure in handing you the enclosed slips which I have cut from one of today's newspapers.[109]

Very often foreign technicians hired to work at the mills ordered parts, machines and equipment, and wrote letters in English to overseas suppliers. In 1882, for example, Bernardo Mascarenhas informed Kerr that George Jates, one of the two English technicians employed at the Cedro mill, would soon order the parts necessary for repairing damaged machines.[110] Américo Teixeira Guimarães, who founded the CCM in 1886, spent several months learning English in order to consult catalogues to select machinery for his mill.[111]

Towards the turn of the century, the process of selecting textile machinery became easier as foreign producers started to take the lead in approaching Brazilian entrepreneurs and began to advertise in local newspapers.[112] Thus, capital goods produced abroad were becoming more easily available and entrepreneurs could select equipment for their mills through Brazilian and foreign representatives of US and British manufacturers without having to go abroad or resort to consulting foreigners, or to spend months studying English or other languages. This development points to the growing importance of the Brazilian market for textile equipment.

The process of selection of electrical equipment did not differ very much from that observed in the case of textile technology. The main difficulty was that when Bernardo Mascarenhas decided to establish an electrical power company in Juiz de Fora in the 1880s, the technology of electricity generation was new, even in the most advanced countries as mentioned above. Few cities in the world were lit by electricity, so there was less scope to observe plants in operation. The installation of the world's first central electric-light power plant, for example, occurred in New York in 1881–82.[113] In Brazil, even the capital Rio de Janeiro was still lit by gas when Bernardo set up his hydroelectric power plant.[114] However, even taking into account the fact that electricity was a science-based technology, the selection of electrical equipment was less dependent on the availability of skilled workers and/or managers than in the case of more intangible technologies.

In 1886, Bernardo Mascarenhas bought the concession to light Juiz de Fora and shortly afterwards he established the CME. The process of selecting the technology for his hydro-electric plant involved much study of electricity. In 1887, the local newspaper *O Pharol* gave the following account of Mascarenhas' dedication to the study of electricity:

> Mr. Mascarenhas, as an enthusiast for electricity, has been studying the matter for a long time in order to discover its mysteries.[115]

Furthermore, Mascarenhas subscribed to specialized magazines, such as *Electrician* and *Electrical World*. Kerr, his friend and agent from Manchester, sent him prospectuses of various producers of electrical equipment: Zipernowski, Deri & Batty (producers of a new system of transformers), Matern Platt, and Elwell Parke & Co. Mascarenhas also read several technical publications such as *The Electric Motor and its Application* and *A Practical Treatise on Electric Lighting*, by J.E. Gordon.[116] In 1887 Mascarenhas wrote to Kerr, asking for more and recent publications on the matter.[117] During the same year he asked the city council of Juiz de Fora to postpone the inauguration of the lighting service for six months, because he needed to make further studies of the matter.[118] At the beginning of 1888 he had finally made up his mind and had decided on the WEC alternating current system, and he sent an order for the equipment together with a detailed plan of the plant.[119]

To sum up, depending on the nature of the technology employed, *mineiro* entrepreneurs resorted to different selection criteria. Technologies of a more intangible nature such as metallurgy, road construction, and transport services were selected mainly on the availability of skilled labour. The selection of more tangible technologies, such as those employed in the textile and electricity-generating industries, depended on different criteria. As the technical knowledge could be found in the form of machinery and equipment, entrepreneurs engaged in visits to other textile mills, both in Brazil and abroad, established direct contacts with foreign machinery producers or their representatives, made use of technical books, or even asked for the help of foreigners based in the province. Furthermore, foreign technicians employed by *mineiro* entrepreneurs were themselves asked to select the appropriate machinery and equipment. However, towards the turn of the century the selection of machinery became easier and more systematic as foreign producers began to establish representatives in the main cities in Brazil and to advertise in the local newspapers.

The User–Supplier Relationship

Those industries which depended most upon foreign technology suffered an additional problem, namely the nature of their relationship with suppliers of machinery and equipment. Most problems were caused by geographic distance, and the cultural and economic differences between users and producers: machines were not supplied exactly as they were ordered, parts went missing on their long journey from manufacturers to would-be industrialists, machines did not perform as advertised, and so on. Among the industries examined in this book, this was particularly true of the textile and electricity-generating industries. Both the iron industry and the CUI depended more on technical knowledge of skilled labour than on the acquisition of machinery.

In the textile industry, the services of representatives and agents of foreign machinery suppliers based in Brazil and abroad did not always make for a smooth relationship between users and foreign suppliers. In 1872, for example, Mascarenhas & Irmãos, owners of the Cedro mill, had several problems with the Rio de Janeiro representative, Guilherme Van Vlick Lidgerwood, of the US manufacturer Author Danfort Paterson, who originally supplied the machinery for the mill. Lidgerwood blamed Mascarenhas for the difficulties with technicians recruited to assemble the machinery. Mascarenhas & Irmãos replied that these difficulties were not their fault. The first technician never arrived, returning from Juiz de Fora as soon as he realized that he had to make the rest of the journey by horse, the man was ill and his illness had never allowed him to ride a horse. The second technician did not possess the qualifications for the job, besides being rude, arrogant and insolent. Even so, contrary to what had been alleged, he was paid in full. Furthermore, Mascarenhas & Irmãos contested the suggestion that missing parts ordered sometime previously, and allegedly sent by the above mentioned representatives, had been stolen on their way to the mill.[120]

As the distance between users and foreign machinery supplies was very great, the chances of goods being lost on their long journey to the hinterland of Minas Gerais were greater than if they had been supplied locally. In 1884, for example, Kerr wrote informing Bernardo Mascarenhas that a case containing pegs was lost in transit.[121] In 1891 Kerr wrote to Theóphilo Marques Ferreira regretting the fact that boxes containing dyeing material and a hydro-extractor had been lost.[122] Part of the machinery of SAIM was also lost on its way to Machado, causing postponement of the beginning of production of the mill.[123]

A further problem concerning foreign suppliers was the question of packing. As machinery had to travel long distances by sea, rail and by muletrain, manufacturers needed to take extra care in packing. Of course, not every producer of machinery was sensitive to the problems of transport in a backward country on the other side of the ocean. In 1885, for example, Kerr wrote regretting the fact that much damage had been done to the machinery in transit.[124] In 1893 the agent wrote again asking if the damage caused to the machinery dispatched was due to carelessness in packing.[125] During the same year Francisco de Paula Mascarenhas informed Theóphilo Marques Ferreira, then general manager of the CCC, that most of the machinery recently received was broken on detraining in Lafaiete and unloading in Sabará.[126]

The supply of imported equipment was also very slow, sometimes taking months and creating embarrassing situations. In 1891, for example, the lighting service of Juiz de Fora was interrupted because of a breakdown of the generating machinery. Domestic lighting was only reestablished two months later when new equipment ordered from the USA finally arrived.[127]

Mistakes in the supply of equipment were not uncommon and also required time to remedy. On 4 January 1884, Francisco de Paula Mascarenhas, manager of the Cachoeira mill, complained that he had opened a box of machinery from England but the contents (wharves for spindles) were not the ones ordered.[128] On 24 March 1884, Kerr wrote to Bernardo Mascarenhas that he regretted the mistake made with the spindle wharves. He had already contacted the producers (Hobson & Barlon), who were going to examine the matter and would hopefully give a full explanation in the course of a few days.[129] On 4 April 1884, Kerr wrote saying that the producers had finally admitted that by some misunderstanding they had made the mistake and were going to supply the same quantity which Mascarenhas had ordered free of cost.[130] It took three months from the day that the mistake was first noticed to the day that the supplier acknowledged it. The delay between the placing of the order and delivery of the correct material must have been much larger. If users and suppliers had been closer to each other the solution would certainly have taken much less time. In 1885 Kerr again regretted that a wrong pair of hearts had been sent by mistake and, as a right one had already been dispatched, he expected it to be there in a fortnight's time.[131]

Sometimes machines did not perform as advertised. In 1889 Bernardo Mascarenhas advised Marques Ferreira, then general manager of the CCC, not to believe everything that the catalogues of machinery producers said, because they tended to exaggerate the performance of their machines.[132] Moreover, machines did not always perform as expected and procuring replacements was a complex and long operation. In 1885, for example, Kerr wrote that he greatly regretted that the governors supplied with a turbine by Gunther had not worked satisfactorily. The poor performance could had been caused by the speed at which the governors were working.[133]

On other occasions foreign suppliers failed to keep their word. In 1893 Henry Rogers Sons & Co., a representative from Rio de Janeiro, wrote that a supplier was refusing to exchange a part which did not fit the machinery of one of the CCC mills, although the supplier had promised to do so before he supplied it. The supplier argued that the part had signs of use and that a long time had passed since it had been sent to Brazil.[134]

On yet other occasions machines were not always supplied according to the specifications stipulated. In 1885 Francisco de Paula Mascarenhas complained that looms received did not satisfy his specifications stipulated in the order.[135] In 1899 Kerr informed Aristides Mascarenhas that the dyeing machine ordered for the Cachoeira mill had been made with only 12 divisions, instead of the 15 originally ordered. The suppliers had never made such a large machine before and they had thought it would be unwise to do so.[136] In 1901 Victor Uslaender & Co., an agent from Rio de Janeiro, wrote that the machine was supplied with a table of 36 ins × 20 ins, instead of 30 ins × 20 ins as ordered. The manufacturer had decided to make the machine larger because he thought it would otherwise not leave enough space for the operative.[137]

There were also times when a foreign supplier did not even guarantee that the equipment supplied would work at all. The first experiments with the equipment supplied by the WEC to the CME to generate electricity were unsuccessful. The supplier did not guarantee anything and expressed reservations about the chances of the equipment ever working. Moreover, the material was not supplied according to the specifications originally drawn up by Bernardo Mascarenhas; the quantity was also insufficient.[138]

Users of foreign technology were also more vulnerable to increases in the prices of materials and machinery because of the length of time between placing an order and delivery, and because any change in exchange rates might represent an increase in their costs. Exchange variations posed a particular problem for Brazilian importers, especially during the late nineteenth century.[139] In 1893, for example, the CME increased the price of domestic lighting by 50 per cent because of the increase in prices, among other things, of imported materials and machinery.[140]

Finally, foreign suppliers were sometimes themselves victims of some of the problems caused by geographic distance and cultural differences. In 1899, for example, the makers of a hardwaste breaking machine complained that the machine had been ready for a long time and that Kerr had done nothing towards having it collected:

> The machine has been in our way now so long and you do not give us any intimation when you will take it that we now give you formal notice that failing receipt from you within 14 days of the requested instructions, we shall dispose of the machine and sue you for Ten Pounds as our damage for breach of contract.[141]

Distance and cultural and economic differences invariably caused problems of communication.

Geographical and cultural distance is a factor which may hinder the interaction of users and producers, and consequently jeorpadize the absorption of a foreign technology.[142] In the past, physical proximity between the producer and user of machinery was a significant factor promoting successful transfer of technology. Easy communication between the producer and user of machinery was important because it fostered and strengthened a complex network of contacts and communication. This promoted a convergence of interests between the user of a machine who appreciates problems connected with its use, and the machinery producer who is acquainted with the problems concerning its production.[143] However, as nineteenth century technologies were produced in places other than Portuguese-speaking countries, and as most firms in Minas Gerais relied on foreign technology and were strongly dependent on foreign skilled labour, problems of communication were aggravated. Because of a scarcity of illustrative material for the other economic sectors, the case of the textile industry will be mainly used to demonstrate some of the problems of communication that businesses in Minas Gerais encountered during the last century.

Although there is no direct evidence for the iron industry and the CUI, it is possible to speculate about the extent of problems in those sectors caused by poor communications. As the technologies used relied heavily on the technical knowledge of personnel, and as there were a large number of foreign entrepreneurs, managers and technicians employed in both the iron industry and the CUI, it is reasonable to believe that the question of communication was crucial for the operation of those technologies. Learning a foreign language was a crucial requisite for both entrepreneurs and workers. Eschwege, founder of the Patriótica foundry, for example, was a German, but when he came to Minas Gerais he could probably already speak Portuguese since he had previously worked in Portugal.[144] On the other hand, Monlevade, founder of the São Miguel de Piracicaba foundry, was a Frenchman who until the year when he came to Brazil lived in France, and it is interesting to note that Monlevade's foundry was only established ten years after his arrival in Minas

Gerais. He spent most of this time studying the deposits of minerals of Minas Gerais[145] and probably had to learn Portuguese before attempting to invest in any kind of business. Schoenewolf, a German foundry master who worked in both the Patriótica and the Morro do Pilar foundries,[146] probably also had had to learn the language before he could effectively manage a foundry in Brazil. Mariano Procópio Ferreira Lage, founder of the CUI, spent some time in the USA and Europe,[147] where he probably learned several languages. This proved important some years later when he organized the CUI, as most of the professionals and skilled workers employed by the company were foreigners.[148]

Nevertheless, this is only speculation and direct evidence of the problem of communication can only be found for the textile industry. *Mineiro* textile entrepreneurs had to learn a foreign language before they could even make their first contacts with machinery producers. When the Cedro mill was established Bernardo Mascarenhas spent a year and a half in the USA learning English while visiting several textile mills to get the know-how on the production of cloth.[149] Learning English would prove to be very important in his future entrepreneurial activities. By the time the Cachoeira mill was established, Bernardo had spent eight months in England studying, working and visiting factories. In Manchester, at Metropolitan Vickers, he met the engineer Robert L. Kerr who became a close friend, his agent and a very useful contact in England.[150] Furthermore, Bernardo's command of English proved crucial by the time the CME was established, as seen above. Américo Teixeira Guimarães – founder of the CCM – had to learn English before sending his first letters to machinery manufacturers in England. It took him several months of hard study before he had a sufficient grasp of the language to carry out these transactions.[151]

Furthermore, not only textile entrepreneurs had to learn a foreign language; foreign workers employed by them also had to acquire language skills, as illustrated by the following letter sent to J.N. Gordon, chairman of the SJDRMC:

> I am returning Mr Jorge Gregor as we do not need an interpreter anymore, since the Americans already understand Portuguese...[152]

Communication problems should not be underestimated since most firms in Minas Gerais relied on foreign technology and depended strongly on foreign skilled workers.

Thus, there were many problems, old and new, in the user–supplier relationship which were created and aggravated by geographic distance and social, cultural and economic differences. The most common of these problems were delays in delivery, adulterated orders, inevitable misunderstandings, loss of goods, lack of sensitivity on the part of the suppliers to the specific circumstances of foreign users, vulnerability to changes in prices due to changes in the exchange rates, and unfulfilled promises. This was particularly true for those industries using embodied technologies, such as the textile and the power industries. The iron industry and the CUI depended more on the accumulated technical knowledge of skilled labour than on the acquisition of machinery.

Another important problem in the relationship between users and producers who did not share common cultural features was the question of communication. Often *mineiro* entrepreneurs had to learn a foreign language before they could make the first contact with technology suppliers, while foreign workers sometimes had to rely on interpreters before they could understand Portuguese properly. Thus, the number of problems faced by the *mineiro* entrepreneurs in their relationship with foreign suppliers is undisputed and shows the importance of physical proximity between users and suppliers for the successful absorption of technology. If the problems related to distance and cultural differences between users and suppliers did not hinder the emergence of some of the industries examined in this work, they certainly delayed their development and increased their costs.

Installation, Maintenance and Adaptation

Selecting and purchasing the right equipment or machinery was neither the hardest nor the least of the problems that *mineiro* entrepreneurs had to overcome in dealing with foreign suppliers and foreign technologies. After obtaining the appropriate equipment and before installing it, transporting it could prove a real handicap. The problems of transporting machinery in the nineteenth century, from their countries of origin to their final destination, cannot be neglected. Very often the lack of suitable means of transport in latecomer economies represented an enormous barrier. Nevertheless, the problem posed by the lack of roads did not affect every industry in the same way. The transport of equipment did not represent a major problem for those industries which employed a more disembodied technology. As mentioned above, metallurgy and road-construction in the nineteenth century depended more on technical competence of skilled labour than on the acquisition of machinery. The basic machinery could be, and actually was, built on the site. Eschwege, for example, helped by a carpenter built most of his foundry's facilities, from the furnaces to the bellows.[153] The installations of the Morro do Pilar foundry were also built on site.[154] Furthermore, the commonest method of production employed by the iron industry in the first three-quarters of the last century – the *cadinho* method – was both indigenous and simple, and did not require complex facilities.[155] The CUI also made most of its equipment on site, as the description of the workshops of the company suggests:

> There are established in Juiz de Fora workshops for a blacksmith, locksmith, carpenter of carriages, carts and coaches, carpenter of bridges and buildings, cabinetmaker, beltmaker and saddler, and painter.[156]

The company also had a brickyard in the Juiz de Fora station which produced bricks and tiles.[157]

Even so, foundries depended on some imported material, as the German foundry master Schoenewolf, who worked in the Morro do Pilar foundry for several years, showed clearly in his report to Eschwege about the planned changes in the facilities of the foundry which included refractory material ordered in England.[158] The hammermills of Eschwege's foundry were also imported from England, since it was virtually impossible to produce them in Brazil,[159] and, as already mentioned, the CUI depended on some imported materials and components. At the time of the construction of the União e Indústria turnpike the company had repeated problems in transporting material bought abroad. In 1856, Mariano Procópio Ferreira Lage complained about the troubles caused by delays in obtaining customs clearance of imported material purchased in Europe. He illustrated very clearly the extent of such problems in the middle of the nineteenth century:

> One day of delay of any object in the customs in Rio de Janeiro may represent a delay of two or three months, if by any chance we miss a muletrain that could bring it.[160]

Thus, although both the iron industry and the CUI were not totally free of the problems caused by the lack of suitable means of transport, which greatly disturbed other businesses, they were not unaffected.

The most affected industries were those that employed technologies embodied in the form of equipment and machinery. Due to the lack of roads, the transport of textile machinery from the port of Rio de Janeiro to the hinterlands of Minas Gerais was full of adventures and obstacles. Machines had to be carried on the back of beasts of burden. Roads were rough and sometimes bridges had to be built along the way.

Bernardo Mascarenhas, for example, arrived in Rio de Janeiro from the USA with 50 tons of machinery in 1871. From there the machinery was transported to Entre Rios by rail, and from Entre Rios to Juiz de Fora in large carts by the CUI. From Juiz de Fora onwards, the machinery was transported in ox-carts. The trip took approximately two months to cover a distance of nearly 250 miles.[161] An eye-witness recalled the caravan passing by and being anticipated by a large number of men fixing and building bridges along the way where the heavy carts had to pass.[162] Further evidence of the lack of basic infrastructure and the difficulties in transporting machinery is given by the proprietors of the Cedro mill in their reply to an inquiry of the president of the Sete Lagoas city council:

> The only difficulty in the acquisition of machines is freight, which is expensive and very slow from Rio de Janeiro to the mill.[163]

Moreover, the lack of suitable means of transport imposed strict limits on the ability of suppliers or agents to dispatch machinery, parts and materials. In 1884 Kerr informed

Bernardo Mascarenhas that he had sent three cases exceeding the weight permissible for transport on the backs of mules because the suppliers could not make them any lighter.[164] Some days later Kerr gave the following account of the problems that had to be overcome when supplying materials to the textile mills located in the hinterland of Minas Gerais:

> With respect to the sizes of cases ordered by you for the dyeing materials I found several of them would have been too heavy for being conveyed on the backs of mules. I therefore have supplied you with smaller cases, making up the quantity to a certain extent by increasing the number of cases. The Brown Catechu is only supplied in solid blocks, and the smallest block I could buy weighed about 3 [?] ... so that I was obliged to purchase the block and get it cut into 3 pieces to suit the weights allowed for the back of mules.[165]

Opening roads and building bridges on the way from Entre-Rios to Machado also seems to have been the destiny of Azarias de Sousa Dias, the founder of the SAIM. A slave who took part in the trip to bring the machinery to Machado, Antônio Moreira de Souza Guerra, better known as Chico Moreira, recalled that the oxen had to be constantly changed in order to continue the exhausting journey. Furthermore, as mentioned above, one of the explanations given for postponing of the beginning of production of the mill was that part of the machinery had been lost during the trip.[166]

As had happened to Bernardo Mascarenhas and his brothers 15 years before, Américo Teixeira Guimarães faced very similar problems when he transported machinery for his mill in Cachoeira dos Macacos, which was not very far from the Cedro mill. To reach Cachoeira dos Macacos, the machinery was transported on the backs of animals and in large ox-drawn carts especially built for carrying machinery. The journey took more than two months from Juiz de Fora, the railhead.[167]

Towards the end of the nineteenth century, the problem of transporting machinery became less acute as the railway was penetrating farther and farther into the hinterlands of Minas Gerais. However, the problems of transport mentioned above did not disappear completely. In the early 1890s, machinery for the CTS was probably transported to either Divinópolis or

Sabará, the closest railway stations at that time, some 25 and 50 miles distance respectively, and from there to Sanct'Anna do São João Acima by ox-carts. This was indeed an improvement, though not the end of serious problems as Zé Carreiro who had participated in the journey as a driver observed:

> Hard time...
> We left family and friends behind. We needed a couple of days to prepare...
> ...it required skill to load the cart. If the loads were not well positioned the cart would tilt forwards or backwards. Tilting forwards would hurt the back of the oxen; backwards would strangle them...
> ...As a rule, we knew the road. We new the pot-holes, the cliffs, the holes... the right places to rest. It was possible to travel up to five leagues per day... There were times of anguish. The pot-holes, for example, were as deep as they were wide and were impossible to cross. The carts and the oxen would sink. It would be a great disaster and the best thing to do was to avoid them, passing by their edges. Nevertheless, there were pot-holes that deceived the driver, even the most experienced. But the biggest danger was the cliffs. There were some of more than a hundred fathoms high, very steep. God help me! I do not like to recall it. When it was raining the surface became very slippery. Saying it like that does not sound dangerous, but it really was. To pass along a road like that required experience. We were always afraid of losing the oxen, the cart or even the load...[168]

Zé Carreiro's description gives a good idea of the obstacles entrepreneurs had to overcome even before starting production. Furthermore, it graphically illustrates the lack of basic infrastructure in Minas Gerais, even at a time when the railway was starting to reach the hinterland of the province.

Although the *mineiro* electrical power companies also employed technologies embodied in equipment, the transport of this equipment did not represent a major obstacle for several reasons. The power companies were established mainly at the turn of the century, a time when the means of transport had improved considerably. The CME, for example, was established on 10 December 1887[169] and the

CFLCL on 26 February 1905.[170] More importantly, however, they were both located in the southern part of Minas Gerais, one of the first regions to be linked to Rio de Janeiro by good means of transport and where there was an extensive network of good roads. The CME was located in Juiz de Fora, which was served by the União e Indústria turnpike from the late 1850s [171] and by the D. Pedro II railway (EFDPII) a few years later.[172] The CFLCL was located very near to Juiz de Fora, in the Mata zone.

Owing to the lack of suitable means of transport, the problems of shipping foreign machinery and equipment from their countries of origin to their final destination represented an enormous barrier, specially for the textile industry.

Once the first difficulties of selecting and purchasing a technology – and in the case of embodied technologies, of transporting it – had been overcome, it had to be installed and put into operation. When the transfer of technology involved countries geographically distant from one another, this implied that skilled labour had also to be procured overseas. Technology is not a set of techniques available independently of the human inputs who utilize it. The capacity to understand and apply technical knowledge is essential for the successful utilization of information incorporated in any 'technological package'.[173] In some countries skilled migrant labour played a critical role not only in setting up a technology but also in its daily operation. Most *paulista* railways, for example, drew heavily on foreign labour for assembling imported material during construction phases and later in maintenance operations. At the outset, *paulista* railways depended entirely upon foreigners for both skilled and unskilled labour, as local supply was scarce. Foreigners, until the turn of the century, virtually monopolized skilled jobs.[174] *Mineiro* entrepreneurs very often also had to rely on foreign technicians to assemble, operate and maintain imported equipment. However, these foreign technicians were neither easy to find nor reliable, and furthermore they were expensive and relationships with them usually proved difficult.

As in the case of the USA, where the transfer of iron and steel technologies took place via the migration of artisans or managers experienced in using the technology,[175] foreign entrepreneurs and ironworkers were extremely important in the establishment of the *mineiro* iron industry. However, the search for these foreign ironworkers was an uncertain enterprise for Brazilian businessmen compared to their US counterparts. Besides demanding high salaries and, sometimes, not possessing the knowledge they claimed, these ironworkers rarely stayed in the same foundry for long. Thus, hiring a foreign technician was usually prohibitively expensive, and this was one of the reasons why the *cadinho* method was so popular.[176]

The largest foundries established in Minas Gerais in the earlier part of the nineteenth century were either owned by foreigners or relied upon foreign technicians. As mentioned above, two of the most successful foundries belonged to foreigners. The Patriótica was established, operated and managed by Eschwege, a German engineer.[177] Moreover, Eschwege counted on the help of a German foundry master, who was considered very competent.[178] Also, as indicated above, the São Miguel de Piracicaba foundry belonged to the French engineer Monlevade and was under his management for more than forty years, obtaining the best results among all the foundries in Minas Gerais.[179] Production at the Morro do Pilar foundry was only possible after Schoenewolf, the German foundry master who worked at the Patriótica foundry, was hired to supervise the work in 1814. His presence was absolutely vital to the successful production of the foundry.[180]

Eschwege stressed the vital role played by foreign ironworkers in setting up an iron foundry in Brazil. They were essential not only for assembling the facilities but also for training the native workforce. However, these foreign technicians earned three times more than Brazilian masters and their travelling expenses were high. There were further problems:

> The foreign masters, who believe themselves to be indispensable, make several demands. Some become idle and others take to drink. As a consequence, they quarrel with their employers, who in the end dismiss them. The work is then done by Brazilians who have only learned a little from the foreign masters. Consequently, the products do not improve and production does not increase with change.

Thus, the entrepreneurs are forced to close down their foundries.[181]

The reliance upon foreigners in the construction and operation of the União e Indústria turnpike was also strong. As in the case of *paulista* railways established in the second half of the nineteenth century, at least at the beginning the CUI depended heavily on foreigners for skilled labour. The road construction was supervised by two French engineers, J.J. Regnier Vigouroux and Theodoro Flagolot, until 1856.[182] In 1857 the French engineers were replaced by a German, Keller, and a Brazilian engineer, Bulhões. During the same year the company also hired Keller's two sons to work as his assistants, who were probably not Brazilians.[183] For the architectural and surveying work foreigners were also employed, namely Carlos Augusto Gambs and Miguel Lallemant, architects, and Adryano H. Mynssen, a surveyor.[184] Moreover, in 1856 Mariano Procópio stated that the company had recruited 20 craftsmen in Hamburg for the workshops.[185] According to the decree of 7 August 1852 which granted the company the concession for the construction of the turnpike, the company established a colony of immigrants in Juiz de Fora in 1858. Among the 667 adults, 389 men and 278 women who lived in the colony in 1860, approximately 196 worked for the company: 48 in the brickyard, 85 in the workshops, 55 in the construction of the road, 5 in the warehouse and 3 as drivers.[186]

The *mineiro* textile industry is full of examples of how crucial foreign technicians were, and how difficult relationships with them might become. The contract for the purchase of machinery for the Cedro mill, for example, included the provision of a technician to assemble and operate the machinery.[187] However, after having reached its final destination after the long journey from the USA where it had been made, to the hinterlands of Minas Gerais where the Cedro mill was located, the machinery was left standing for months waiting for a technician to assemble it. As already mentioned, the first technician who came from the USA in accordance with the contract never arrived. Then, two other technicians were hired, Barnes and Nicholson. Barnes left the company five months after his arrival: he did not have the qualifications he claimed and his relationship with the Mascarenhas family rapidly deteriorated.[188] Nicholson stayed longer in the company and his wife became responsible for training the weavers. Furthermore, at least in the first years, every master in the mill apart from the blacksmith and carpenter masters was hired abroad, preferably in the country where the machinery had been bought.[189] In 1879, two Englishmen, George Jates and Nathan Holt, experts in weaving and spinning, were recruited by Kerr to work at the Cedro mill. Nathan Holt was dismissed in 1882 because of his rudeness and carelessness, which had caused considerable damage to the machinery. Obviously, there are two sides of the story and this is only the version of the employer. The worker's version, as usual, is not available. George Jates also left in 1882 and the company hired another foreign technician, John Smith, in the same year.[190]

At the beginning, the Cachoeira mill also relied on foreign technicians to supervise work. In 1876 the Cachoeira mill hired an Englishman, William Hutchinson, for two years to set up and operate the mill and train the workforce. In 1879 another two foreign machinists, John and William Lomas, and a foreign weaver, Andrew White, were hired to replace William Hutchinson who had returned to England. The first machinist left the company to visit England in 1882 but would not promise to return. In the same year William Lomas and Andrew White ran away during the night, but there is no information about the reasons which motivated them to do it. Nevertheless, based on the number of problems with foreign workers that employers reported, it is reasonable to believe that the attitude of *mineiro* employers towards their workforce was harsh. In 1883 James Winders, another Englishman, was hired to work at the mill.[191]

The employment of, and the search for foreign technicians, as well as the problems of retaining foreign workers, continued throughout the century and remained at the beginning of this century. James Winders continued to be employed at the CCC after the merger of the Cedro and the Cachoeira mills until 1889 despite the numerous problems he caused. In 1888 Francisco de Paula Mascarenhas wrote to Bernardo Mascarenhas giving the following account of James Winders' misbehaviour:

During my absence, while I was travelling to São Sebastião, several regrettable events occurred caused by James' drunkenness... Last Saturday, with the excuse of a row between Linney and his wife James assaulted her... On Sunday, James got drunk and assaulted his wife once again, causing a great scandal and too much screaming, and intended to shoot her with a gun and a rifle; meanwhile, an employee of the mill went there to save the poor woman and he was also assaulted by James. The insulted man grasped the Englishman and beat him badly, but not as much as he deserved.[192]

However, there is no information about Winders' story. In 1884 Kerr wrote saying that he had made enquiries about an experienced and skilful dyer and that he had found that such workers expected to earn from £5 to £6 per week, plus free accommodation.[193] Although there is no information about the salary of a Brazilian machinist during this year, comparison between the salaries of James Nicholson and his wife in 1872, and that of a Brazilian machinist five year later is illustrative of the differences between the salaries paid to foreigners and Brazilians. In the first case, James Nicholson received 10$000 mil-réis per day, plus food and accommodation, and his wife 4$000 mil-réis. In the second case, a Brazilian machinist in 1877 received 5$000 mil-réis, without food or accommodation.[194] In December 1886 Kerr wrote saying that it would be very difficult to recruit a mechanic in England who would understand carding, spinning and weaving, and who would also be capable of erecting machinery and keeping it in good order.[195]

Moreover, William Hutchinson's long story with the CCC illustrates well not only the difficulties of recruiting skilled foreign labour, but also the difficulty of retaining it. In 1883 William Hutchinson was invited to work for the company once again, but he decided not to go back to Brazil because his wife would not agree to accept the decision.[196] In September 1886 Kerr wrote saying that he had spoken to William Hutchinson, who would consider the matter of rejoining the CCC and would reply in the course of a few days.[197] Three months later Kerr wrote that Hutchinson was reluctant to travel to Brazil unless the company was willing to offer him great inducements to leave home again.[198] However, it seems that the CCC decided to pay the 'great inducements' that Hutchinson was requesting, as in 1889 he rejoined the company for a two-year contract. In 1891 William Hutchinson returned to England and left his son, Herbert, in his place together with a relative, also William, who had come out with him two years previously. Both of them continued working for the company until 1894 when they returned for good to England. In 1892 William Hutchinson was once again recruited to set up machinery recently acquired for the São Vicente mill. He stayed until October 1894.[199] However, in the following year he again refused to return to Brazil because his family opposed his leaving England.[200] Kerr tried to recruit another machinist whose services would cost £6 per week.[201] Eventually the company decided to hire John Lomas who was employed at the São Sebastião mill, but he left the company after a few months and the company failed to hire another foreign technician.[202] Only in 1901 after the representatives in Brazil of Henry Rogers, Sons & Co., an English manufacturer of textile machinery, were informed that the CCC needed a technician and offered an operative from their own factory in England was the problem resolved.[203]

The employment of foreign technicians can also be noted in other textile mills in Minas Gerais. In 1893 Manoel José de Souza Moreira wrote to Aristides Mascarenhas, chairman of the CCC, requesting the help of a foreign technician for assembling machinery at the CTS.[204] At the CCM an English technician was hired to install machinery, but his relationship with the manager of the mill, Américo Teixeira Guimarães, soon deteriorated and the Englishman returned home early.[205] In 1875 the Brazil Industrial, a textile mill established in Juiz de Fora, hired five technicians in England just to assemble the machinery.[206]

Although Bernardo Mascarenhas had a good knowledge of electricity and was able to draw up detailed plans for his electrical power plant, he also had to rely upon foreign technicians during installation. At the beginning of 1889 the equipment ordered from WEC began to arrive together with two North American technicians.[207] However, they did not possess the necessary skills, as Bernardo stated in his letter to the agents of WEC.[208] The CME continued to rely on foreign technicians throughout the century, and in 1893 the company informed its customers that the increase in the price of the domestic lighting service was due, among other things, to the increase in the salaries of its foreign employees[209] probably due to exchange rate fluctuations.

Thus, *mineiro* business enterprises relied heavily on foreigners for setting up and putting into operation foreign technologies. However, once installed, it was often necessary to adapt imported equipment or processes of production to local conditions. This was often necessary because of differences in physical or climatic factors on the inputs used,[210] and the availability of factors of production among different countries. Techniques which were efficient in one environment might not be so in another.[211] The problems of adaptation did not apply only to the operation of equipment and machinery, but also with regard to managerial procedures. And the problems of adaptation were often neither simple nor trivial, in some cases requiring relatively sophisticated inputs of skills or information drawing on the experience of other local firms. It might also not be possible to undertake adaptation without the assistance of from governments, educational institutions or even specialised consultants. However, it was often one of the most important technological activities which a firm could implement. Indeed, empirical studies in Latin America have shown that the primary source of technological change within firms arose from an accretion of these relatively minor trouble-shooting efforts to adapt equipment and procedures to local conditions.[212]

During the nineteenth century, all of the *mineiro* firms examined in this book carried out a surprising amount of minor adaptations and modifications. The development of the *cadinho* method of production is clear evidence of this. The *cadinho* process derived from modifications applied by Eschwege and other foreign experts, based on the Swedish method of iron-making, to a more primitive technique first introduced into Brazil by African slaves. Eschwege's main contribution was the application of water to power the bellows and the hammermill.[213] Nevertheless, the simplicity of the *cadinho* method meant that scope for further modification was very limited. Lack of skilled personnel rendered the *cadinho* foundry the only feasible method of production in Minas Gerais, and attempts to employ more complex methods usually failed.

Manuel Ferreira da Câmara, for example, attempted to establish a foundry of large proportions in the first decade of the last century. He planned to build three blast furnaces, but in the end built only one because there was not enough water power and wood available in the neighbourhood for the operation of more than one blast furnace, one forge and one hammermill. Later, Câmara decided to build two small Swedish furnaces to replace the blast furnace. The original structure had been damaged as the result of early experimental firings when the inexperience of the workforce led to high temperatures which destroyed the walls. Nevertheless, the Swedish furnaces could not operate effectively because of the scarcity of water power. In 1814, Schoenewolf, a German foundry-master who had worked at the Morro do Pilar foundry for several years, described the failure of attempts to adapt and repair the bellows of the forge:

> When I arrived, the hammermill and the forge were already built... as well as the two bellows made of leather, which were put into action by strings instead of chains.
>
> Mr Câmara assured me that the bellows produced enough air. However, the first experiment showed that the quantity of air was so irregular that it was not possible to refine...
>
> Mr Câmara tried to repair it... lost his patience and transferred the managership to his brother, who had never seen an iron foundry before...
>
> The manager attempted several innovations... without changing the final result.

In the end, Schoenewolf changed the whole lay-out of the hammermill and reconstructed the bellows according to Eschwege's specifications. Furthermore, Câmara had decided not to use a blast furnace before the arrival of skilled personnel requested from the government. Altogether, he requested 14 people, among them smelters, refiners, moulder-masters and so on.[214] Further evidence of limits to the capacity of adaptation and modification is given by Eschwege, who imported the hammermills from England as it was nearly impossible to produce them locally.[215]

As shown above, although the CUI depended more on the technical knowledge of skilled labour than on the acquisition of machinery, the company also relied strongly on imported tools and materials for the construction of roads, carriages and carts.[216] Nevertheless, the importation of these materials did not represent a reliance on any specific technology embodied in machines or equipment: the importation of these implements were due to the impossibility of obtaining them locally. But, apart from the imported materials and tools mentioned above, the company produced almost everything else it needed in workshops at Juiz de Fora. The facilities there included a smithy, carriage shop, harness and leather working depot, and a paintshop.[217] In the company report of 1856, Mariano Procópio Ferreira Lage pointed out the strategic importance of these workshops for the CUI due to the lack of local resources, the difficulty of obtaining them where the central station was established (Juiz de Fora), and the necessity for the company not to depend on imports for everything it needed for its daily running.[218] Thus, the establishment of the various workshops in the Juiz de Fora station may be seen as part of the company's policy to create, in the long run, a local capacity of routine maintenance, repairs work, and the provision of spare parts.

Supply problems also encouraged textile entrepreneurs to invest in workshops, to provide maintenance and repair facilities and to manufacture locally some spare parts, and even to adapt and modify the imported machinery. At the CCC, for example, some form of equipment adaptation and modification was carried out. As the supply of imported parts could not be guaranteed the company employed several skilled craftsmen in its forges to replace broken parts. Manoel Peculista, a slave acquired by the Cedro mill, for example, was considered an excellent forger, and he was probably employed to manufacture spare parts and tools.[219] Further evidence of the adaptation process is found in the company's correspondence. In 1884, Francisco de Paula Mascarenhas, manager of the Cachoeira mill, wrote to Bernardo Mascarenhas saying that he had to halt spinning operations pending repairs.[220] In 1885, he wrote again saying that:

I am returning the axles of the turbines, which have given me too many troubles, because the manufacturers did not calculate the brackets of the three large hangers in relation to the position of the pulleys of the turbines. The brackets they sent were too large... Nevertheless, by moving the pulleys from one side to the other I managed to sort everything out.[221]

During the same year, Francisco reported that the new weaving machine lacked the rear card and that he was going to make a new one of wire or bamboo to replace it, until a new card was ordered from England.[222] A month later he reported that they had worked until night-fall the preceding day trying to fix the turbines. They forged iron and put it on the edge of the axle to see if the turbines would work without the 'thrust collars' which were badly damaged.[223] In the following year Francisco wrote to Theóhilo Marques Ferreira saying that James could go as soon as he finished the loom parts which were going to be modified.[224] A month later Francisco de Paula Mascarenhas reported that he had made some alterations in the spindles and that the alterations had yielded a 70 per cent increase in production.[225]

This was not a simple adaptation and alteration, but an impressive improvement revealing a surprising ability to refine a foreign technology. In 1904, Dario Diniz Mascarenhas, manager of the Cachoeira mill, informed Caetano Mascarenhas that in the beginning the machinery had worked with Brazilian belts but they broke very often. Subsequently, new English belts were ordered but these continued to break though not as frequently as locally-manufactured belts, probably because of their width. Hence, new modified belts would be required from England.[226] This episode demonstrates how, by trial and error, *mineiro* businessmen both adapted imported technology to local needs and were able to devise more specific technical instructions for foreign suppliers. Indeed, companies when possible ordered machinery according to their own specifications. However, this kind of adaptation and modification required a sophisticated degree of interaction between user and supplier, and no doubt the availability of an English agent was an important element in this interaction. In 1884, for example, Kerr wrote saying that he had dispatched the special looms and jacquards that the CCC had ordered.[227] Nevertheless, these modifications were expensive, as Kerr observed,[228] but such orders of non-standard equipment must have been considered worthwhile. In 1885 Kerr wrote again informing Bernardo Mascarenhas that:

> I send you a new catalogue by Mr Gunther, and on page 35 you will see the same kind of governors on the same principle but altered a little in the design and construction, since yours were made for Cachoeira.[229]

In the following year he reported that the modifications made on the weft bobbins had been prompted by Bernardo's suggestions. Nevertheless, they cost rather more,[230] further evidence that modifications to standard equipment cost a company dear. Another point to be stressed is that these extra costs had to be covered at a time when the mil-réis was depreciating rapidly against foreign currencies. In these circumstances special orders were doubly costly; equipment would take longer to supply by which time prices would have risen.[231] In the same year James Leffel & Co. wrote saying that:

> We carefully note all the specifications, also the drawings which you sent, and have forwarded the same to our shops to have a suitable turbine constructed.[232]

Thus, the adaptations and modifications carried out by the CCC were not restricted to the company's workshops. On several occasions the company ordered equipment according to its own specifications directly from the foreign manufacturer.

There is also evidence of adaptations and modifications of equipment and machinery carried out by the CME. The original plan drawn by Bernardo Mascarenhas and sent to WEC gave detailed specifications for the manufacture of equipment for the electrical power plant.[233] Bernardo followed with a detailed description of the location and distance of the power plant in relation to the city of Juiz de Fora and how the electricity would be distributed to the different points of the city. Furthermore, he gave precise specifications for the manufacture of the lamps and bulbs, and the conductor cables to be used in the distribution of the electricity.[234] Bernardo's plans demonstrate the extent of his technical knowledge previous to the establishment of the CME.

Moreover, close to the day fixed by the contract between the company and the city council of Juiz de Fora for the inauguration of the lighting service, the experiments carried out on the equipment did not yield positive results. As mentioned earlier, the supplier would not guarantee the equipment which in any case did not exactly follow the stipulated specifications. To overcome these difficulties Bernardo had to improvise an axle and to extend the generator pulleys. He finally succeeded and on 5 September 1889 the lighting service was inaugurated.[235] In this event it is important to point out the importance of the existence of a local technical ability to deal with foreign, newly-developed technology. Entrepreneurial skill and initiative enabled operating difficulties to be resolved by adapting equipment.

Thus, owing to poor communications the problems of transporting foreign machinery and equipment from their countries of origin to their final destination represented an enormous barrier, specially for the textile industry. Machinery and equipment had to be carried on the backs of beasts of burden, and roads and bridges had to be built along the way. It required special attention on the part of foreign suppliers to the packing and assembling of equipment as shipment was long and difficult. However, these problems of transport became less acute with the arrival of the railway by the end of the nineteenth century, although difficulties related to the transport of machinery and equipment continued to persist. Nevertheless, some sectors of the *mineiro* economy were not as badly affected as the textile industry. Most of the equipment, machinery and facilities used by the iron industry and the CUI were built on-site. The electricity-generating companies, in their turn, were established mainly after the turn of the century when the means of transport had improved considerably in an area with an extensive network of good roads.

Further, *mineiro* business enterprises relied strongly on foreigners. They were vital not only for introducing new technology, but also for operating equipment. In the iron industry, foreign ironworkers and foreign entrepreneurs played a critical role during the earlier part of the nineteenth century. The reliance of the CUI upon foreigners for the construction and operation of the turnpike was also great and the company recruited engineers, architects and craftsmen abroad. Foreign technicians were no less crucial to the textile industry. They assembled the machinery, supervised production and trained the workforce. Finally, the electricity-generating industry was no exception and foreign personnel were also used in the CME. However, foreign skilled personnel were difficult to find and expensive, and personal relationships with them usually proved difficult.

In addition, the successful transfer of foreign technology requires a local capacity for adaptation and modification – adjusting technology to a new socio-economic environment. This capacity of adaptation and modification can be observed in nineteenth-century Minas Gerais, particularly in the iron industry with the development of the *cadinho* method. This native method of production was the result of modifications, based on the Swedish method of production, introduced by foreign technicians. Nevertheless, the simplicity of the *cadinho* method meant that the possibility of extensive refinement was limited, but the lack of skilled personnel made the *cadinho* foundry the only feasible means of production for the *mineiro* entrepreneur. Attempts to employ more complex methods of production usually failed, so Minas Gerais was compelled to use a 'dead-end' technology.

Even though the CUI relied on imported tools and materials for the construction of roads, carriages and carts, the company depended more on technical knowledge of trained personnel than on the acquisition of machinery and equipment. Thus, it seems inappropriate to speak of a process of adaptation of technology in a strict sense. *Mineiro* textile entrepreneurs were prompted by problems in their relationship with foreign suppliers to invest in workshops thereby gaining the capability to repair, modify and even manufacture machinery. Finally, the adaptation and modification of equipment and machinery can also be observed at the CME which employed a newly-developed technology with all the technical difficulties that this involved.

CONCLUSION

Most business enterprises in nineteenth-century Minas Gerais relied strongly on foreign technology and the main sources of technology were Great Britain and the USA. The only exception in the first three-quarters of the nineteenth century was the iron industry which employed an indigenous process of production. Nevertheless, this indigenous technology imposed strict limits on the development of the industry which virtually disappeared when it had to compete against foreign products at the end of the century. In terms of the process of selection of technology, *mineiro* entrepreneurs resorted to different strategies to acquire the minimum level of technological skill required. These included long periods of study abroad, visits to similar establishments in Brazil and overseas, direct and indirect contacts with foreign producers of machinery, the use of technical books, and even the help of foreigners resident in Minas Gerais. Furthermore, the geographic distance and cultural and socio-economic differences between users and foreign suppliers of technologies aggravated existing problems and created new problems in their relationship. The most common problems were, among others, delays in delivery, adulterated orders, inevitable misunderstandings, loss of goods, lack of sensitivity on the part of suppliers to the specific circumstances of foreign customers, unfulfilled promises, and so on.

Moreover, as a consequence of the dependence of most *mineiro* firms upon foreign technologies and foreign skilled personnel, communication problems were not a negligible difficulty. Entrepreneurs had to learn a foreign language before they could make their first contacts with machinery producers, while foreign workers had to rely on interpreters before they could understand Portuguese properly. Very often, due to the lack of suitable means of transport, transporting foreign machinery to Minas Gerais proved to be a real hardship. Machines had to be carried on the backs of beasts of burden, and roads and even bridges had to be built. The penetration of the railway into the hinterland of Minas Gerais at the end of the nineteenth century helped to ease this problem, although it was not completely resolved. Moreover, *mineiro* business enterprises relied heavily on foreign technicians not only to set up equipment but also to operate it. Nevertheless, these foreign technicians were difficult to find. They were often unreliable, expensive, and relationships with them usually proved difficult. Finally, although some capacity of adaptation and modification can be observed in nineteenth-century Minas Gerais, this capacity had strict limits.

This examination of technology – availability and adaptation – reveals Minas Gerais to have been an inhospitable environment for the entrepreneur. *Mineiro* firms relied strongly on foreign technologies and skilled personnel. The process of adaptation and modification was too narrow to be characterized as a specific *mineiro* way of manufacturing. The existing informal and spontaneous technological innovative system was not developed enough to take the process of technological assimilation farther in the direction of a profound modification of existing foreign technologies, or to create a more complex indigenous technological alternative. The narrowness of the capacity of the nineteenth-century *mineiro* economy to absorb and refine imported technology was due to a lack of skills and entrepreneurship, which was confirmed by the failure to develop a capital goods industry.

Conclusion

This research strongly supports the view that economic development of backward countries does not necessarily follows the same path taken by advanced economies. The business environment in nineteenth-century Minas Gerais differed from that of the more advanced countries in several important respects.

The 'self-made man' stereotype of a businessman, coming from the bottom of the social ladder and acting virtually alone, hardly applies to the case of the *mineiro* businessman. He usually came from the upper classes and business was more often than not a family venture. Families were also important in providing funds, personnel and political influence, which was often needed to secure economic advantages and/or to prevent potential competition.

Furthermore, strategies and the internal organization of the firms were determined in large proportions by considerations not related with the market. They were mainly the result of the social context in which firms were operating and of the attempt to make up for relative backwardness. Thus, in many cases firms were forced to produce/distribute themselves what in the more developed countries was provided by an existing and well-developed chain of suppliers/distributors. Strategies and structures were also determined in large part by political considerations both within the controlling family and in the firm's relationship with the state and other business regulators. As family ventures, sooner or later firms had to face the question of having to accomodate within their structures a growing number of family members and shareholders'descendants. The relationship with the state was important not only for securing economic advantages, as mentioned before, but also for securing the intervention of the state whenever *mineiro* entrepreneurs failed or were unable to establish the necessary infrastructure by themselves.

The lack of indigenous technology and a capital-goods industry imposed solutions to problems that entrepreneurs in more technologically advanced countries rarely had to worry about. Local entrepreneurs were often faced with the problem of making use of foreign technical packages that were not entirely suited to local resources, to the scale of the businesses or to market requirements. The challenge of handling and adapting these foreign packages posed, therefore, unique and paramount difficulties.

Finally, due to the limits imposed by the backwardness of the business environment, national private firms continued to be restricted to the lighter, less-dynamic and more labour-intensive sectors of the economy until the last decade of this century. Brazilian firms were unable to break up the vicious circle of lack of competitiveness imposed by the less-dynamic business environment, or to reduce the gap between themselves and firms from more advanced countries. Thus, from the 1950s onwards, when foreign multinational firms started to establish in large numbers in Brazil, Brazilian firms had to specialize in order to survive even in the smaller and less-dynamic Brazilian market.

The structural limits on the development of national private capital would later require the state to intervene in the economy, turn itself into a producer, and invest in those sectors where foreign capital was reluctant to invest, such as the capital-goods industry. Foreign capital would not and could not offset the structural limits of the Brazilian business community. It invested in the more dynamic and more capital-intensive sectors, where they could secure oligopolistic profits. This industrial specialization was to persist until the end of the twentieth century, leading to a pattern of business development in which the national private, the state, and foreign capitals controlled different sectors according to each one's competitive forces,[1] a pattern that had no counterpart in the more advanced economies.

Notes

1 Nineteenth-Century Brazilian and *Mineiro* Economic History

1. W. Dean, 'Economy', in L. Bethell (ed.), *Brazil: Empire and Republic, 1822–1930* (Cambridge, 1989), p. 218.
2. C. Furtado, *Formação Econômica do Brasil*, 16th edn (São Paulo, 1979), p. 90.
3. *Ibid.*, pp. 89–92.
4. L. Bethell and J.M. Carvalho, '1822–1850', in L. Bethell (ed.), *Brazil: Empire and Republic, 1822–1930* (Cambridge, 1989), pp. 14–20.
5. Furtado, *Formação Econômica do Brasil*, *op.cit.*, pp. 93–4.
6. Dean, 'Economy', *op.cit.*, p. 219.
7. Bethell and Carvalho, *op.cit.*, pp. 55–112.
8. Furtado, *Formação Econômica do Brasil*, *op.cit.*, pp. 96–8.
9. Bethell and Carvalho, *op.cit.*, pp. 45–6.
10. P.C. Mello and R.W. Slenes, 'Análise Econômica da Escravidão no Brasil', in P. Neuhaus (ed.), *Economia Brasileira: Uma Visão Histórica* (Rio de Janeiro, 1980), p. 91.
11. *Ibid.*, p. 91.
12. Bethell and Carvalho, *op.cit.*, p. 46.
13. Mello and Slenes, *op.cit.*, p. 109.
14. L.C. Soares, 'Urban Slavery in XIXth-Century Rio de Janeiro', University of London, unpublished Ph.D. thesis, 1988, pp. 145–273.
15. Bethell and Carvalho, *op.cit.*, p. 46.
16. *Ibid.*, p. 46.
17. *Ibid.*, pp. 94–109. For further discussion about the abolition of the trans-Atlantic slave trade to Brazil see L. Bethell, *The Abolition of the Brazilian Slave Trade. Britain and the Slave Trade Question, 1807–1869* (Cambridge, 1970); R. Conrad, *The Destruction of Brazilian Slavery:1850–1888*, (Berkeley, 1972), chapter 2; and R. Conrad, *World of Sorrow: The African Slave Trade to Brazil* (Baton Rouge, 1986).
18. Dean, 'Economy', *op.cit.*, p. 255.
19. Furtado, *Formação Econômica do Brasil*, *op.cit.*, p. 114.
20. *Ibid.*, p. 113.
21. A.P. Canabrava, 'A Grande Laboura', in S. B. Holanda (ed.), *História Geral da Civilização Brasileira – II. O Brasil Monárquico*, vol. VI 4th edn (São Paulo, 1985), pp. 87–102.
22. Furtado, *Formação Econômica do Brasil*, *op.cit.*, p. 113.
23. R. Graham, '1850–1870', in L. Bethell (ed.), *Brazil: Empire and Republic, 1822–1930* (Cambridge, 1989), p. 116.
24. V.N. Pinto, 'Balanço das Transformações Econômicas no Século XIX', in C.G. Mota (ed.), *Brasil em Perspectiva* 17th edn (Rio de Janeiro, 1988), p. 139.

25. C. Prado Júnior, *História Econômica do Brasil*, 36th edn (São Paulo, 1988), p. 192.
26. E. Viotti da Costa, *Da Monarquia à República: Momentos Decisivos* (São Paulo, 1987), pp. 210–1.
27. L.C.T.D. Prado, 'Commercial Capital, Domestic Market and Manufacturing in Imperial Brazil: The Failure of Brazilian Economic Development in the nineteenth Century', University of London, unpublished Ph.D. thesis, 1991, p. 217.
28. Graham, '1850–1870', *op.cit.*, p. 146.
29. Prado Júnior, *op.cit.*, p. 192.
30. C.M. Lewis, *Public Policy and Private Initiative: Railway Building in São Paulo, 1860–1889* (London, 1991), pp. 4–13.
31. Prado, *op.cit.*, pp. 234–71.
32. Graham, '1850–1870', *op.cit.*, p. 148.
33. The Paraguayan War is the war which Brazil, Argentina and Uruguay waged against Paraguay for 5 years (1865–70), and which was the most serious international crisis in Brazilian history. The war turned out to be long and tough, demanding a large amount of resources. In the end Brazil won the war, but paid a high price for it. Moreover, Paraguay could not pay even a small part of the war debt. Prado Júnior, *op.cit.*, pp. 193–4. For further details about the Paraguayan War see N.W. Sodré, *Formação Histórica do Brasil*, 10th edn (Rio de Janeiro, 1979), pp. 228–34; Graham, '1850–1870', *op.cit.*, pp. 150–8; and A. Sousa Júnior, 'Guerra do Paraguai', in S. B. Holanda VI (ed.), *História Geral da Civilização Brasileira* (São Paulo, 1985), pp. 299–314.
34. Prado, *op.cit.*, pp. 271–2, 285–7.
35. Prado Júnior, *op.cit.*, pp. 194–5.
36. Directoria Geral de Estatistica, *Relatórios e Trabalhos Estatísticos* (Rio de Janeiro, 1872).
37. Dean, 'Economy', *op.cit.*, p. 235.
38. Furtado, *Formação Econômica do Brasil*, pp. 117–22.
39. M.L. Lamounier, 'Between Slavery and Free Labour: Experiments with Free Labour and Patterns of Slave Emancipation in Brazil and Cuba c.1830–1888', University of London, unpublished Ph.D. thesis, 1993, pp. 183–4.
40. Lamounier, *op.cit.*, pp. 184–98.
41. Viotti da Costa, *Da Monarquia à República*, *op.cit.*, pp. 243–4.
42. Dean, 'Economy', *op.cit.*, pp. 235–6.
43. Sodré, *op.cit.*, p. 251.
44. Dean, 'Economy', *op.cit.*, pp. 235–6.
45. B. Fausto, 'Society and Politics', in L. Bethell (ed.), *Brazil: Empire and Republic, 1822–1930* (Cambridge, 1989), pp. 257–8.
46. Dean, 'Economy', *op.cit.*, pp. 236–7.
47. Furtado, *Formação Econômica do Brasil*, *op.cit.*, p. 114.
48. Lewis, *op.cit.*, pp. 35–51.
49. Dean, 'Economy', *op.cit.*, p. 226.
50. *Ibid.*, pp. 228–30.
51. C.M. Peláez, *Economia Brasileira Contemporânea: Origens e Conjuntura Atual*, (São Paulo, 1987), p. 37.

188   *Notes*

52. Holloway, *op.cit.*, p. 37, 56–61.
53. Dean, 'Economy', *op.cit.*, pp. 228–30.
54. S. Silva, *Expansão Cafeeira e Origem da Indústria no Brasil* (São Paulo, 1976), pp. 77–81.
55. W. Cano, *Raízes da Concentração Industrial em São Paulo*, 3rd. edn (São Paulo, 1990), pp. 69–86.
56. J.M. Cardoso de Mello, *O Capitalismo Tardio: Contribuição à Revisao Crítica da Formação e Desenvolvimento da Economia Brasileira* (São Paulo, 1982), p. 99.
57. Silva, *op.cit.*, pp. 77–81.
58. W. Dean, *A Industrialização de São Paulo, 1880–1945* (São Paulo, 1971), pp. 15–6.
59. W. Suzigan, *Indústria Brasileira: Origens e Desenvolvimento* (São Paulo, 1986), p. 349.
60. C. Furtado, *Análise do 'Modelo' Brasileiro*, 7th edn (Rio de Janeiro, 1982), p. 16.
61. J.D. Wirth, *Minas Gerais in the Brazilian Federation, 1889–1937* (Stanford, 1977), pp. 1–5.
62. P.I. Singer, *Desenvolvimento Econômico e Evolução Urbana: Evolução Econômica de São Paulo, Blumenau, Porto Alegre, Belo Horizonte e Recife* (São Paulo, 1968), pp. 199–203.
63. F. Iglésias, 'Minas Gerais', in S.B. Holanda (ed.), *História Geral da Civilização Brasileira*, vol. IV 4th edn (São Paulo, 1985), pp. 368–9.
64. Singer, *op.cit.*, pp. 204–6.
65. *Ibid.*, pp. 206–7.
66. Iglésias, 'Minas Gerais', *op.cit.*, pp. 368–9.
67. J.H. Lima, *Café e Indústria em Minas Gerais, 1870–1920* (Petrópolis, 1981), p. 13.
68. Singer, *op.cit.*, p. 209.
69. R.B. Martins and M.C.S. Martins, 'As Exportações de Minas Gerais no Século XIX', in *Seminário Sobre a Economia Mineira* (Diamantina, 1982), September, p. 117.
70. Lima, *op.cit.*, p. 14.
71. Martins and Martins, *op.cit.*, pp. 109–10.
72. Wirth, *op.cit.*, p. 45.
73. Iglésias, 'Minas Gerais', *op.cit.*, p. 393.
74. Wirth, *op.cit.*, p. 45.
75. F. Iglésias, *Política Econômica do Governo Provincial Mineiro, 1835–1889* (Rio de Janeiro, 1958), pp. 90–3.
76. Wirth, *op.cit.*, pp. 49–50.
77. D.C. Libby, *Transformação e Trabalho em uma Economia Escravista: Minas Gerais no Século XIX* (São Paulo, 1988), pp. 257–69.
78. Wirth, *op.cit.*, p. 11.
79. Libby, *op.cit.*, pp. 134–5.
80. F.A.M. Gomes, *História da Siderurgia no Brasil* (Belo Horizonte/São Paulo, 1983), p. 35.
81. Banco de Desenvolvimento de Minas Gerais, *Diagnóstico da Economia Mineira*, I, (Belo Horizonte, 1968), pp. 64–5.

82. R.B. Martins, 'A Indústria Têxtil Doméstica de Minas Gerais no Século XIX', in *Anais do II Seminário sobre a Economia Brasileira* (Belo Horizonte, 1983), pp. 81–4.
83. D.A. Giroletti, 'A Modernização Capitalista em Minas Gerais: A Formação do Operariado Industrial e de uma Nova Cosmovisão', Universidade Federal do Rio de Janeiro/Museu Nacional, unpublished Ph.D. thesis, Rio de Janeiro, 1987, pp. 16–109; and Libby, *Transformação e Trabalho*, *op.cit.*, pp. 225–39.
84. Lima, *op.cit.*, p. 82.
85. *Ibid.*, p. 82.
86. Companhia União e Indústria, *Relatório da Assembléia Geral dos Acionistas* (Rio de Janeiro, 1861), p. 5.
87. Singer, *op.cit.*, p. 210.
88. Iglesias, *Política Econômica do Governo Provincial Mineiro*, *op.cit.*, p. 165.
89. Wirth, *op.cit.*, pp. 57–8.
90. Singer, *op.cit.*, p. 213.
91. Wirth, *op.cit.*, pp. 3–5.
92. *Ibid.*, pp. 23–4.

2 The Entrepreneur

1. L.C.T.D. Prado, 'Commercial Capital, Domestic Market and Manufacturing in Imperial Brazil: The Failure of Brazilian Economic Development in the nineteenth Century', University of London, unpublished Ph.D. thesis, 1991, pp. 174–83.
2. C. Furtado, *The Economic Growth of Brazil: A Survey from Colonial to Modern Times* (Los Angeles, 1965), pp. 124–5.
3. *Ibid.*, p. 125.
4. *Ibid.*, pp. 124–6.
5. Mainly represented by W. Dean, *A Industrialização de São Paulo* (São Paulo, 1971), and J. Gorender, *A Burguesia Brasileira*, 6th edn (São Paulo, 1986).
6. Mainly represented by J.M. Cardoso de Mello, *O Capitalismo Tardio: Contribuição à Revisão Crítica da Formação e Desenvolvimento da Economia Brasileira* (São Paulo, 1982) and W. Cano, *Raízes da Concentração Industrial em São Paulo*, 3rd edn (São Paulo, 1977).
7. H. Lydall, *The Entrepreneurial Factor in Economic Growth* (London, 1992), pp. 82–3.
8. *Ibid.*, pp. 84–6.
9. See Dean, *op.cit.*
10. F.C. Prestes Motta, *Empresários e Hegemonia Política* (São Paulo, 1979), p. 41.
11. F.A.M. Gomes, *História da Siderurgia no Brasil* (Belo Horizonte/São Paulo, 1983), pp. 79–85.
12. Dean, *op.cit.*
13. D.C. Libby, *Transformação e Trabalho em uma Economia Escravista: Minas Gerais no Século XIX* (São Paulo, 1988), p. 149.
14. *Ibid.*, pp. 163–9.

15. W. Suzigan, *Indústria Brasileira: Origem e Desenvolvimento* (São Paulo, 1986), pp. 258–9.
16. For a further discussion of iron and textile technologies see Chapter 4.
17. Libby, *op.cit.*, p. 154.
18. For a further discussion about the participation of immigrants in the industrialization of Juiz de Fora see A. Esteves, *Álbum do Município de Juiz de Fora* (Belo Horizonte, 1914); D.A. Giroletti, *A Industrialização de Juiz de Fora: 1850–1930* (Juiz de Fora, 1988); P. Oliveira, *História de Juiz de Fora* (Juiz de Fora, 1966); L.J. Stehling, 'Trajetória da Indústria em Juiz de Fora', in *Revista do Instituto Histórico e Geográfico de Juiz de Fora*, vol. 2, no. 2 (Juiz de Fora, 1966), pp. 30–7; and L.A.V. Arantes, 'As Origens da Burguesia Industrial em Juiz de Fora, 1858/1912', Universidade Federal Fluminense, unpublished M.Sc. thesis, Niterói, 1991.
19. Arantes, *op.cit.*, pp. 87–121.
20. Lydall, *op.cit.*, p. 83.
21. Arantes, *op.cit.*, pp. 88–9.
22. See Dean, *op.cit.* and Gorender, *op.cit.*
23. Arantes, *op.cit.*, p. 98.
24. *Ibid.*, p. 160.
25. *Ibid.*, p. 35.
26. Companhia União e Indústria, *Relatório da Assembléia Geral dos Acionistas* (Rio de Janeiro, 1857), pp. 38–9.
27. C.M. Lewis, *Public Policy and Private Initiative: Railway Building in São Paulo, 1860–1889*, (London, 1991), pp. 35–55. For a further discussion about the building and the financing of the Paulista railways see also F.A.M. Saes, *As Ferrovias de São Paulo, 1870–1940* (São Paulo, 1981).
28. P. Tamm, *Uma Dinastia de Tecelões*, 2nd edn (Belo Horizonte, 1960), pp. 64–9.
29. G. Guimarães, *Francisco José de Andrade Botelho* (Belo Horizonte, 1950), p. 14.
30. M.L.P. Costa, *A Fábrica de Tecidos de Machado, 1871–1917* (Belo Horizonte, 1989), p. 25.
31. M.T.R.O. Versiani, 'The Cotton Textile Industry of Minas Gerais, Brazil: Beginnings and Early Development, 1868–1906', University of London, unpublished Ph.D. thesis, 1991, pp. 50–1.
32. G.M. Mascarenhas, *Centenário da Fábrica do Cedro, 1872–1972* (Belo Horizonte, 1972), pp. 93–118.
33. S.J. Stein, *Origens e Evolução da Indústria Têxtil no Brasil, 1850–1950* (Rio de Janeiro, 1950), p. 216.
34. Versiani, *op.cit.*, pp. 81–2.
35. *Ibid.*, pp. 75–6.
36. *Ibid.*, p. 76.
37. *Ibid.*, p. 76.
38. *Ibid.*, p. 77.
39. Tamm, *op.cit.*, p. 25.
40. A.M. Vaz, *Cia. Cedro e Cachoeira: História de uma Empresa Familiar, 1883–1987* (Belo Horizonte, 1990), pp. 102–3.

41. Versiani, *op.cit.*, p. 88.
42. N.A.M. Freitas, 'Cia. Têxtil Cachoeira dos Macacos: Empresa que deu Origem a uma Cidade', Fundação Mineira de Arte Aleijadinho/Escola Superior de Artes Plásticas, mimeo., Belo Horizonte, 1990, p. 17.
43. Versiani, *op.cit.*, p. 88.
44. *Ibid.*, pp. 86–8.
45. *Ibid.*, pp. 89–91.
46. N.L. Mascarenhas, *Bernardo Mascarenhas: o Surto Industrial de Minas Gerais* (Rio de Janeiro, 1954), pp. 123–5.
47. Versiani, *op.cit.*, p. 91.
48. *Ibid.*, p. 92.
49. *Ibid.*, p. 82.
50. M.A.G. Souza, *História de Itaúna* (Belo Horizonte, 1986), I, p. 101–94.
51. Versiani, *op.cit.*, p. 128.
52. Companhia Industrial Pitanguense, 'Estatutos', (1893) in *Minas Gerais*, 5 January 1894, pp. 7–8; and Companhia Industrial Pitanguense, 'Ata da Assembléia Geral Institutiva' (1893) in *Minas Gerais*, 5 January 1894, p. 7.
53. Companhia Industrial Pitanguense, 'Lista Nominativa dos Srs. Subscritores' (1894), in *Minas Gerais*, 5 January 1894, p. 7.
54. Versiani, *op.cit.*, p. 168.
55. Tamm, *op.cit.*, p. 87.
56. Versiani, *op.cit.*, pp. 169–70.
57. *Ibid.*, pp. 174–5.
58. Companhia Progresso Fabril, 'Ata da Sessão da Assembléia Geral dos Acionistas para a Constituição da mesma Companhia' (1893), in *Minas Gerais*, 23 May 1893, pp. 6–8.
59. Mascarenhas, *Centenário da Fábrica do Cedro, op.cit.*, p. 118 and Versiani, *op.cit.*, p. 165.
60. Companhia Industrial São Domingos, 'Ata da Assembléia de Instalação' (1894), in *Minas Gerais*, 21 February 1894, p. 7.
61. Companhia Industrial São Domingos, 'Lista dos Acionistas' (1894), in *Minas Gerais*, 21 February 1894, p. 7.
62. Versiani, *op.cit.*, pp. 172–4.
63. Companhia Tecidos Mineiros, 'Relação dos Acionistas' (1894), in *Minas Gerais*, 11 February 1894, p. 6.
64. Versiani, *op.cit.*, pp. 128–243.
65. Lydall, *op.cit.*, pp. 80–9.
66. A.M.F.C. Monteiro, 'Empreendedores e Investidores em Indústria Têxtil no Rio de Janeiro: 1878–1895', Universidade Federal Fluminense, unpublished M.Sc. thesis, Niterói, 1985, pp. 98–101.
67. *Ibid.*, pp. 120–3.
68. *Ibid.*, pp. 132–4.
69. *Ibid.*, pp. 143–7.
70. *Ibid.*, pp. 156–9.
71. *Ibid.*, pp. 169–76.
72. *Ibid.*, pp. 182–3.
73. *Ibid.*, pp. 193–4.
74. *Ibid.*, pp. 208–13.

75. *Ibid.*, pp. 223–9.
76. *Ibid.*, pp. 239–43.
77. *Ibid.*, pp. 252–4.
78. See Ministério da Agricultura, Indústria e Commercio, *Recenseamento do Brazil Realizado em 1 de Setembro de 1920*, vol. IV, (Rio de Janeiro, 1924), 2nd part, p. 48 and Directoria Geral de Estatística, *Relatorio Annexo ao do Ministerio dos Negocios do Imperio de 1876* (Rio de Janeiro, 1877), p. 15.
79. Prado, *op.cit.*, pp. 180–3.
80. See Dean, *op.cit.*, pp. 25–40.
81. Letter from Bernardo Mascarenhas reproduced in Mascarenhas, *Bernardo Mascarenhas*, p. 118.
82. The members of the Mascarenhas family and the number of shares that each one held were: Bernardo Mascarenhas (400), Policena da Silva Mascarenhas (100), Francisco Mascarenhas (78), Vitor Mascarenhas (50), Caetano Mascarenhas (50), Viriato Diniz Mascarenhas (35), Theóphilo Marques Ferreira (30), Elvira Diniz Mascarenhas (25), Pacífico Mascarenhas (20), Antônio Diniz Mascarenhas (20), Altivo Diniz Mascarenhas (15), and Antônio Augusto Mascarenhas (10) – see P. Oliveira, *Companhia Mineira de Eletricidade: Pioneira da Iluminação Hidrelétrica na América do Sul* (Juiz de Fora, 1969), p. 27.
83. Among the original shareholders of the CME it is possible to identify the names of the following local businessmen: Francisco Baptista de Oliveira, the Baron of Santa Helena who together with Francisco Baptista de Oliveira founded the first bank in Minas Gerais, the Banco Territorial e Mercantil de Minas; João Baptista de Oliveira e Souza, Francisco Baptista de Oliveira's father; Frederico Ferreira Lage, and Alfredo Ferreira Lage – sons of Mariano Procópio Ferreira Lage founder of the CUI. Companhia Mineira de Eletricidade, 'Ata da Primeira Reunião dos Acionistas da Companhia Mineira de Eletricidade, Instalação da Assembléia Geral e Constituição da Sociedade', reproduced in *ibid.*, pp. 25–6.
84. 'O Falecimento do Dr Norberto Custodio Ferreira', in *Jornal Cataguases* (Cataguases), 17 February 1935, p. 1.
85. 'Dr José Monteiro Ribeiro Junqueira', in *Gazeta de Leopoldina* (Leopoldina), 19 May 1946.
86. L.S. Costa, *Cataguases Centenária: Dados para a sua História* (Cataguases, 1977), p. 541.
87. *Panorama do Setor de Energia Elétrica no Brasil*, ed. R.F. Dias, L.M.M. Cabral, P.B.B. Cachapuz, and S.T.N. Lamarrão (Rio de Janeiro, 1988), pp. 34–5.
88. *Ibid.*, pp. 34–9.
89. W.L. Bastos, *Mariano Procópio Ferreira Lage: Sua Vida, Sua Obra, Descendência, Genealogia*, 2nd edn (Juiz de Fora, 1991).
90. *Ibid.*, p. 204.
91. R.F. Burton, *Viagem aos Planaltos do Brasil (1868)*, I (São Paulo, 1941), p. 147.
92. Bastos, *Mariano Procópio Ferreira Lage*, *op.cit.*, p. 16.

Notes

93. 'Receipt to Mariano Procópio Ferreira Lage signed by J.A. Brito, 29 March 1849', Biblioteca Nacional – Sessão de Manuscritos – Catálogo de Documentos Biográficos – Pasta C 1034–57.
94. 'Letter to Mariano Procópio Ferreira Lage from the Minister and Secretary of the Affairs of the Empire, the 22 April 1871'. Biblioteca Nacional – Sessão de Manuscritos – Catálogo de Documentos Biográficos – Pasta C 1034–57.
95. Bastos, *Mariano Procópio Ferreira Lage*, *op.cit.*, pp. 172–3.
96. Vaz, *op.cit.*, pp. 34–40.
97. *Ibid.*, pp. 48–51, 71.
98. D.A. Giroletti, 'Formação do Empres rio Industrial', Universidade Federal de Minas Gerais, mimeo., Belo Horizonte, 1991, p. 4.
99. Tamm, *op.cit.*, pp. 87–151.
100. *Ibid.*, pp. 87–151.
101. W.L. Bastos, *Francisco Baptista de Oliveira um Pioneiro: Sua Vida, Sua Obra, Sua Descendência, Genealogia* (Juiz de Fora, 1967), pp. 144–69.
102. Companhia Cachoeira dos Macacos, 'Ata da Assembléia Geral dos Subscritores de Ações da Sociedade Anonyma Cachoeira dos Macacos para Constituição da mesma', reproduced in Freitas, *op.cit.*, p. 23.
103. *Gazeta de Leopoldina* (Leopoldina), 19 May 1946.
104. 'O Falecimento do Dr Norberto Custodio Ferreira', in *Jornal Cataguases* (Cataguases), 17 February 1935, p. 1.
105. Reproduced in Guimarães, *op.cit.*, p. 14.
106. *Ibid.*, pp. 11–31.
107. Versiani, *op.cit.*, pp. 50–1.
108. Monteiro, *op.cit.*, p. 122.
109. P. Cammack, 'State and Federal Politics in Minas Gerais, Brazil', University of Oxford, unpublished Ph.D. thesis, Oxford, 1980, pp. 55–6.
110. P.L. Payne, *British Entrepreneurship in the Nineteenth Century*, 2nd. edn (London, 1988), p. 21.
111. Giroletti, *Formação do Empresário Industrial*, *op.cit.*, pp. 3–15.
112. Cammack, *op.cit.*, p. 57.
113. Dean, *op.cit.*
114. See Cano, *op.cit.*, chapter II; Cardoso de Mello, *op.cit.*, pp. 96–106; and Z.M.C. Mello, *Metamorfoses da Riqueza: São Paulo, 1845–1895* (São Paulo, 1985), chapters II and IV.
115. Cammack, *op.cit.*, pp. 43–50.
116. Arantes, *op.cit.*, pp. 41–5.
117. Bastos, *Mariano Procópio Ferreira Lage*, *op.cit.*, pp. 15–270.
118. Companhia União e Indústria, *Relatório da Assembléia Geral dos Acionistas* (1861), p. 7.
119. Mariano Procópio Ferreira Lage, then, listed the names of the following farmers: Candido Alves Coutinho, Joaquim Gomes Leal and Antonio Gomes de Siqueira, and their neighbours, interested in the construction of the branch from the Parahybuna station upto the farm owned by Francisco Gomes de Oliveira; the Baron of Prados and his neighbours, interested in the construction of the branch from Jaguary where there were large coffee farms to the Simao Pereira station; Gervasio Antonio da Silva and Manoel José Pires, interested

194 *Notes*

in the construction of the branch from the Espírito Santo parish to
the Mathias station; and Marcellino Gonçalves da Costa and his son
José Anastacio da Costa Lima, interested in the construction of the
branch from the São Francisco parish to the Juiz de Fora station. See
Companhia União e Indústria, *Relatório da Assembléia Geral dos Acionistas* (1861), p. 7, pp. 17–8.

120. Lewis, *op.cit.*, pp. 35–55.
121. Companhia União e Indústria, *Relatório da Assembléia Geral dos Acionistas*, (1865), p. 5.
122. A. Gerschenkron, *Economic Backwardness in Historical Perspective: a book
of essays* (Cambridge, 1962).
123. See Giroletti, *A Industrialização de Juiz de Fora, 1850–1930, op.cit.*, pp.
27–31.
124. *Ibid.*, p. 47.
125. *Ibid.*, p. 50.
126. J.H. Lima, *Café e Indústria em Minas Gerais (1870–1920)* (Petrópolis,
1981), pp. 101–2.
127. Arantes, *op.cit.*, p. 159.
128. Giroletti, *Industrialização de Juiz de Fora, op.cit.*, p. 92.
129. For a further discussion of the concept of the 'bourgeois immigrant'
see Dean, *op.cit.*, pp. 59–81.
130. Arantes, *op.cit.*, pp. 87–8.
131. *Ibid.*, pp. 98–9.
132. *Ibid.*, p. 100.
133. *Ibid.*, p. 100.
134. *Ibid.*, p. 101.
135. *Ibid.*, p. 102.
136. According to Libby, most of the iron foundries were situated within
the Metalúrgica region. Libby, *op.cit.*, pp. 152–60.
137. W.L. von Eschwege, *Pluto Brasiliensis*, II (Berlin, 1833; reprinted Belo
Horizonte/São Paulo, 1979), p. 203.
138. *Ibid.*, p. 247.
139. Gomes, *História da Siderurgia no Brasil, op.cit.*, pp. 79–85.
140. Libby, *op.cit.*, p. 183.
141. *Ibid.*, p. 151.
142. *Ibid.*, p. 152.
143. *Ibid.*, p. 207.
144. Suzigan, *op.cit.*, pp. 258–9.
145. *Ibid.*, p. 259.
146. Lydall, *op.cit.*, p. 83.
147. *Ibid.*, p. 82.
148. J.A. Paula, 'Dois Ensaios sobre a Gênese da Industrialização em
Minas Gerais: a Siderurgia e a Indústria Têxtil', in *Anais do II Seminário sobre a Economia Mineira* (Belo Horizonte, 1983), p. 31.
149. See J.B. Say, *Tratado de Economia Política* (São Paulo, 1983) and F.
Quesnay, *Quesnay's 'Tableau Économique'* (London, 1972).
150. Companhia Cedro e Cachoeira, 'Caixa de Correspondências Recebidas no. 2', 'Letter from Antônio Cândido Mascarenhas to Joaquim
Pereira Lopes, 3 August 1870'.

151. Vaz, *op.cit.*, pp. 42–3.
152. See R.F. Hébert and A.N. Link, *The Entrepreneur: Mainstream Views and Radical Critiques* (New York, 1982); M. Casson, *The Entrepreneur: An Economic Theory* (Oxford, 1982); H. Barreto, *The Entrepreneur in Microeconomic Theory: Disappearance and Explanation* (New York, 1989); M. Binks and P. Vale, *Entrepreneurship and Economic Change* (London, 1990); and Lydall, *op.cit.*; R. Cantillon, *Essai sur la Nature du Commerce en Général* (London, 1931); Quesnay, *op.cit.*; A.R.J. Turgot, *Reflexions on the Formation and the Distribution of Riches*, (New York, 1971); Say, op.cit.; K. Marx, *Capital*, vol. I (London, 1988); M. Weber, *The Protestant Ethic and the Spirit of Capitalism*, 20th edn (London, 1989); J.A. Schumpeter, *A Teoria do Desenvolvimento Econômico* (São Paulo, 1982); I.M. Kirzner, *Competition and Entrepreneurship* (Chicago, 1973).
153. Tamm, *op.cit.*, p. 86.
154. *Ibid.*, pp. 87, 100–2, 109–10.
155. *Ibid.*, pp. 87–208.
156. Vaz, *op.cit.*, p. 93.
157. Guimarães, *op.cit.*.
158. B.S. Veiga, *Almanach Sul Mineiro* (Campanha, 1874), p. 148.
159. *Ibid.*, pp. 146–51.
160. Versiani, *op.cit.*, pp. 50–2.
161. *Ibid.*, pp. 81–2.
162. *Ibid.*, pp. 75–6.
163. *Ibid.*, pp. 76–7, 89, 91–3.
164. Vaz, *op.cit.*, p. 34.
165. *Ibid.*, pp. 34–40.
166. *Ibid.*, pp. 102–3.
167. Companhia Cachoeira dos Macacos, 'Ata da Assembléia Geral dos Subscritores de Ações da Sociedade Anonyma Cachoeira dos Macacos para Constituição da mesma', reproduced in Freitas, *op.cit.*, p. 23.
168. Versiani, *op.cit.*, p. 88.
169. *Ibid.*, pp. 86–8.
170. *Ibid.*, p. 91.
171. Vaz, *op.cit.*, pp. 42–3.
172. *Ibid.*, p. 43.
173. Mascarenhas, *Bernardo Mascarenhas*, *op.cit.*, pp. 79–86, 123–9.
174. Versiani, *op.cit.*, p. 82.
175. Souza, *op.cit.*, pp. 101–15, 123–7, 194–98.
176. *Ibid.*, pp. 170–3.
177. Versiani, *op.cit.*, pp. 128–243.
178. *Ibid.*, pp. 167–71.
179. Companhia Industrial Pitanguense, 'Lista Nominativa dos Srs. Subscritores' (1894), in *Minas Gerais*, 5 January 1894, p. 7.
180. Versiani, *op.cit.*, p. 165.
181. Companhia Progresso Fabril, 'Estatutos' (1893), in *Minas Gerais*, 23 May 1893, pp. 7–8.
182. Versiani, *op.cit.*, pp. 174–5.
183. Companhia Industrial São Domingos, 'Ata da Assembléia de Instalação' (1894), in *Minas Gerais*, 21 February 1894, p. 7.

184. Monteiro, *op.cit.*, pp. 98–101.
185. *Ibid.*, pp. 120–3.
186. *Ibid.*, pp. 143–7.
187. *Ibid.*, pp. 156–9.
188. *Ibid.*, pp. 169–76.
189. *Ibid.*, pp. 182–3.
190. *Ibid.*, pp. 193–4.
191. *Ibid.*, pp. 208–13.
192. *Ibid.*, pp. 223–9.
193. *Ibid.*, pp. 239–43.
194. *Ibid.*, pp. 252–4.
195. Suzigan in his work about the origins of the Brazilian industry comes to the same conclusions regarding the origin of the funds invested in the *mineiro* and the *carioca* textile industries. For a brief discussion about the origins of the capital invested in the textile industry established in different parts of Brazil until the beginning of the twentieth century see Suzigan, *op.cit.*, pp. 122–45, and Stein, *op.cit.*, pp. 41–3.
196. Vaz, *op.cit.*, pp. 42–3.
197. The members of the Mascarenhas family are: Bernardo Mascarenhas, Policena da Silva Mascarenhas (Bernardo's mother), Francisco Mascarenhas, Vitor Mascarenhas, Caetano Mascarenhas, Viriato Diniz Mascarenhas, Theóphilo Marques Ferreira, Elvira Diniz Mascarenhas, Pacífico Mascarenhas, Antônio Diniz Mascarenhas, Altivo Diniz Mascarenhas, and Antônio Augusto Mascarenhas – see Oliveira, *Companhia Mineira de Eletricidade*, *op.cit.*, p. 27.
198. *Ibid.*, p. 27.
199. Bastos, *Mariano Procópio Ferreira Lage*, *op.cit.*, p. 21.
200. *Ibid.*, p. 27.
201. *Ibid.*, p. 22.
202. *Ibid.*, pp. 23–5.
203. 'O Falecimento do Dr Norberto Custódio Ferreira', in *Jornal Cataguases* (Cataguases), 17 February 1935, p. 1.
204. 'Dr José Monteiro Ribeiro Junqueira', in *Gazeta de Leopoldina* (Leopoldina), 19 May 1946.
205. Costa, *op.cit.*, p. 541.
206. 'Dr José Monteiro Ribeiro Junqueira', in *Gazeta de Leopoldina* (Leopoldina), 19 May 1946.
207. In 1905, for example, Leopoldina was the eighth largest producer of coffee in the Mata zone. See Lima, *op.cit.*, p. 36.
208. D. McDowall, *The Light: Brazilian Traction, Light and Power Company Limited, 1899–1945* (Toronto, 1988), pp. 48–79.

3 The *Mineiro* Firm

1. See M. Weber, *The Theory of Social and Economic Organization* (New York, 1947).
2. See A.D. Chandler, *The Visible Hand: The Managerial Revolution in American Business* (Cambridge, Mass., 1977); A.D. Chandler, 'The

United States Seedbed of Managerial Capitalism' in A.D. Chandler and H. Deams (eds), *Managerial Hierarchies: Comparative Perspectives on the Rise of Modern Industrial Enterprises* (Cambridge, Mass., 1980); and T.K. McCraw, *The Essential Alfred Chandler: Essays toward a Historical Theory of Big Business* (Boston, 1991).

3. J.A. Paula, 'Dois Ensaios sobre a Gênese da Industrializaçagão em Minas Gerais: a Siderurgia e a Indústria Têxtil', in *Anais do II Semin rio sobre a Economia Mineira* (Belo Horizonte, 1983), p. 38.
4. D.C. Libby, *Transformação e Trabalho em uma Economia Escravista: Minas Gerais no Século XIX* (São Paulo, 1988), pp. 147–8.
5. Paula, *op.cit.* pp. 32–3.
6. Libby, *op.cit.* pp. 148–9.
7. M. Atkinson and C. Barber, *The Growth and Decline of the South Wales Iron Industry, 1760–1880* (Cardiff, 1987), pp. 4–6.
8. F.A.M. Gomes, *História da Siderurgia no Brasil* (Belo Horizonte/São-Paulo, 1983), p. 148.
9. W.L. von Eschwege, *Pluto Brasiliensis* vol. II (Berlin, 1833; reprinted Belo Horizonte/São Paulo, 1979), p. 261.
10. Paula, *op.cit.* p. 37.
11. J.C. Costa Sena, 'Viagem de Estudos Metallurgicos no Centro da Provincia de Minas', in *Annaes da Escola de Minas* (Ouro Preto, 1881), no. 1, pp. 117–41.
12. *Ibid.*, p. 112.
13. Eschwege, *op.cit.* pp. 247–52.
14. *Ibid.*, pp. 207–13.
15. Gomes, *História da Siderurgia no Brasil, op.cit.*, pp. 141–6.
16. C.M. Peláez, *História da Industrialização Brasileira: Crítica à Teoria Estruturalista no Brasil* (Rio de Janeiro, 1972), p. 145.
17. Gomes, *História da Siderurgia no Brasil* pp. 146–7.
18. According to Libby, there is evidence that the industry was heavily concentrated in the Metalúrgica region in 1821. This concentration is confirmed in the period 1854–58, when 80 per cent of the foundries were located in the Metalúrgica – Mantiqueira region. The same trend was found for the period 1863–66, although the information is incomplete and scattered. Libby, *op.cit.* pp. 152–60.
19. *Ibid.*, p. 165.
20. *Ibid.*, p. 168.
21. Gomes, *História da Siderurgia no Brasil, op.cit.*, p. 111.
22. Libby, *op.cit.* p. 168.
23. Eschwege, *op.cit.* pp. 209–13.
24. Libby, *op.cit.* pp. 163–4.
25. Eschwege, *op.cit.* pp. 247–54.
26. Libby, *op.cit.* p. 162.
27. P. Ferrand, 'A Indústria de Ferro no Brasil (Provincia de Minas Geraes)', in *Annaes da Escola de Minas* (Ouro Preto, 1885) no. 4, pp. 167–85.
28. A.D. Chandler, *Strategy and Structure: Chapters in the History of the American Industrial Enterprise* 7th edn (Cambridge, Mass., 1991), p. 21.

29. Companhia União e Indústria, *Relatório da Assembléia Geral dos Acio-
    nistas* (1861), p. 5.
30. Ministério dos Negócios de Agricultura, Comércio e Obras Publicas,
    'Instruções expedidas ao Conselheiro M.C. Galvão, encarregando-o
    de estudos relativamente às propostas da companhia União e Indús-
    tria concernentes à Estrada de Ferro de Pedro II' no. 1, Secção 3, 10
    October, 1868, reproduced in A.O. Esteves, 'Mariano Procópio', in
    Revista do Instituto Histórico e Geográfico Brasileiro vol. 230, January –
    March, 1956, pp. 232–3.
31. Estrada de Ferro D. Pedro II, 'Relatório do Ano de 1869 Apresen-
    tado ao Ilmo. e Exmo. Sr. Conselheiro Diogo Velho Cavalcanti de
    Albuquerque, Ministro e Secretário de Estado dos Negócios da Agri-
    cultura, Comércio e Obras Públicas por Mariano Procópio Ferreira
    Lage, Director da mesma Estrada', reproduced in *ibid.*, p. 250.
32. Chandler, *Strategy and Structure*, *op.cit.*, p. 21.
33. As note 31, p. 251.
34. *Ibid.*, p. 250.
35. Companhia União e Indústria, *Relatório da Assembléia Geral dos Acio-
    nistas* (1856), pp. 13–5.
36. Esteves, *op.cit.* pp. 138–9.
37. Companhia União e Indústria, *Relatório da Assembléia Geral dos Acio-
    nistas* (1857), pp. 1–3.
38. D.A. Giroletti, 'Companhia e a Rodovia União e Indústria e o Desen-
    volvimento de Juiz de Fora, 1850 a 1900', Universidade Federal de
    Minas Gerais, mimeo, Belo Horizonte, 1980, p. 30.
39. Companhia União e Indústria, *Relatório da Assembléia Geral dos Acio-
    nistas* (1860), p. 7.
40. *Ibid.* (1866), annexe 12.
41. *Ibid.* (1865), pp. 5–6.
42. *Ibid. 1869*, pp. 3–4.
43. Giroletti, *op.cit.* pp. 18–19.
44. A.C. El-Kareh, *Filha Branca de Mãe Preta: A Companhia de Estrada de
    Ferro D. Pedro II, 1855–1865* (Petrópolis, 1982), pp. 57–8.
45. Libby, *op.cit.* pp. 216–25.
46. *Ibid.*, p. 233.
47. *Panorama do Setor de Energia Elétrica no Brasil*, ed. R.F. Dias, L.M.M.
    Cabral, P.B.B. Cachapuz and S.T.N. Lamarrão (Rio de Janeiro,
    1988), pp. 48–54.
48. P. Oliveira, *Companhia Mineira de Eletricidade: Pioneira da Iluminação
    Hidrelétrica na América do Sul* (Juiz de Fora, 1969), pp. 35–44.
49. Companhia Força e Luz Cataguazes-Leopoldina, *80 Anos Companhia
    Força e Luz Cataguazes-Leopoldina: Uma Luz* (1988), pp. 1–4.
50. *Panorama do Setor de Energia Elétrica no Brasil op.cit.*, pp. 34–41.
51. Companhia Força e Luz Cataguazes-Leopoldina, 'Relatorio do Ger-
    ente' (1909), p. 6.
52. *Ibid.* (1910), p.8.
53. Oliveira, *Companhia Mineira de Eletricidade op.cit.*, pp. 27–8, 39, 49–50.
54. Suplemento Minas Gerais, 'Companhia Força e Luz Cataguazes-Leo-
    poldina' (Cataguazes, 1913).

55. The Banking Almanac, Directory, Year Book and Diary (London, 1889), p. 563.
56. F.A.M. Gomes, 'A Eletrificaçagão no Brasil', in *Caderno História e Energia* (São Paulo, 1986), no. 2, October, p. 8.
57. Eschwege, *op.cit.* p. 258.
58. *Ibid.*, p. 250.
59. *Ibid.*, p. 253.
60. *Ibid.*, p. 259.
61. *Ibid.*, p. 259.
62. Gomes, *História da Siderurgia no Brasil op.cit.*, p. 120.
63. Eschwege, *op.cit.* pp. 253–4.
64. Costa Sena, *op.cit.* p. 125.
65. Esteves, *op.cit.* p. 12.
66. Costa Sena, *op.cit.* pp. 117–41.
67. Libby, *op.cit.* p. 144.
68. Eschwege, *op.cit.*, pp. 58–9.
69. Companhia União e Indústria, *Relatório da Assembléia Geral dos Acionistas* (1864), annexes 8 and 9.
70. El-Kareh, *op.cit.* p. 121.
71. Companhia União e Indústria, *Relatório da Assembléia Geral dos Acionistas* (1863), pp. 11–12.
72. Libby, *op.cit.* p. 233.
73. N.A.M. Freitas, 'Cia. Têxtil Cachoeira dos Macacos: Empresa que deu Origem a uma Cidade', Fundação Mineira de Arte Aleijadinho/ Escola Superior de Artes Plásticas, mimeo, Belo Horizonte, 1990, pp. 27–9.
74. Letter from Bernardo Mascarenhas of 24 January 1883 to Mascarenhas, Barbosa & Cia., reproduced in N.L. Mascarenhas, *Bernardo Mascarenhas: o Surto Industrial de Minas Gerais* (Rio de Janeiro, 1954), p. 71.
75. A.M. Vaz, *Cia. Cedro e Cachoeira: História de uma Empresa Familiar, 1883–1987* (Belo Horizonte, 1990), p. 245.
76. Companhia Cedro e Cachoeira, 'Caixa de Correspondências Bernardo Mascarenhas, 1883–1899 – no. 148', 'Letter from Francisco de Paula Mascarenhas to Bernardo Mascarenhas, 26 April 1887'.
77. Companhia Cedro e Cachoeira, 'Caixa de Correspondências Recebidas no. 21', 'Letter from Rodolpho Alves, March 1887'.
78. See Chandler, *The Visible Hand op.cit.*, parts III and IV.
79. Vaz, *op.cit.* pp. 220–6.
80. Companhia Cedro e Cachoeira, 'Relatório da Diretoria' (1889), pp. 1–2.
81. *Ibid.*, p.30.
82. Vaz, *op.cit.* p. 246.
83. Companhia Cedro e Cachoeira, 'Caixa de Correspondências Recebidas no. 41', 'Letter from Rodolpho, Irmão & Mattos, 12 April 1895'.
84. Companhia Cedro e Cachoeira, 'Caixa de Correspondências Recebidas no. 42', 'Letter from Eugenio Azevedo & Companhia to Aristides J. Mascarenhas, 5 August 1895'.

85. Vaz, *op.cit.* pp. 245–6.
86. S.J. Stein, *Origens e Evolução da Indústria Têxtil no Brasil, 1850–1950* (Rio de Janeiro, 1950), p. 38, 80.
87. Vaz, *op.cit.* pp. 245–61.
88. Freitas, *op.cit.* pp. 27–9.
89. Companhia Cedro e Cachoeira, 'Caixa de Correspondências Recebidas no. 26', 'Letter from M.J. Clemence to Theóphilo Marques Ferreira, 7 December 1889'.
90. Letter from M.J. Clemence to Américo Teixeira Guimarães on 25 October 1889, reproduced in Freitas, *op.cit.* p. 123.
91. Companhia Cedro e Cachoeira, 'Caixa de Correspondências Recebidas no. 30', 'Letter from M.J. Clemence to Theóphilo Marques Ferreira, 4 June 1891'.
92. *Ibid.*, 31 July 1891.
93. Companhia Cedro e Cachoeira, 'Caixa de Correspondências Recebidas no. 51', 'Letter from M.J. Clemence to Aristides J. Mascarenhas, 3 June 1899'.
94. Freitas, *op.cit.* pp. 8–9.
95. Companhia Cedro e Cachoeira, 'Relatório e Quadro Demonstrativo de Lucros Apresentado pelo Dr. Francisco Bahia da Rocha, Gerente da Fábrica de SãoVicente' (1895).
96. Letter from Manoel Pimenta Figueiredo to the general manager of the Companhia Cedro e Cachoeira on 15 July 1898, reproduced in D. Giroletti, *Fábrica Convento Disciplina* (Belo Horizonte, 1991), p. 67.
97. Companhia Cedro e Cachoeira, 'Caixa de Correspondências Recebidas no. 16', 'Letter from Francisco de Paula Mascarenhas to Bernardo Mascarenhas, 23 July 1884'.
98. Companhia Cedro e Cachoeira, 'Caixa de Correspondências Recebidas no. 36', 'Letter from Américo Teixeira Guimarães to Francisco de Paula Mascarenhas, 27 August 1893'.
99. Companhia Cedro e Cachoeira, 'Relatório da Diretoria', *op.cit.* (1889).
100. G.M. Mascarenhas, *Centenário da Fábrica do Cedro, 1872–1972* (Belo Horizonte, 1972), p. 145.
101. Vaz, *op.cit.* p. 226.
102. Report of the technical specifications of the equipment to be supplied by the Westinghouse Company, reproduced in Oliveira, *Companhia Mineira de Eletricidade* pp. 29–31.
103. Companhia Mineira de Eletricidade, 'Relatório da Diretoria' (1892), reproduced in *Ibid.*, pp. 38–9.
104. *Ibid.*, p. 39.
105. *Ibid.*, p. 44.
106. Companhia Mineira de Eletricidade, 'Relatório da Diretoria' (1901), reproduced in *Ibid.*, p. 44.
107. Companhia Força e Luz Cataguazes-Leopoldina, *80 Anos Companhia Força e Luz Cataguazes-Leopoldina: Uma Luz* (1988), pp. 1–4.
108. Companhia Força e Luz Cataguazes-Leopoldina, 'Relatorio da Diretoria' (1909), pp. 3–4.
109. M.F. Neto, 'Os Frutos da Diversificação', in *Administração e Serviços* June 1982.

110. *Panorama do Setor de Energia Elétrica no Brasil*, *op.cit.*, pp. 34–41.
111. Libby, *op.cit.* p. 137.
112. The cruzado was the old Portuguese currency and the official Brazilian currency during the colonial period. A.B.H. Ferreira, *Novo Dicionário da Língua Portuguesa* 2nd edn (Rio de Janeiro, 1986), p. 504.
113. Eschwege, *op.cit.* p. 247.
114. Paula, *op.cit.* p. 31.
115. Gomes, *História da Siderurgia no Brasil op.cit.* pp. 141–7.
116. Eschwege, *op.cit.* p. 208.
117. *Ibid.*, p. 209.
118. *Ibid.*, p. 210.
119. *Ibid.*, p. 248.
120. *Ibid.*, p. 251.
121. Gomes, *História da Siderurgia no Brasil*, *op.cit.*, p. 109.
122. *Ibid.*, p. 109.
123. *Ibid.*, pp. 141–2.
124. Paula, *op.cit.* p. 38.
125. Gomes, *História da Siderurgia no Brasil*, *op.cit.*, p. 144.
126. Libby, *op.cit.* pp. 151–2.
127. Costa Sena, *op.cit.* pp. 140–1.
128. Paula, *op.cit.* p. 31.
129. Eschwege, *op.cit.* pp. 209–13.
130. *Ibid.*, pp. 247–54.
131. D.A. Giroletti, 'A Companhia e a Rodovia União e Indústria e o Desenvolvimento de Juiz de Fora, 1850 a 1900', Universidade Federal de Minas Gerais, mimeo, Belo Horizonte, 1980, pp. 18–9.
132. Companhia União e Indústria, *Relatório da Assembléia Geral dos Acionistas* (1857), pp. 38–9.
133. *Ibid.* (1856), p. 14.
134. *Ibid.*
135. Esteves, *op.cit.* pp. 149–52.
136. Companhia União e Indústria, *Relatório da Assembléia Geral dos Acionistas* (1866).
137. Esteves, *op.cit.* p. 224.
138. El-Kareh, *op.cit.* pp. 78–9.
139. Esteves, *op.cit.* p. 240.
140. Companhia União e Indústria, *Relatório da Assembléia Geral dos Acionistas* (1865, 1869, 1870, 1875).
141. Companhia Cedro e Cachoeira, 'Estatutos' (Cedro, 1883), pp. 7–8.
142. D.M. Mascarenhas, *Genealogia da Família Mascarenhas, 1824–1989* (Belo Horizonte, 1990), p. 183.
143. Mascarenhas, *Centenário da Fábrica do Cedro*, *op.cit.*, p. 140.
144. Vaz, *op.cit.* p. 95.
145. *Ibid.*, p. 150.
146. Mascarenhas, *Centenário da Fábrica do Cedro*, *op.cit.*, p. 245–7.
147. Vaz, *op.cit.* p. 151.
148. Mascarenhas, *Centenário da Fábrica do Cedro*, *op.cit.*, pp. 245–6.
149. Mascarenhas, *Genealogia da Família Mascarenhas*, *op.cit.*, p. 205.

202 *Notes*

150. Letter from Dario Diniz Mascarenhas to Theóphilo Marques Ferreira, 17 July 1892, reproduced in Giroletti, *Fábrica Convento e Disciplina, op.cit.,* p. 223.
151. Companhia Cedro e Cachoeira, 'Caixa de Correspondências Recebidas no. 16', 'Letter from Francisco de Paula Mascarenhas to Bernardo Mascarenhas, 16 June 1884'.
152. Companhia Cedro e Cachoeira, 'Caixa de Correspondências Recebidas no. 17', 'Letter from Francisco de Paula Mascarenhas to Bernardo Mascarenhas, 20 May 1885'.
153. Companhia Cedro e Cachoeira, 'Caixa de Correspondências Recebidas no. 41', 'Letter from Dario Diniz Mascarenhas to Francisco de Paula Mascarenhas, 7 February 1885'.
154. Companhia Cedro e Cachoeira, 'Caixa de Correspondências Recebidas no. 16', 'Letter from Francisco de Paula Mascarenhas to Bernardo Mascarenhas, 16 June 1884'.
155. *Ibid.,* 15 September 1884.
156. *Ibid.,* 13 June 1884.
157. Companhia Cedro e Cachoeira, 'Caixa de Correspondências Recebidas no. 16', 'Letter from Francisco de Paula Mascarenhas to Theóphilo Marques Ferreira, 2 September 1884'.
158. Companhia Cedro e Cachoeira, 'Caixa de Correspondências Recebidas no. 17', 'Letter from Francisco de Paula Mascarenhas to Bernardo Mascarenhas, 14 January 1885'.
159. Companhia Cedro e Cachoeira, 'Caixa de Correspondências Recebidas no. 41', 'Letter from Dario Diniz Mascarenhas to Francisco de Paula Mascarenhas, 7 February 1895'.
160. Companhia Cedro e Cachoeira, 'Caixa de Correspondências Recebidas no. 17', 'Letters from Francisco de Paula Mascarenhas to Bernardo Mascarenhas, 24 February 1885 and 25 April 1885'.
161. Companhia Cedro e Cachoeira, 'Caixa de Correspondências Caetano Mascarenhas, 1883–1912 – no. 149', 'Letter from Caetano Mascarenhas to José J. Fernandes Ramos, 23 March 1900'.
162. Companhia Cedro e Cachoeira, 'Caixa de Correspondências Caetano Mascarenhas, 1883–1912 – no. 149', 'Letter from Dario Diniz Mascarenhas to Caetano Mascarenhas, 16 January 1904'.
163. Companhia Cedro e Cachoeira, 'Caixa de Correspondências Recebidas no. 16', 'Letter from Francisco de Paula Mascarenhas to Bernardo Mascarenhas, 13 June 1884'.
164. Companhia Cedro e Cachoeira, 'Caixa de Correspondências Recebidas no. 17', 'Letter from Francisco de Paula Mascarenhas to Bernardo Mascarenhas, 14 April 1885'.
165. Mascarenhas, *Centenário da Fábrica do Cedro, op.cit.,* pp. 245–7.
166. Companhia Cachoeira de Macacos, 'Evoluçao da Cia. Têxtil Cachoeira de Macacos, 1886–1967', mimeographed notes distributed by the company.
167. Freitas, *op.cit.,* p. 27.
168. Companhia Cedro e Cachoeira, 'Caixa de Correspondências Recebidas no. 26', 'Letter from Américo Teixeira Guimarães to Theóphilo Marques Ferreira, 2 May 1889'.

169. Companhia Cedro e Cachoeira, 'Caixa de Correspondências Recebidas no. 36', 'Letter from Américo Teixeira Guimarães to Francisco de Paula Mascarenhas, 27 August 1893'.
170. M.A.G. Souza, *História de Itaúna* (Belo Horizonte, 1986), vol. I, p. 124.
171. Companhia de Tecidos Santanense, 'Estatutos' (1891).
172. The 15 shareholders holding at least 50 shares on 31 December 1895 were: Manoel José de Souza Moreira (670), Manoel Gonçalves de Souza Moreira (385), José Gonçalves de Souza Moreira (240), Francisco Gonçalves de Souza (210), Augusto Gonçalves de Souza Moreira (150), Vicente Gonçalves de Souza (150), Antônio Pereira de Mattos (150), Francisco Baeta Coelho (100), Antônio Maximiano de Campos (50), José Gonçalves de Souza (50), Joao Gonçalves de Souza (50), Francisco Manoel Franco (50), Francisco Bahia da Rocha (50), Rogério Candido de Andrade (50) and Thomaz Antônio d'Andrade (50). Companhia de Tecidos Santanense, 'Lista Nominativa dos Acionistas da Companhia' (1895), reproduced in J.W.T. Mello, *Santanense: Revoluçao Filosófica e Industrial em Sanct'Anna do São Joao Acima* (Belo Horizonte, 1991), pp. 252–3.
173. *Ibid.*, pp. 228–9.
174. Companhia de Tecidos Santanense, 'Ata da Assembléia Geral Ordinária dos Acionistas' (24 March 1899).
175. Letter from Bernardo Mascarenhas reproduced in Mascarenhas, *Bernardo Mascarenhas*, *op.cit.*, p. 118.
176. Oliveira, *Companhia Mineira de Eletricidade*, *op.cit.*, p. 48.
177. The members of the Mascarenhas family and the number of shares that each one held were: Bernardo Mascarenhas (400), Policena da Silva Mascarenhas (100), Francisco Mascarenhas (78), Vitor Mascarenhas (50), Caetano Mascarenhas (50), Viriato Diniz Mascarenhas (35), Theóphilo Marques Ferreira (30), Elvira Diniz Mascarenhas (25), Pacífico Mascarenhas (20), Antônio Diniz Mascarenhas (20), Altivo Diniz Mascarenhas (15) and Antônio Augusto Mascarenhas (10). *Ibid.*, p. 27.
178. *Ibid.*, p. 27.
179. Companhia Mineira de Eletricidade, 'Estatutos' (1888), reproduced in *O Pharol* (Juiz de Fora), 15 January 1888.
180. Oliveira, *Companhia Mineira de Eletricidade*, *op.cit.*, p. 27.
181. *Ibid.*, p. 41.
182. Mascarenhas, *Bernardo Mascarenhas*, *op.cit.*, p. 134.
183. Letter from Bernardo Mascarenhas to the Westinghouse Electric M. Company, reproduced in *ibid.*, p. 141.
184. Companhia Força e Luz Cataguazes-Leopoldina, 'Ata da 1a. Reunião da Diretoria' (1905).
185. L.S. Costa, *Cataguases Centenária: Dados para a sua História* (Cataguases, 1977), p. 541.
186. Companhia Força e Luz Cataguazes-Leopoldina, 'Ata da 25a. Reunião da Diretoria' (1909).
187. Costa, *op.cit.* p. 542.
188. Neto, *op.cit.*,

189. Companhia Força e Luz Cataguazes-Leopoldina, 'Ata da 27a. Reunião da Diretoria' (1910).
190. Companhia Força e Luz Cataguazes-Leopoldina, 'Ata da 29a. Reunião da Diretoria' (1910).
191. Companhia Força e Luz Cataguazes-Leopoldina, 'Relatório do Gerente' (1910), p. 9.

4 Technology

1. P. O'Brien, 'The Mainsprings of Technological Progress in Europe, 1750–1850', in P. Mathias and J.A. Davis (eds), *Innovation and Technology in Europe: From the Eighteenth Century to the Present Day* (Oxford, 1991), p. 6.
2. J.L. Anderson, *Explaining Long-Term Economic Change* (London, 1991), p. 41.
3. J.A. Schumpeter, *A Teoria do Desenvolvimento Econômico* 3rd. edn (São Paulo, 1988), p. 50.
4. P. Temin, *Casual Factors in American Economic Growth in the Nineteenth Century* (London, 1986), p. 31.
5. N. Rosenberg, *Inside the Black Box: Technology and Economics* (New York, 1990), pp. 5–6; and O'Brien, *op.cit.* pp. 7–9.
6. Anderson, *op.cit.* p. 44.
7. N. Rosenberg, *Perspectives on Technology* (New York, 1976), pp. 75–6.
8. C.T. Stewart and Y. Nihei, *Technology Transfer and Human Factors* (Lexington, 1987), p. 2.
9. A.C. Samli, 'Introduction', in A.C. Samli (ed.), *Technology Transfer: Geographic, Economic, Cultural, and Technical Dimensions* (Westport, 1985), pp. xv-xvii.
10. Stewart and Nihei, *op.cit.* p. 2.
11. D.J. Jeremy, 'Introduction: Some of the Larger Issues Posed by Technology Transfer', in D. J. Jeremy (ed.), *International Technology Transfer: Europe, Japan and the USA, 1700–1914* (Aldershot, 1991), pp. 1–3.
12. Rosenberg, *Inside the Black Box op.cit.*, pp. 246–7.
13. See N. Rosenberg, *Technology and American Economic Growth* (New York, 1972), pp. 59–86.
14. C. Freeman, 'Japan: A New National System of Innovation?', in G. Dosi, C. Freeman, R. Nelson, G. Silverberg and L. Soete (eds), *Technical Change and Economic Theory* (London, 1988), pp. 330–46.
15. A. Gerschenkron, *Economic Backwardness in Historical Perspective: A Book of Essays* (London, 1962), p. 8.
16. Rosenberg, *Inside the Black Box op.cit.*, pp. 247–9.
17. J. M Katz, 'Domestic Technology Generation in LDCs: A Review of Research Findings', in J. M. Katz (ed.), *Technology, Generation in Latin American Manufacturing Industries* (London, 1937), pp. 13–55.
18. Rosenberg, *Perspectives on Technology op.cit.*, pp. 154–68.
19. W. Suzigan, *Indústria Brasileira: Origem e Desenvolvimento* (São Paulo, 1986), pp. 122–3.

20. D.S. Landes, *The Unbound Prometheus: Technological Change and Industrial Development in Western Europe from 1750 to the Present* (Cambridge, 1969), pp. 41, 211–15.
21. D.J. Jeremy and D.H. Stapleton, 'Transfers between Culturally-Related Nations: The Movement of Textile and Railroad Technologies between Britain and The United States, 1780–1840', in D. J. Jeremy (ed.), *International Technology Transfer: Europe, Japan and the USA, 1700–1914* (Aldershot, 1991), pp. 31–9.
22. Landes, *op.cit.* pp. 211–15.
23. T.K. Derry and T.I. Williams, *A Short History of Technology: From the Earliest Times to A.D. 1900* (Oxford, 1960), p. 582.
24. Companhia Cedro e Cachoeira, 'Caixa de Correspondências no.2', 'Contract between Van Vlick Lidgerwood and Mascarenhas & Irmãos, 27 September 1870'.
25. Companhia Cedro e Cachoeira, 'Copiador de Cartas de 1881 – Mascarenhas Irmaos', 'Letter from Mascarenhas Irmãos to the president of the Sete Lagoas City Council, 13 March 1882'.
26. Letter from Bernardo Mascarenhas on 13 April 1874 from Manchester, reproduced in G.M. Mascarenhas, *Centenário da Fábrica do Cedro, 1872–1972* (Belo Horizonte, 1972), pp. 97–8.
27. Letter from Bernardo Mascarenhas on 18 December 1874 from New York, reproduced in *ibid.*, pp. 99–100.
28. Companhia Cedro e Cachoeira, 'Relatório da Diretoria' (1883), p. 2.
29. Companhia Cedro e Cachoeira, 'Caixa de Correspondências no.16', 'Letter from Max Nothmann, 1 July 1884'.
30. *Ibid.*, no. 21, 21 May 1887.
31. Companhia Cedro e Cachoeira, 'Caixa de Correspondências no.30', 'Letter from Robert L. Kerr to Theóphilo Marques Ferreira, 6 August 1891'.
32. Companhia Cedro e Cachoeira, 'Caixa de Correspondências no.36', 'Letter from Robert L. Kerr to Francisco de Paula Mascarenhas, 29 September 1893'.
33. Companhia Cedro e Cachoeira, 'Caixa de Correspondências no.41', 'Letter from James Leffel & Co. to Francisco de Paula Mascarenhas, 19 January 1895'.
34. Companhia Cedro e Cachoeira, 'Caixa de Correspondências no.50', 'Letter from Robert L. Kerr to Aristides Mascarenhas, 23 February 1899'.
35. Companhia Cedro e Cachoeira, 'Caixa de Correspondências no.58', 'Letter from Robert L. Kerr to Caetano Mascarenhas, 27 November 1901'.
36. Companhia Cedro e Cachoeira, 'Caixa de Correspondências no.50', 'Letter from Victor Uslaender, 27 January 1899'.
37. Companhia Cedro e Cachoeira, 'Caixa de Correspondências no.14', 'Letter from Max Nothmann, 19 November 1883'.
38. Companhia Cedro e Cachoeira, 'Caixa de Correspondências no.57', 'Letter from Blum & Company, 24 July 1901'.
39. N.L. Mascarenhas, *Bernardo Mascarenhas: O Surto Industrial de Minas Gerais* (Rio de Janeiro, 1954), p. 125.

40. N.A.M. Freitas, 'Cia. Têxtil Cachoeira de Macacos: Empresa que deu Origem a uma Cidade', Fundação Mineira de Arte Aleijadinho/Escola Superior de Artes Plásticas, mimeo, Belo Horizonte, 1990, p. 27.
41. M.A.G. Souza, *História de Itaúna* (Belo Horizonte, 1986), vol. I, p. 126.
42. M.L.P. Costa, *A Fábrica de Tecidos de Machado* (Belo Horizonte, 1989), p. 35.
43. B.S. Veiga, *Almanack Sul Mineiro* (Campanha, 1874), p. 148.
44 Costa, *op.cit.* p. 35.
45. S.J. Stein, *Origens e Evolução da Indústria Têxtil no Brasil, 1850–1950* (Rio de Janeiro, 1950), p. 51.
46. J.M. Katz, 'Domestic Technology Generation in LDCs: A Review of Research Findings', in J. M. Katz (eds.), *Technology Generation in Latin American Manufacturing Industries* (London, 1987), pp. 28–30.
47. H. Uchida, 'The Transfer of Electrical Technologies from the United States and Europe to Japan, 1869–1914', in D. J. Jeremy (ed.), *International Technology Transfer: Europe, Japan and the USA, 1700–1914* (Aldershot, 1991), pp. 219–30.
48. Gerschenkron, *op.cit.* p. 8.
49. Uchida, *op.cit.* pp. 219–30.
50. *Ibid.*, pp. 219–30.
51. P. Oliveira, *Companhia Mineira de Eletricidade: pioneira da iluminação hidrelétrica na América do Sul* (Juiz de Fora, 1969), pp. 29–31.
52. Companhia Mineira de Eletricidade, *O Pharol* (Juiz de Fora), 27 March 1891.
53. *Ibid.*, 8 August 1896.
54. *Panorama do Setor de Energia Elétrica no Brasil* ed. R.F. Dias, L.M.M. Cabral, P.B.B. Cachapuz and S.T.N. Lamarrão (Rio de Janeiro, 1988), p. 32.
55. Suplemento Minas Gerais, *Companhia Força e Luz Cataguazes-Leopoldina* (Cataguazes, 1913).
56. Derry and Williams, *op.cit.* pp. 429–30.
57. *Ibid.*, p. 431.
58. R.J. Forbes, 'Roads to c 1900', in C. Singer, E.J. Holmyard, A.R. Hall and T.I. Williams (eds), *A History of Technology, vol. IV (Oxford, 1958), p. 531.*
59. Derry and Williams, *op.cit.* p. 433.
60. W.L. Bastos, *Mariano Procópio Ferreira Lage: Sua Vida, Sua Obra, Descendência, Genealogia* (Juiz de Fora, 1991), pp. 23–9.
61. Forbes, *op.cit.* pp. 536–7.
62. Companhia União e Indústria, *Relatório da Assembléia Geral dos Acionistas* (1857), pp. 21–3.
63. I. McNeil, 'Roads, Bridges and Vehicles', in I. McNeil (ed.), *An Encyclopaedia of the History of Technology* (London, 1990), pp. 438–9.
64. Companhia União e Indústria, *Relatório da Assembléia Geral dos Acionistas* (1857), p. 23.
65. *Ibid.* (1856) p. 22.
66. W.L. von Eschwege, *Pluto Brasiliensis* vol. II (Berlin, 1833; reprinted Belo Horizonte/São Paulo, 1979), p. 203.
67. Libby, *op.cit.* p. 152.
68. Eschwege, *op.cit.* p. 203.

69. *Ibid.*, p. 205.
70. Libby, *op.cit.* pp. 147–8.
71. J.A. Paula, 'Dois Ensaios sobre a Gênese da Industrialização em Minas Gerais: a Siderurgia e a Indústria Têxtil', in Anais do II Seminário sobre a Economia Mineira (Belo Horizonte, 1983), p. 34.
72. Eschwege, *op.cit.* pp. 207–14, 247–54.
73. J.C. Costa Sena, 'Viagem de Estudos Metallurgicos no Centro da Provincia de Minas', in *Annaes da Escola de Minas*, no.1 (Ouro Preto, 1881), pp. 134–5.
74. *Ibid.*, pp. 117–41.
75. F.A.M. Gomes, *História da Siderurgia no Brasil* (Belo Horizonte, 1983), p. 84.
76. Eschwege, *op.cit.* p. 211.
77. Libby, *op.cit.* pp. 159–60.
78. C.A. Oliveira, 'A Metallurgia de Ferro em Minas', in Annaes da Escola de Minas, no.5 (Ouro Preto, 1902), p. 79.
79. *Ibid.*, p. 76.
80. J.R. Harris, *The British Iron Industry, 1700–1850* (London, 1988), pp. 12–13.
81. For a detailed account of the history of the technological development of the British iron industry in the nineteenth century see M. Atkinson and C. Barber, *The Growth and Decline of the South Wales Iron Industry, 1760–1880* (Cardiff, 1987) chapter 3, and Harris, *op.cit.*
82. C.K. Hyde, 'Iron and Steel Technologies Moving Between Europe and the United States, before 1914', in D. J. Jeremy (ed.), *International Technology Transfer: Europe, Japan and the USA, 1700–1914* (Aldershot, 1991), pp. 51–2; and W.K.V. Gale, 'Ferrous Metals', in I. McNeil (ed.), *An Encyclopaedia of the History of Technology* (London, 1990), pp. 153–76.
83. Gale, *op.cit.* p. 167.
84. Rosenberg, *Technology and American Economic Growth op.cit.*, pp. 77–8.
85. F.P. Oliveira, 'Estudos Siderúrgicos na Provincia de Minas', in *Annaes da Escola de Minas de Ouro Preto*, no.3 (Ouro Preto, 1884), pp. 108–9.
86. Libby, *op.cit.* pp. 148–9.
87. Gomes, *op.cit.* p. 112.
88. Costa Sena, *op.cit.* pp. 117–41.
89. Gomes, *op.cit.* p. 110.
90. Suzigan, *op.cit.* pp. 277–8.
91. Gomes, *op.cit.* pp. 303–50.
92. Rosenberg, *Perspectives on Technology, op.cit.*, pp. 154–68.
93. R. Kaplinsky, 'Technology Transfer, Adaptation and Generation: A Framework for Evaluation', in M. Chatterji (ed.), *Technology Transfer in the Developing Countries* (London, 1990), pp. 19–20.
94. Rosenberg, *Technology and American Economic Growth op.cit.*, p. 77.
95. Gomes, *op.cit.* pp. 79–85.
96. Eschwege, *op.cit.* p. 250.
97. Gomes, *op.cit.* p. 109.
98. *Ibid.*, p. 109.
99. *Ibid.*, pp. 109–13.

100. Libby, *op.cit.* p. 137.
101. Eschwege, *op.cit.* p. 207.
102. *Ibid.*, p. 208.
103. *Ibid.*, p. 210.
104. Bastos, *op.cit.* pp. 15–16.
105. Companhia União e Indústria, *Relatório da Assembléia Geral dos Acio-nistas* (1857), p. 21.
106. A.M. Vaz, Cia. *Cedro e Cachoeira: História de uma Empresa Familiar, 1883–1987* (Belo Horizonte, 1990), p. 50.
107. Mascarenhas, *Bernardo Mascarenhas op.cit.*, p. 37.
108. Letter from Bernardo Mascarenhas on 18 December 1874 from New York, reproduced in *ibid.*, pp. 64–6.
109. Companhia Cedro e Cachoeira, 'Caixa de Correspondências no.15', 'Letter from Robert L. Kerr to Bernardo Mascarenhas, 17 April 1884'.
110. D.A. Giroletti, *Fábrica Convento Disciplina* (Belo Horizonte, 1991), p. 85.
111. Freitas, *op.cit.* p. 27.
112. Stein, *op.cit.* p. 50.
113. *The Longman Encyclopedia* p. 328.
114. Mascarenhas, *Bernardo Mascarenhas op.cit.*, p. 89.
115. Companhia Mineira de Eletricidade, *O Pharol*, vol.12 (Juiz de Fora), 12 November 1887.
116. Mascarenhas, *Bernardo Mascarenhas op.cit.*, 15–16.
117. Letter from Bernardo Mascarenhas to Robert L. Kerr on 21 February 1887, reproduced in *ibid.*, p. 93.
118. *Ibid.*, p. 115.
119. Gomes, *op.cit.* pp. 5–6.
120. Companhia Cedro e Cachoeira, 'Copiador de Cartas da Fábrica do Cedro – 18/10/1872 a 10/04/1879', 'Letter from Mascarenhas & Irmãos to Meilford de Lidgerwood, 18 February 1873'.
121. Companhia Cedro e Cachoeira, 'Caixa de Correspondências no.15', 'Letter from Robert L. Kerr to Bernardo Mascarenhas, 28 February 1884'.
122. Companhia Cedro e Cachoeira, 'Caixa de Correspondências no.29', 'Letter from Robert L. Kerr to Theóphilo Marques Ferreira, 24 April 1891'.
123. Costa, *op.cit.* pp. 35–6.
124. Companhia Cedro e Cachoeira, 'Caixa de Correspondências no.18', 'Letter from Robert L. Kerr to Bernardo Mascarenhas, 10 July 1885'.
125. Companhia Cedro e Cachoeira, 'Caixa de Correspondências no.35', 'Letter from Robert L. Kerr to Theóphilo Marques Ferreira, 2 March 1893'.
126. Companhia Cedro e Cachoeira, 'Caixa de Correspondências no.35', 'Letter from Francisco de Paula Mascarenhas to Theóphilo Marques Ferreira, 13 January 1893'.
127. Companhia Mineira de Eletricidade, *O Pharol* (Juiz de Fora), 27 March 1891.

128. Companhia Cedro e Cachoeira, 'Caixa de Correspondências no.15', 'Letter from Francisco de Paula Mascarenhas to Bernardo Mascarenhas, 4 January 1884'.
129. Companhia Cedro e Cachoeira, 'Caixa de Correspondências no.15', 'Letter from Robert L. Kerr to Bernardo Mascarenhas, 24 March 1884'.
130. *Ibid.*, 4 April 1884.
131. *Ibid.*, no. 18, 18 September 1885.
132. Companhia Cedro e Cachoeira, 'Caixa de Correspondências – Bernardo Mascarenhas, 1883–1899 – no.148', 'Letter from Bernardo Mascarenhas to Theóphilo Marques Ferreira, 20 April 1889'.
133. Companhia Cedro e Cachoeira, 'Caixa de Correspondências no.18', 'Letter from Robert L. Kerr to Bernardo Mascarenhas, 30 October 1885'.
134. Companhia Cedro e Cachoeira, 'Caixa de Correspondências no. 36', 'Letter from Henry Rogers Sons & Co. to Francisco de Paula Mascarenhas, 5 August 1893'.
135. Companhia Cedro e Cachoeira, 'Caixa de Correspondências no. 17', 'Letter from Francisco de Paula Mascarenhas to Bernardo Mascarenhas, 22 April 1885'.
136. Companhia Cedro e Cachoeira, 'Caixa de Correspondências no. 51', 'Letter from Robert L. Kerr to Aristides Mascarenhas, 15 June 1899'.
137. Companhia Cedro e Cachoeira, 'Caixa de Correspondências no. 58', 'Letter from Victor Uslaender & Co., 11 December 1901'.
138. Mascarenhas, *Bernardo Mascarenhas, op.cit.*, p. 140.
139. For a more detailed account of exchange rate variations in nineteenth-century Brazil see E.A. Cardoso, 'Exchange Rates in nineteenth-Century Brazil: An Econometric Model', in *The Journal of Development Studies*, vol. 19, no. 2, January 1983 pp. 170–8.
140. Companhia Mineira de Eletricidade, 'Letter from Bernardo Mascarenhas to the president of the City Council of Juiz de Fora on 7 June 1893'.
141. Companhia Cedro e Cachoeira, 'Caixa de Correspondências no. 51', 'Letter to Robert L. Kerr, 11 August 1899'.
142. B.A. Lundvall, 'Innovation as an Interactive Process: From User–Producer Interaction to the National System of Innovation', in G. Dosi, C. Freeman, R. Nelson, G. Silverberg and L. Soete (eds), *Technical Change and Economic Theory* (London, 1988), pp. 349–66.
143. Rosenberg, *Perspectives on Technology, op.cit.*, p. 168.
144. Gomes, *op.cit.* p. 79.
145. *Ibid.*, p. 109.
146. Eschwege, *op.cit.* p. 208.
147. Bastos, *op.cit.* p. 23.
148. See Companhia União e Indústria, *Relatório da Assembléia Geral dos Acionistas* (1856), pp. 13–4; (1857), p. 21; and (1866), annexe no. 12.
149. Mascarenhas, *Bernardo Mascarenhas, op.cit.*, p. 37.
150. *Ibid.*, pp. 63–4.
151. Freitas, *op.cit.* p. 27.

152. Companhia Cedro e Cachoeira, 'Copiador de Cartas da Fábrica do Cedro – 18/10/1872 a 10/04/1879', 'Letter from Mascarenhas & Irmãos to J.N. Gordon, 6 November 1872'.
153. Eschwege, *op.cit.* p. 248.
154. *Ibid.*, p. 208.
155. Libby, *op.cit.* pp. 147–8.
156. Companhia União e Indústria, *Relatório da Assembléia Geral dos Acionistas* (1857), p. 23.
157. Bastos, *op.cit.* pp. 40–1.
158. Eschwege, *op.cit.* p. 210.
159. Gomes, *op.cit.* p. 84.
160. Companhia União e Indústria, *Relatório da Assembléia Geral dos Acionistas* (1856), p. 22.
161. Vaz, *op.cit.* p. 50.
162. *Ibid.*, p. 50.
163. Companhia Cedro e Cachoeira, 'Copiador de Cartas de 1881 – Mascarenhas & Irmãos', 'Letter from Mascarenhas Irmãos to the president of the Sete Lagoas District Council, 13 March 1882'.
164. Companhia Cedro e Cachoeira, 'Caixa de Correspondências no. 16', 'Letter from Robert L. Kerr to Bernardo Mascarenhas, 8 July 1884'.
165. Companhia Cedro e Cachoeira, 'Caixa de Correspondências no. 16', 'Letter from Robert L. Kerr to Bernardo Mascarenhas, 31 July 1884'.
166. Costa, *op.cit.* pp. 35–6.
167. Freitas, *op.cit.* p. 27.
168. J.W.T. Mello, *Santanense: Revolução Filosófica e Industrial em Sanct'Anna do São João Acima* (Belo Horizonte, 1991), p. 142.
169. Mascarenhas, *Bernardo Mascarenhas*, *op.cit.*, p. 120.
170. Companhia Força e Luz Cataguazes-Leopoldina, *80 Anos da Companhia Força e Luz Cataguazes-Leopoldina: Uma Luz sobre a História* (1985), p. 1.
171. Bastos, *op.cit.* p. 30.
172. F. Iglésias, *Política Econômica do Governo Provincial Mineiro: 1835–1889* (Rio de Janeiro, 1958), p. 165.
173. Rosenberg, *Perspectives on Technology*, *op.cit.*, pp. 154–68.
174. R.H. Mattoon, 'Railroads, Coffee, and Big Business in São Paulo Brazil', in *Hispanic American Historical Review*, vol. 57, no. 2, May 1977, pp. 289–93.
175. Hyde, *op.cit.* pp. 52–70.
176. Libby, *op.cit.* p. 141.
177. Eschwege, *op.cit.* pp. 247–54.
178. Gomes, *op.cit.* p. 83.
179. Libby, *op.cit.* p. 149.
180. Eschwege, *op.cit.*, p. 208.
181. *Ibid.*, pp. 257–8.
182. A.O. Esteves, 'Mariano Procópio: Trabalhos Originais', in *Revista do Instituto Histórico e Geográfico Brasileiro*, vol.230 (Rio de Janeiro, 1856), pp. 149–52.
183. Companhia União e Indústria, *Relatório da Assembléia Geral dos Acionistas* (1857), p. 21.

Notes 211

184. D.A. Giroletti, 'A Companhia e a Rodovia União e Indústria e o Desenvolvimento de Juiz de Fora, 1850 a 1900', Universidade Federal de Minas Gerais, mimeo, Belo Horizonte, 1980, p. 27.
185. Companhia União e Indústria, *Relatório da Assembléia Geral dos Acionistas* (1856), p. 13.
186. Giroletti, 'A Companhia e a Rodovia União e Indústria', pp. 31–7.
187. Companhia Cedro e Cachoeira, 'Caixa de Correspondências no. 2', 'Contract of purchase of machinery signed by Mascarenhas & Irmãos and Gme. Van Vlick Lidgerwood, 27 September 1870'.
188. Companhia Cedro e Cachoeira, 'Copiador de Cartas da Fábrica do Cedro – 18/10/1872 a 10/04/1879', 'Letter from Mascarenhas & Irmãos to Meilford de Lidgerwood, 18 February 1873'.
189. Vaz, *op.cit.* p. 53.
190. Giroletti, *Fábrica Convento Disciplina op.cit.*, pp. 84–6.
191. *Ibid.*, pp. 86–8.
192. Letter from Francisco de Paula Mascarenhas to Bernardo Mascarenhas on 9 June 1888, reproduced in *ibid.*, pp. 89–90.
193. Companhia Cedro e Cachoeira, 'Caixa de Correspondências no. 16', 'Letter from Robert L. Kerr to Bernardo Mascarenhas, 8 July 1884'.
194. Vaz, *op.cit.* p. 201.
195. Companhia Cedro e Cachoeira, 'Caixa de Correspondências no. 20', 'Letter from Robert L. Kerr to Bernardo Mascarenhas, 11 December 1886'.
196. Companhia Cedro e Cachoeira, 'Caixa de Correspondências no. 14', 'Letter from William Hutchinson to Robert L. Kerr, 7 January 1883'.
197. Companhia Cedro e Cachoeira, 'Caixa de Correspondências no. 20', 'Letter from Robert L. Kerr to Bernardo Mascarenhas, 2 August 1886'.
198. *Ibid.*, 11 December 1886.
199. Giroletti, *Fábrica Convento Disciplina, op.cit.*, pp. 94–5.
200. Companhia Cedro e Cachoeira, 'Caixa de Correspondências no. 41', 'Letter from Robert L. Kerr to Francisco de Paula Mascarenhas, 23 May 1895'.
201. *Ibid.*, no. 42, 8 August 1895.
202. Giroletti, *Fábrica Convento Disciplina op.cit.*, p. 96.
203. Companhia Cedro e Cachoeira, 'Caixa de Correspondências no. 56', 'Letter from Henry Rogers, Sons & Co. of Brazil to Companhia Cedro e Cachoeira, 28 May 1901'.
204. Companhia Cedro e Cachoeira, 'Caixa de Correspondências no. 35', 'Letter from Manoel José de Souza Moreira to Aristides Mascarenhas, 24 April 1893'.
205. Freitas, *op.cit.* p. 27.
206. Stein, *op.cit.* p. 52.
207. Oliveira, *Companhia Mineira de Eletricidade, op.cit.*, p. 31.
208. Letter from Bernardo Mascarenhas, reproduced in Mascarenhas, *Bernardo Mascarenhas op.cit.*, p. 141.
209. Companhia Mineira de Eletricidade, 'Declaração da Companhia Mineira de Eletricidade', 'Letter issued by the Companhia Mineira

de Eletricidade informing its customers the increase in the price of the domestic lighting service, 10 June 1893'.
210. Kaplinsky, *op.cit.* pp. 19–26.
211. Rosenberg, *Technology and American Economic Growth*, *op.cit.*, p. 61.
212. Kaplinsky, *op.cit.* pp. 19–26.
213. Libby, *op.cit.* pp. 137–8.
214. Eschwege, *op.cit.* pp. 208–11.
215. Gomes, *op.cit.* p. 84.
216. Companhia União e Indústria, *Relatório da Assembléia Geral dos Acionistas* (1856), p. 22.
217. *Ibid.*, (1857), p. 23.
218. *Ibid.*, (1856), pp. 15–16.
219. Giroletti, *Fábrica Convento Disciplina*, *op.cit.*, pp. 61–2.
220. Companhia Cedro e Cachoeira, 'Caixa de Correspondências no. 16', 'Letter from Francisco de Paula Mascarenhas to Bernardo Mascarenhas, 2 June 1884'.
221. *Ibid.*, no. 17 12 May 1885.
222. *Ibid.*, no. 18, 24 September 1885.
223. *Ibid.*, no. 17, October 1885.
224. Companhia Cedro e Cachoeira, 'Caixa de Correspondências no. 19', 'Letter from Francisco de Paula Mascarenhas to Theóphilo Marques Ferreira, 18 May 1886'.
225. *Ibid.*, 28 May 1886.
226. Companhia Cedro e Cachoeira, 'Caixa de Correspondências Caetano Mascarenhas, 1883–1912 – no. 149', 'Letter from Dario Diniz Mascarenhas to Caetano Mascarenhas, 16 January 1904'.
227. Companhia Cedro e Cachoeira, 'Caixa de Correspondências no. 16', 'Letter from Robert L. Kerr to Bernardo Mascarenhas, 18 July 1884'.
228. *Ibid.*
229. *Ibid.*, no. 18, 30 October 1885.
230. *Ibid.*, no. 19, 16 July 1886.
231. *Ibid.*, no. 18, 18 September 1885.
232. Companhia Cedro e Cachoeira, 'Caixa de Correspondências no. 41', 'Letter from James Leffel & Co. to Francisco de Paula Mascarenhas, 19 January 1895'.
233. Mascarenhas, *Bernardo Mascarenhas*, *op.cit.*, pp. 131–2.
234. *Ibid.*, pp. 132–4.
235. *Ibid.*, pp. 140–8.

Conclusion

1. For a discussion of the pattern of business development in the twentieth century in Brazil see P. Evans, *Dependent Development: The Alliance of Multinational, State and Local Capital in Brazil* (Princeton, 1979)

Bibliography

PRIMARY SOURCES

Manuscripts

Companhia Cachoeira dos Macacos, 'Livro de Registro de Empregados, 1926–1931'.

Companhia Cachoeira dos Macacos, 'Livro de Registro de Empregados, 1935'.

Companhia Cedro e Cachoeira, 'Relatório da Diretoria' (1883–1889).

Companhia Cedro e Cachoeira, 'Caixa de Correspondências Bernardo Mascarenhas, 1883–1899 – no. 148'.

Companhia Cedro e Cachoeira, 'Caixa de Correspondências Recebidas' (1872–1901).

Companhia Cedro e Cachoeira, 'Relatório e Quadro Demonstrativo de Lucros Apresentado pelo Dr Francisco Bahia da Rocha, Gerente da Fábrica de São Vicente' (1895).

Companhia Cedro e Cachoeira, 'Estatutos da Companhia Cedro e Cachoeira' (1883, 1891).

Companhia Cedro e Cachoeira, 'Estatutos da Fábrica do Cedro' (1872).

Companhia Cedro e Cachoeira, 'Copiador de Cartas da Fábrica do Cedro, 18/10/1872 a 10/04/1879'.

Companhia Cedro e Cachoeira, 'Copiador de Cartas, 1872–1879 – Mascarenhas & Irmãos'.

Companhia Cedro e Cachoeira, 'Copiador de Cartas de 1881 – Mascarenhas & Irmãos'.

Companhia Cedro e Cachoeira, 'Copiador de Cartas, 1878–1880 – Mascarenhas & Barbosa'.

Companhia Cedro e Cachoeira, 'Caixa de Correspôndências Caetano Mascarenhas, 1883–1912 – no. 149'.

Companhia Cedro e Cachoeira, 'Quarto Relatório apresentado Assembléia Geral dos Acionistas da Companhia Cedro & Cachoeira, em 15 de Março de 1887'.

Companhia Força e Luz Cataguazes-Leopoldina, 'Ata da 1a., Reunião da Diretoria' (1905).

Companhia Força e Luz Cataguazes-Leopoldina, 'Ata da 25a., Reunião da Diretoria' (1909).

Companhia Força e Luz Cataguazes-Leopoldina, 'Ata da 27a., Reunião da Diretoria' (1909).

Companhia Força e Luz Cataguazes-Leopoldina, 'Ata da 29a., Reunião da Diretoria' (1910).

Companhia Força e Luz Cataguazes-Leopoldina, 'Relatorio da Diretoria' (1911).

Companhia Força e Luz Cataguazes-Leopoldina, 'Relatório do Gerente' (1909–10).

213

214   *Bibliography*

Companhia Mineira de Eletricidade, 'Letter from Bernardo Mascarenhas to the president of the City Council of Juiz de Fora, 7 June 1893'.
Companhia Mineira de Eletricidade, 'Declaração da Companhia Mineira de Eletricidade'. 'Letter issued by the Companhia Mineira de Eletricidade informing its customers the increase in the price of the domestic lighting service, 10 June 1893'.
Companhia de Tecidos Santanense, 'Estatutos' (1891).
Companhia de Tecidos Santanense, 'Ata da Primeira Assembléia Geral Extraordinária dos Acionistas, 19 December 1891'.
Companhia de Tecidos Santanense, 'Registro de Empregados' (n.d.).
Companhia de Tecidos Santanense, 'Ata da Assembléia Ordinária dos Acionistas' (1893, 1894, 1899).
Companhia de Tecidos Santanense, 'Lista Nominativa dos Acionistas da Companhia' (1895).
'Receipt to Mariano Procópio Ferreira Lage signed by J.A. Brito, 29 March 1849', Biblioteca Nacional – Sessão de Manuscritos – Catálogo de Documentos Biográficos – Pasta C 1034–57.
'Letter to Mariano Procópio Ferreira Lage from the Minister and Secretary of the Affairs of the Empire, 22 April 1871'. Biblioteca Nacional – Sessão de Manuscritos – Catálogo de Documentos Biográficos – Pasta C 1034–57.

Printed

Official Publications

Directoria Geral de Estatistica, *Relatórios e Trabalhos Estatísticos* (Rio de Janeiro, 1872).
Diretoria Geral de Estatística, *Relatórios Annexo ao do Minsiterio dos Negocios do Imperio de 1876* (Rio de Janeiro, 1877).
Ministerio da Agricultura, Industria e Commercio, Directoria Geral de Estatistica, *Recenseamento do Brazil realizado em 1 de Setembro de 1920: Resumo Historico dos Inqueritos Censitarios Realizados no Brazil*, vol. I (Rio de Janeiro, 1922).
Ministério da Agricultura, Indústria e Commercio, *Recenseamento do Brazil Realizado em 1 de Setembro de 1920*, vol. IV (Rio de Janeiro, 1924), 2nd Part.
Ministerio da Agricultura, Commercio e Obras Publicas, *Relatório da Repartição dos Negocios da Agricultura, Commercio, Obras Publicas: Relatorio da Inspecção Geral das Obras Publicas do Municipio da Corte* (Rio de Janeiro, 1862).
Ministerio da Agricultura, Commercio e Obras Publicas, *Relatorio da Repartição dos Negocios da Agricultura, Commercio e Obras Publicas* (Rio de Janeiro, 1868–1869).
Parliamentary Papers, *Consular Reports*, LXIII (1861).

Company Reports

Companhia Cachoeira de Macacos, 'Evolução da Cia. Têxtil Cachoeira de Macacos, 1886–1967', mimeographed notes distributed by the company.

Companhia Força e Luz Cataguazes-Leopoldina, *80 Anos Companhia Força e Luz Cataguazes-Leopoldina: Uma Luz* (1988).

Companhia União e Indústria, *Relatório da Assembléia Geral dos Acionistas* (1856, 1857, 1860, 1861, 1862, 1863, 1864, 1865, 1866, 1869, 1870, 1872, 1875).

Contemporary Works

R.F. Burton, *Viagem aos Planaltos do Brasil (1868)*, vol. I (São Paulo, 1941).
J.C. Costa Sena, 'Viagem de Estudos Metallurgicos no Centro da Provincia de Minas', in *Annaes da Escola de Minas*, no. 1 (Ouro Preto, 1881), pp. 117–41.
P. Ferrand, 'A Indústria de Ferro no Brasil (Provincia de Minas Geraes)', in *Annaes da Escola de Minas*, no. 4 (Ouro Preto, 1885), pp. 167–88.
M.D. Graham, *Journal of a Voyage to Brazil and Residence There, During Part of the Years 1821, 1822, 1823* (London, 1824).
C.A. Oliveira, 'A Metallurgia de Ferro em Minas', in *Annaes da Escola de Minas*, no. 5 (Ouro Preto, 1902).
F.P. Oliveira, 'Estudos Siderúrgicos na Provincia de Minas', in *Annaes da Escola de Minas de Ouro Preto*, no. 3 (Ouro Preto, 1884).
The Banking Almanac, Directory, Year Book and Diary (London, 1889).
B.S. Veiga, *Almanach Sul Mineiro* (Campanha, 1874).

Newspapers and Periodicals

Gazeta de Leopoldina (Leopoldina), 24 March 1907; 19 May 1946.
Jornal Cataguases (Cataguases), 12 March 1906; 8 August 1908; 19 July 1908; 17 February 1935.
Minas Gerais, 23 May 1893; 5 January 1894; 11 February 1894; 21 February 1894.
O Pharol (Juiz de Fora), 15 January 1888; 27 March 1891; 8 August 189; 27 August 1897.
Suplemento Minas Gerais, *Companhia Força e Luz Cataguazes-Leopoldina* (Cataguazes, 1913).

SECONDARY SOURCES

C. Abel and C.M Lewis, 'General Introduction', in C. Abel and C.M. Lewis (eds), *Latin America: Economic Imperialism and the State* (London, 1991), pp. 1–25.
J.L. Anderson, *Explaining Long-Term Economic Change* (London, 1991).
História Empresarial Vivida, ed. Cleber Aquino (São Paulo, 1987).
L.A.V. Arantes, 'As Origens da Burguesia Industrial em Juiz de Fora', 1858/1912, Universidade Federal Fluminense, unpublished M.Sc. thesis, Niterói, 1991.
M. Atkinson and C. Barber, *The Growth and Decline of the South Wales Iron Industry, 1760–1880* (Cardiff, 1987).

216 Bibliography

R.K. Aufhauser, 'Slavery and Technological Change', in *Journal of Economic History*, vol. 34 (March, 1974), pp. 36–50.

Banco de Desenvolvimento de Minas Gerais, *Diagnóstico da Economia Mineira*, vol. I (Belo Horizonte, 1968).

R.C. Barquin, 'Some Introductory Notes on the Transfer of Technology', in D. Soen (ed.), *Industrial Development and Technology Transfer* (London, 1981), pp. 101–4.

H. Barreto, *The Entrepreneur in Microeconomic Theory: Disappearance and Explanation* (New York, 1989).

W.L. Bastos, *Mariano Procópio Ferreira Lage: Sua Vida, Sua Obra, Descendência, Genealogia*, 2nd edn (Juiz de Fora, 1991).

W.L. Bastos, *Francisco Baptista de Oliveira um Pioneiro: Sua Vida, Sua Obra, Sua Descendência, Genealogia* (Juiz de Fora, 1967).

L. Bethell, *The Abolition of the Brazilian Slave Trade. Britain and the Slave Trade Question, 1807–1869* (Cambridge, 1970).

L. Bethell and J.M. Carvalho, '1822–1850', in L. Bethell (ed.), *Brazil: Empire and Republic, 1822–1930* (Cambridge, 1989), pp. 45–112.

Brazilian Embassy/London, *Brazil's Energy and Heavy Industries*, no. 15 (London, 1977).

L.C. Bresser Pereira, *Empresários e Administradores no Brasil* (São Paulo, 1974).

A.P. Canabrava, 'A Grande Laboura', in S.B. Holanda (ed.), *História Geral da Civilização Brasileira – II. O Brasil Monárquico*, 4th edn vol. VI (São Paulo, 1985), pp. 85–137.

P. Cammack, 'State and Federal Politics in Minas Gerais, Brazil', Univerity of Oxford, unpublished Ph.D. thesis, Oxford, 1980.

W. Cano, *Raízes da concentração industrial em São Paulo*, 3rd edn (São Paulo, 1990).

R. Cantillon, *Essai sur la Nature du Commerce en Général* (London, 1931).

E.A. Cardoso, 'Desvalorizações Cambiais, Indústria e Café: Brasil, 1862–1906', in *Revista Brasileira de Economia*, vol. xxxv, no. 2 (1981), pp. 85–106.

E.A. Cardoso, 'Exchange Rates in Nineteenth-Century Brazil: An Econometric Model', in *Journal of Development Studies*, vol. 19, no. 2, January 1983, pp. 170–8.

F.H. Cardoso, *Empresário Industrial e Desenvolvimento Econômico* (São Paulo, 1964).

F.H. Cardoso, *Ideologias de la Burgesia Industrial en Sociedades Dependientes (Argentina y Brasil)* (Mexico, 1971).

F.H. Cardoso and E. Faletto, *Dependência e Desenvolvimento na América Latina: Ensaio de Interpretação Sociológica*, 6th edn (Rio de Janeiro, 1981).

F.H. Cardoso and E. Faletto, *Dependency and Development in Latin America* (London, 1979).

J.M. Cardoso de Mello, *O Capitalismo Tardio: Contribuição à Revisão Crítica da Formação e Desenvolvimento da Economia Brasileira* (São Paulo, 1982).

M. Casson, *The Entrepreneur: An Economic Theory* (Oxford, 1982).

C. Castro, *As Empresas Estrangeiras no Brasil, 1860–1913* (Rio de Janeiro, 1979).

A.D. Chandler, 'The United States Seedbed of Managerial Capitalism', in A.D. Chandler and H. Deams (eds), *Managerial Hierarchies: Comparative Perspectives on the Rise of Modern Industrial Enterprises* (Cambridge, Mass., 1980), pp. 9–40.

A.D. Chandler, *The Visible Hand: The Managerial Revolution in American Business* (Cambridge, Mass., 1977).

A.D. Chandler, *Strategy and Structure: Chapters in the History of the American Industrial Enterprise*, 7th edn (Cambridge, Mass, 1991).

R. Conrad, *The Destruction of Brazilian Slavery:1850–1888* (Berkeley, 1972).

R. Conrad, *World of Sorrow: The African Slave Trade to Brazil* (Baton Rouge, 1986).

M.L.P. Costa, *A Fábrica de Tecidos de Machado* (Belo Horizonte, 1989).

L.S. Costa, *Cataguases Centenária: Dados para a sua História* (Cataguases, 1977).

C. Dahlman and L. Westphal, 'The Transfer of Technology: Factors in the Acquisition of Technology', in *Finance and Development*, December 1983, pp. 6–9.

W. Dean, *A industrialização de São Paulo* (São Paulo, 1971).

W. Dean, 'Economy', in L. Bethell (ed.), *Brazil: Empire and Republic, 1822–1930* (Cambridge, 1989), pp. 217–56.

W. Dean, *Rio Claro: A Brazilian Plantation System, 1820–1920* (Stanford, 1976).

W. Dean, 'The Planter as Entrepreneur: The Case of São Paulo', in *Hispanic America Historical Review*, vol. xxxvi, no. 2 (1966), pp. 138–52.

A. Delfim Netto, *O Problema do Café no Brasil* (São Paulo, 1959).

T.K. Derry and T.I. Williams, *A Short History of Technology: From the Earliest Times to A.D. 1900* (Oxford, 1960).

R.F. Dias, L.M.M. Cabral, P.B.B. Panorama do Setor de Energia Elétrica no Brasil, Cachapuz and S.T.N. Lamarrão (eds) (Rio de Janeiro, 1988).

E. Diniz, *Empresário, Estado e Capitalismo no Brasil, 1930–45* (São Paulo, 1978).

M.C. Eakin, *The St John d'El Rey Mining Company and the Morro Velho Gold Mine* (Durham, 1989).

P.L. Eisenberg, *A Mentalidade dos Fazendeiros no Congresso Agrícola de 1878* (São Paulo, 1990).

A.C. El-Kareh, *Filha Branca de Mãe Preta: A Companhia de Estrada de Ferro D. Pedro II, 1855–1865* (Petrópolis, 1982).

F. Engels, *The Condition of the Working Class in England* (London, 1987).

W.L. von Eschwege, *Pluto Brasiliensis*, vol. II (Berlin, 1833; reprinted Belo Horizonte/São Paulo, 1979).

A.O. Esteves, *Album do Município de Juiz de Fora* (Belo Horizonte, 1914).

A.O. Esteves, 'Mariano Procópio', in *Revista do Instituto Histórico e Geográfico Brasileiro*, vol. 230, January–March, 1956, pp. 7–398.

P. Evans, *Dependent Development: the Alliance of Multinational, State and Local Capital in Brazil* (Princeton, 1979).

A. Faria, *Mauá* (Rio de Janeiro, 1926).

B. Fausto, 'Society and Politics', in L. Bethell (ed.), *Brazil: Empire and Republic, 1822–1930* (Cambridge, 1989), pp. 257–307.

A.B.H Ferreira, *Novo Dicionário da Língua Portuguesa*, 2nd edn (Rio de Janeiro, 1986).

R.J. Forbes, 'Roads to c 1900', in C. Singer, E.J. Holmyard, A.R. Hall, and T.I. Williams (eds), *A History of Technology* vol. IV (Oxford, 1958), pp. 520–47.

M.S.C. Franco, *Homens Livres na Ordem Escravocrata* (São Paulo, 1969).

A.G. Frank, *Capitalism and Underdevelopment in Latin America: Historical studies of Chile and Brazil* (New York, 1967).

C. Freeman, 'Japan: A New National System of Innovation?' in G. Dosi, C. Freeman, R. Nelson, G. Silverberg and L. Soete (eds), *Technical Change and Economic Theory* (London, 1988), pp. 330–48.

N.A.M. Freitas, 'Cia. Têxtil Cachoeira dos Macacos: Empresa que deu Origem a uma Cidade', Fundação Mineira de Arte Aleijadinho/Escola Superior de Artes Plásticas, mimeo, Belo Horizonte, 1990.

W. Fritsch, *External Constraints on Economic Policy in Brazil, 1889–1930* (London, 1988).

C. Furtado, *Analise do 'Modelo' Brasileiro*, 7th edn (Rio de Janeiro, 1982).

C. Furtado, *Formação Econômica do Brasil*, 16th edn (São Paulo, 1979).

C. Furtado, *The Economic Growth of Brazil: A Survey from Colonial to Modern Times* (Los Angeles, 1965).

W.K.V. Gale, 'Ferrous Metals', in I. McNeil (ed.), *An Encyclopaedia of the History of Technology* (London, 1990), pp. 146–85.

A. Gerschenkron, *Economic Backwardness in Historical Perspective: A Book of Essays* (London, 1962).

D.A. Giroletti, *A Industrialização de Juiz de Fora: 1850–1930* (Juiz de Fora, 1988).

D.A. Giroletti, 'A Modernização Capitalista em Minas Gerais: A Formação do Operariado Industrial e de uma Nova Cosmovisão', Universidade Federal do Rio de Janeiro/Museu Nacional, unpublished Ph.D. thesis, Rio de Janeiro, 1987.

D.A. Giroletti, 'A Formação do Empresário Industrial', Universidade Federal de Minas Gerais, mimeo, Belo Horizonte, 1991.

D.A. Giroletti, *Fábrica Convento Disciplina* (Belo Horizonte, 1991).

D.A. Giroletti, 'A Companhia e a Rodovia União e Indústria e o Desenvolvimento de Juiz de Fora, 1850 a 1900', Universidade Federal de Minas Gerais, mimeo, Belo Horizonte, 1980.

F.A.M. Gomes, *História da Siderurgia no Brasil* (Belo Horizonte/São Paulo, 1983).

F.A.M. Gomes, 'A Eletrificação no Brasil', in *Caderno História e Energia*, no. 2 (São Paulo, 1986), October.

J. Gorender, *A Burguesia Brasileira*, 6th edn (São Paulo, 1986).

J. Gorender, *O Escravismo Colonial* (São Paulo, 1978).

R. Graham, *Britain and the Onset of Modernization in Brazil, 1850–1914* (Cambridge, 1968).

R. Graham, '1850–1870', in L. Bethell (ed.), *Brazil: Empire and Republic, 1822–1930* (Cambridge, 1989), pp. 113–60.

G. Guimarães, *Francisco José de Andrade Botelho* (Belo Horizonte, 1950).

L. Hannah, 'Visible and Invisible Hands in Great Britain', in A.D. Chandler and H. Demas (eds), *Managerial Hierarchies: Comparative Perspectives on the Rise of Modern Industrial Enterprises* (Cambridge, Mass., 1980), pp. 41–76.

L. Hannah, *The Rise of the Corporate Economy*, 2nd edn (London, 1983).

J.R. Harris, *The British Iron Industry, 1700–1850* (London, 1988).

R.F. Hébert and A.N. Link, *The Entrepreneur: Mainstream Views and Radical Critiques* (New York, 1982).

W.T. Hogan, *Economic History of the Iron and Steel Industry in the United States* (Lexington, 1971).

S.B. Holanda, *Raízes do Brasil*, 21st edn (Rio de Janeiro, 1982).

T.H. Holloway, *The Brazilian Coffee Valorization of 1906: Regional Politics and Economic Dependence* (Madison, 1975).

E. Hopkins, *A Social History of the English Working Classes, 1815–1945* (London, 1979).

C.K. Hyde, 'Iron and Steel Technologies Moving Between Europe and the United States, Before 1914', in D.J. Jeremy (ed.), *International Technology Transfer: Europe, Japan and the USA, 1700–1914* (Aldershot, 1991), pp. 51–73.

O. Ianni, *Industrialização e Desenvolvimento Social no Brasil* (Rio de Janeiro, 1963).

F. Iglésias, 'Minas Gerais', in S.B. Holanda (ed.), *História Geral da Civilização Brasileira – II. O Brasil Monárquico*, 4th edn, vol. IV (São Paulo, 1985), pp. 364–412.

F. Iglésias, *Política Econômica do Governo Provincial Mineiro: 1835–1889* (Rio de Janeiro, 1958).

H. Jaguaribe, *Desenvolvimento Econômico e Desenvolvimento Político* (Rio de Janeiro, 1962).

D.J. Jeremy, 'Introduction: Some of the Larger Issues Posed by Technology Transfer', in D.J. Jeremy (ed.), *International Technology Transfer: Europe, Japan and the USA, 1700–1914* (Aldershot, 1991), pp. 1–5.

D.J. Jeremy and D.H. Stapleton, 'Transfers between Culturally-Related Nations: The Movement of Textile and Railroad Technologies between Britain and The United States, 1780–1840', in D.J. Jeremy (ed.), *International Technology Transfer: Europe, Japan and the USA, 1700–1914* (Aldershot, 1991), pp. 31–48.

R. Kaplinsky, 'Technology Transfer, Adaptation and Generation: A Framework for Evaluation', in M. Chatterji (ed.), *Technology Transfer in the Developing Countries* (London, 1990), pp. 19–26.

J.M. Katz, 'Domestic Technology Generation in LDCs: A Review of Research Findings', in J.M. Katz (ed.), *Technology Generation in Latin American Manufacturing Industries* (New York, 1987), pp. 13–55.

I.M. Kirzner, *Competition and Entrepreneurship* (Chicago, 1973).

J. Kocka, 'The Modern Industrial Enterprise in Germany', in A.D. Chandler and H. Deams (eds), *Managerial hierarchies: Comparative Perspectives on the Rise of Modern Industrial Enterprises* (Cambridge, Mass., 1980), pp. 77–116.

L. Kowarick, *Trabalho e Vadiagem: a Origem do Trabalho Livre no Brasil* (São Paulo, 1987).

M.L. Lamounier, 'Between Slavery and Free labour: Experiments with Free Labour and Patterns of Slave Emancipation in Brazil and Cuba c.1830–1888', University of London, unpublished Ph.D. thesis, 1993.

D.S. Landes, *The Unbound Prometheus: Technological Change and Industrial Development in Western Europe from 1750 to the Present* (Cambridge, 1969).

C.M. Lewis, *Public Policy and Private Initiative: Railway Building in São Paulo, 1860–1889* (London, 1991).

C.M. Lewis, 'Historia Económica y Historia Empresarial: Tendencias recientes en la Literatura Brasileña, c.1850–1945' (mimeo, paper presented at XXVII Asemblea CLADEA, La Gerencia en la América Latina: Experiencias Comparativas, Universidad de los Andes, Bogotá, Octubre 21 a 24 de 1992).

D.C. Libby, *Trabalho Escravo e Capital Estrangeiro no Brasil: O Caso de Morro Velho* (Belo Horizonte, 1984).

D.C. Libby, *Transformação e Trabalho em uma Economia Escravista: Minas Gerais no Século XIX* (São Paulo, 1988).

J.H. Lima, *Café e Indústria em Minas Gerais (1870–1920)* (Petrópolis, 1981).

The Longman Encyclopaedia.

B.A. Lundvall, 'Innovation as an Interactive Process: From User-Producer Interaction to the National System of Innovation', in G. Dosi, C. Freeman, R. Nelson, G. Silverberg, and L. Soete (eds), *Technical Change and Economic Theory* (London, 1988), pp. 349–69.

H. Lydall, *The Entrepreneurial Factor in Economic Growth* (London, 1992).

A. Martins Filho and R.B. Martins, 'Slavery in a Non-export economy: Nineteenth-Century Minas Gerais Revisited', in *Hispanic American Historical Review*, vol. 63(3) pp. 537–68, 1983.

R.B. Martins, 'A Indústria Têxtil Doméstica de Minas Gerais no Século XIX', in *Anais do II Seminário sobre a Economia Brasileira* (Belo Horizonte, 1983), pp. 77–94.

R.B. Martins, 'Growing in Silence: The Slave Economy of Nineteenth-Century Minas Gerais', Vanderbilt University, unpublished Ph.D. thesis, Nashville, 1980.

R.B. Martins, 'Minas Gerais, Século XIX: Tráfico e Apego à Escravidão numa Economia Não-Exportadora', in *Estudos Econômicos*, vol. 13(1), pp. 181–209, January–April, 1983.

R.B. Martins and M.C.S. Martins, 'As Exportações de Minas Gerais no Século XIX', in *Seminário Sobre a Economia Mineira* (Diamantina, 1982), September, pp. 105–20.

K. Marx, *Capital*, vol. I (London, 1988).

D.M. Mascarenhas, *Genealogia da Família Mascarenhas, 1824–1989* (Belo Horizonte, 1990).

G.M. Mascarenhas, *Centenário da Fábrica do Cedro, 1872–1972* (Belo Horizonte, 1972).

N.L. Mascarenhas, *Bernardo Mascarenhas: o Surto Industrial de Minas Gerais* (Rio de Janeiro, 1954).

P. Mathias, *The First Industrial Nation: The Economic History of Britain, 1700–1914*, 2nd edn (London, 1983).

R.H. Mattoon, 'Railroads, Coffee and Big Business in São Paulo Brazil', in *Hispanic American Historical Review*, lvii, no. 2 (1977), pp. 273–92.

T.K. McCraw, *The Essential Alfred Chandler: Essays Toward a Historical Theory of Big Business* (Boston, 1991).

D. McDowall, *The Light: Brazilian Traction, Light and Power Company Limited, 1899–1945* (Toronto, 1988).

H. Mcleod, *Religion and the Working Class in Nineteenth-Century Britain* (London, 1984).

I. McNeil, 'Roads, Bridges and Vehicles', in I. McNeil (ed.), *An Encyclopaedia of the History of Technology,* (London, 1990).

J.W.T. Mello, *Santanense: Revolução Filosófica e Industrial em Sanct'Anna do São João Acima* (Belo Horizonte, 1991).

P.C. Mello and R.W. Slenes, 'Análise Econômica da Escravidão no Brasil', in P. Neuhaus (ed.), *Economia Brasileira: Uma Visão Histórica* (Rio de Janeiro, 1980), pp. 89–122.

Z.M.C. Mello, *Metamorfoses da Riqueza: São Paulo, 1845–1895* (São Paulo, 1985).

H.P. Melo, *O Café e a Economia Fluminense: 1889/1920* (Rio de Janeiro, 1993).

J.S. Mill, *Principles of Political Economy With Some Other Applications to Social Philosophy* (New York, 1987).

A.M.F.C. Monteiro, 'Empreendedores e Investidores em Indústria Têxtil no Rio de Janeiro: 1878–1895', Universidade Federal Fluminense, unpublished M.Sc. thesis, Niterói, 1985.

M.F. Neto, 'Os Frutos da Diversificaçao', in *Administração e Serviços,* June 1982.

O. Nogueira de Matos, *Café e Ferrovias: A Evolução Ferroviária de São Paulo e o Desenvolvimento da Cultura Cafeeira* (São Paulo, 1974).

P. O'Brien, 'The Mainsprings of Technological Progress in Europe, 1750–1850', in P. Mathias and J.A. Davis (eds), *Innovation and Technology in Europe: From the Eighteenth Century to the Present Day,* (Oxford, 1991), pp. 6–17.

K. Odaka, 'Redundancy Utilized: The Domestic Economics of Female Domestic Servants in Pre-War Japan', in J. Hunter (ed.), *Japanese Women Working* (Lava, 1993), pp. 16–36.

F. Oliveira, *A Economia Brasileira: Crítica à Razão Dualista* (Petropolis, 1988).

F. Oliveira, *A Economia da Dependência Imperfeita* (Rio de Janeiro, 1980).

P. Oliveira, *Companhia Mineira de Eletricidade: Pioneira da Iluminação Hidrelétrica na América do Sul* (Juiz de Fora, 1969).

P. Oliveira, *História de Juiz de Fora* (Juiz de Fora, 1966).

J.A. Paula, 'Dois Ensaios sobre a Gênese da Industrialização em Minas Gerais: a Siderurgia e a Indústria Têxtil', in *Anais do II Seminário sobre a Economia Mineira* (Belo Horizonte, 1983), pp. 19–73.

P.L. Payne, *British Entrepreneurship in the Nineteenth Century,* 2nd edn (London, 1988).

C.M. Peláez, *Economia Brasileira Contemporânea: Origens e Conjuntura Atual* (São Paulo, 1987).

C.M. Peláez, *História da Industrialização Brasileira: Crítica à Teoria Estruturalista no Brasil* (Rio de Janeiro, 1972).

M.T.S. Petrone, 'Imigração', in S.B. Holanda (ed.), *História Geral da Civilização Brasileira – III. O Brasil Republicano,* 4th edn, vol. IX (São Paulo, 1985), pp. 93–133.

V.C. Piccini, 'Deve-se Formar Empresários?', in *Anais da IX Reunião da ANPAD* (Florianópolis, 1985).

V.N. Pinto, 'Balanço das Transformaçoes Econômicas no Século XIX', in C.G. Mota (ed.), *Brasil em Perspectiva*, 17th edn (Rio de Janeiro, 1988).

L.C.T.D. Prado, 'Commercial Capital, Domestic Market and Manufacturing in Imperial Brazil: The Failure of Brazilian Economic Development in the XIXth Century', University of London, unpublished Ph.D. thesis, 1991.

C. Prado Júnior, *Formação do Brasil Contemporâneo*, 5th edn (São Paulo, 1957).

C. Prado Júnior, *História Econômica do Brasil*, 36th edn (São Paulo, 1988).

F.C. Prestes Motta, *Empresários e Hegemonia Política* (São Paulo, 1979).

D.S. Pugh and D.J. Hickson, *Writers on Organizations*, 4th edn (London, 1989).

F. Quesnay, *Quesnay's 'Tableau Économique'* (London, 1972).

D. Ricardo, *Principles of Political Economy and Taxation* (Cambridge, 1992).

E.W. Ridings, 'Business Associationalism, the Legitimation of Enterprise, and the Emergence of a Business Elite in Nineteenth-Century Brazil', in *Business History Review*, vol. 63 (Winter 1989), pp. 757–96.

N. Rosenberg, *Inside the Black Box: Technology and Economics* (New York, 1990).

N. Rosenberg, *Perspectives on Technology* (New York, 1976).

N. Rosenberg, *Technology and American Economic Growth* (New York, 1972).

W.W. Rostow, *The Stages of Economic Growth; A Non-communist Manifesto*, 3rd edn (New York, 1990).

F.A.M. Saes, *As Ferrovias de São Paulo, 1870–1940* (São Paulo, 1981).

F.A.M. Saes, *A Grande Empresa de Serviços Públicos na Economia Cafeeira* (São Paulo, 1986).

A.C. Samli, 'Introduction', in A.C. Samli (ed.), *Technology Transfer: Geographic, Economic, Cultural, and Technical Dimensions* (Westport, 1985), pp. xv–xviii.

T. Santos, *Dependencia y Cambio Social* (Mexico, 1970).

J.B. Say, *Tratado de Economia Política* (São Paulo, 1983).

J.A. Schumpeter, *A Teoria do Desenvolvimento Econômico*, 3rd edn (São Paulo, 1982).

S. Silva, *Expansão Cafeeira e Origem da Indústria no Brasil* (São Paulo, 1976).

P.I. Singer, *Desenvolvimento Econômico e Evolução Urbana: Evolução Econômica de São Paulo, Blumenau, Porto Alegre, Belo Horizonte e Recife* (São Paulo, 1968).

R.W. Slenes, 'Os Múltiplos de Porcos e Diamantes: A Economia Escravista de Minas Gerais no Século XIX', in *Caderno IFCH-UNICAMP*, vol. 17.

A. Smith, *Inquiry Into the Nature and Causes of the Wealth of the Nations* (Harmondsworth, 1970).

L.C. Soares, *A Manufatura na Formação Econômica e Social Escravista no Sudeste: Um Estudo das Atividades Manufatureiras na Região Fluminense, 1840–1880* (Niterói, 1980).

L.C. Soares, 'Urban Slavery in Nineteenth-Century Rio de Janeiro', University of London, unpublished Ph.D. thesis, 1988.

N.W. Sodré, *Formação Histórica do Brasil*, 10th edn (Rio de Janeiro, 1979).

N.W. Sodré, *História da Burguesia Brasileira* (Rio de Janeiro, 1964).

M.A.G. Souza, *História de Itaúna*, vol. I (Belo Horizonte, 1986).

A. Sousa Júnior, 'Guerra do Paraguai', in S.B. Holanda (ed.), *História Geral da Civilização Brasileira – II O Brasil Monárquico*, vol. VI (São Paulo, 1985), pp. 299–314.

J. Souza Martins, *Conde Matarazzo, o Empresário e a Empresa: Estudo de Sociologia do Desenvolvimento*, 2nd edn (São Paulo, 1976).

J. Souza Martins, *O Cativeiro da Terra* (São Paulo, 1979).

H.A. Spalding, *Organized Labor in Latin America: Historical Studies of Urban Workers in Dependent Societies* (New York, 1977).

L.J. Stehling, 'Trajetória da Indústria em Juiz de Fora', in *Revista do Instituto Histórico e Geográfico de Juiz de Fora*, vol. 2, no. 2 (Juiz de Fora, 1966), pp. 30–7.

S.J. Stein, *Origens e Evolução da Indústria Têxtil no Brasil, 1850–1950* (Rio de Janeiro, 1979).

S.J. Stein, *Vassouras: A Brazilian Coffee County, 1850–1900* (Cambridge, Mass., 1957).

C.T. Stewart and Y. Nihei, *Technology Transfer and Human Factors* (Lexington, 1987).

W. Suzigan, *Indústria Brasileira: Origem e Desenvolvimento* (São Paulo, 1986).

J.E. Sweigart, *Coffee Factorage and the Emergence of a Brazilian Capital Market, 1850–1888* (London, 1987).

T. Szmrecsanyi, 'Agrarian Bourgeoisie, Regional Government and the Origins of São Paulo's Modern Sugar Industry', paper presented at the Symposium on Elites and Economic Management in Latin America, XIX and XXth Centuries, 47th International Congress of Americanists, Tulane 1990.

P. Tamm, *Uma Dinastia de Tecelões*, 2nd edn (Belo Horizonte, 1960).

M.C. Tavares, *Da Substituição de Importações ao Capitalismo Financeiro: Ensaios sobre Economia Brasileira*, 11th edn (Rio de Janeiro, 1983).

P. Temin, *Casual Factors in American Economic Growth in the Nineteenth Century*, (London, 1986).

E.P. Thompson, *The Making of the Working Class* (London, 1980).

S. Topik, 'Recent Studies on the Economic History of Brazil', in *Latin American Research Review*, vol. XXIII, no. 1 (1988), pp. 175–95.

A.R.J. Turgot, *Reflexions on the Formation and the Distribution of Riches* (New York, 1971).

H. Uchida, 'The Transfer of Electrical Technologies from the United States and Europe to Japan, 1869–1914', in D.J. Jeremy (ed.), *International Technology Transfer: Europe, Japan and the USA, 1700–1914* (Aldershot, 1991), pp. 219–41.

A.M. Vaz, *Cia. Cedro e Cachoeira: História de uma Empresa Familiar, 1883–1987* (Belo Horizonte, 1990).

B.S. Veiga, *Almanack Sul Mineiro* (Campanha, 1874).

M.T.R.O. Versiani, 'The Cotton Textile Industry of Minas Gerais, Brazil: Beginnings and Early Development, 1868–1906', University of London, unpublished Ph.D. thesis, 1991.

A. Villanova Villela and W. Suzigan, *Política do Governo e Crescimento da Economia Brasileira, 1889–1945* (Rio de Janeiro, 1973).

E. Viotti da Costa, *Da Monarquia à República: Momentos Decisivos* (São Paulo, 1987).

E. Viotti da Costa, 'O Escravo na Grande Lavoura', in S.B. Holanda (ed.), *História Geral da Civilização Brasileira – II. O Brasil Monárquico*, vol. V (São Paulo, 1985), pp. 135–88.

E. Viotti da Costa, '1870–1889', in L. Bethell (ed.), *Brazil: Empire and Republic, 1822–1930* (Cambridge, 1989), pp. 161–213.

M. Weber, *The Protestant Ethic and the Spirit of Capitalism*, 20th edn (London, 1989).

M. Weber, *The Theory of Social and Economic Organization* (New York, 1964).

E.V.D. Weid and A.M.R. Bastos, *O Fio da Meada: Estratégia de Expansão de uma Indústria Têxtil, Companhia América Fabril – 1878/1930* (Rio de Janeiro, 1986).

J.D. Wirth, *Minas Gerais in the Brazilian Federation, 1889–1937* (Stanford, 1977).

Index

232 *Index*